STEPPING FORWARD IN FAITH

Redeemer University College
1974 - 1994

written by
Henry R. De Bolster

STEPPING FORWARD IN FAITH
REDEEMER UNIVERSITY COLLEGE 1974 - 1994

Copyright © 2001, Henry R. De Bolster

ISBN: 1-55306-293-0

**For more information or
to order additional copies, please contact:**

Redeemer University College Bookstore
777 Garner Road East
Ancaster, ON L9K 1J4
(905) 648-9575 Fax (905) 648-2134
e-mail: books@redeemer.on.ca

Guardian Books is an imprint of *Essence Publishing,* a Christian Book Publisher dedicated to furthering the work of Christ through the written word. For more information, contact:
44 Moira Street West, Belleville, Ontario, Canada K8P 1S3.
Phone: 1-800-238-6376 Fax: (613) 962-3055
E-mail: info@essencegroup.com
Internet: www.essencegroup.com

Printed in Canada
by

This book is dedicated to
all those who participated in the
establishment and development of
Redeemer University College:
members of the feasibility study committee;
members of the OCCA board;
the pioneer and subsequent students;
members of the administration, faculty and staff;
members of the board of governors;
members of the board of Redeemer Foundation;
members of the senate;
members of the many committees;
the volunteers;
and the many supporters of the College.

Thank you for your support,
dedication and tireless work.

Rev. Henry R. De Bolster,
B.A., B.D., M.Div.

Rev. Henry R. De Bolster, B.A., B.D., M.Div.

Table of Contents

Preface & Acknowledgements

It has been seven years since I retired as president of Redeemer College. Immediately after my retirement, I was asked by the Mt. Hamilton Christian Reformed Church to help with their difficulties and to function, together with Rev. James Van Weelden, as their interim pastor. I served in this capacity for almost five years. During those years, that congregation required my full attention and I had no time to think about writing the story of Redeemer College as I had experienced that story.

However, when I was no longer in the active ministry, I began to realise that it was necessary to tell others the great things the Lord had done—from the moment that the feasibility study began until my retirement—for these things should not be forgotten. Several people encouraged me to write my experiences of those early years. Some even told me that I owed the College a book about the years of my involvement. Because I am not a writer, it took me some time to decide to begin my research and writing. Writing is a difficult task, and I admire all those who have given their time and energy to put their thoughts on paper

If it had not been for the promises of several people to help me, I might not have had the courage to write this book. Therefore, I want to thank those who encouraged me, read the manuscript, gave helping suggestions and edited the various drafts which made the book a reality. They are: my former assistant, Mrs. Margaret Buma, who was always ready to listen, to advise and to encourage me throughout all those years; Dr. Justin Cooper, my academic right hand and my successor as president of Redeemer University College, who checked the manuscript for historical accuracy because he was involved with the venture of faith from the beginning; Dr.

Dick Kranendonk, who gave the best years of his life to the College, and who also prepared the manuscript for publication, and Mrs. Henny Kranendonk, his spouse, who put the final touches to the manuscript; Dr. Theodore Plantinga, the first Executive Director of the Ontario Christian College Association (OCCA), the predecessor of Redeemer College, and presently professor of philosophy at Redeemer University College; and last, but not least, Dr. Al Wolters, professor of religion and theology and classical studies at the College, the person who informed me of my appointment as the first president of the College. To all these people I say, thank you so much for your time and willingness to be of such great help. Without their assistance this book would not have been published.

I want to take this opportunity to thank the many volunteers who helped over the years, who promoted the College and who were always willing to come to the College for board, senate, foundation and committee meetings. I think of the many donors who, with their large and small gifts, expressed their confidence in the work of the College. Your generosity was awe-inspiring. Thank you very much.

Thanks to Robert Kranendonk, an alumnus of the College, who designed the cover, and who digitally edited the pictures to be included. Finally, I want to thank my wife of fifty years, Cobie, for reading the first draft and for giving me her first impressions.

I have written a personal account from my perspective as chairman of the feasibility study group, president of OCCA, and founding president of Redeemer College. Naturally, such an account is coloured by my interpretation. I have done my best to be fair and factual, but if I have committed an injustice to anyone, I apologise. It was not done intentionally. Any errors or omissions are, of course, my responsibility.

The publication of this book would not have been possible without a grant from the Redeemer Foundation. I want to thank the Foundation most heartily.

Above all, I thank the Lord who gave me health, strength, determination and inspiration throughout the years of my involvement with the College and during the writing of this book.

There was trauma and delight in recalling many of the events. May God richly bless you as you read the history of this miraculous institution. I believe that Redeemer College was created and upheld by the sovereign hand of the Lord. May He receive the glory for the story I was privileged to write.

Henry R. De Bolster
Hamilton, Ontario
July 2001

ONE

How It All Began

I clearly remember the day that Mr. Andy Langendoen came to see me in the parsonage in St. Catharines. It was in the year 1974. Andy was doing well. His business had been growing, and he wanted to do something special for Christian education, in addition to his support for the local grade school and high school. Andy wanted to study the possibility of starting a Christian college in the province of Ontario, but he could not do that by himself. He decided to come to me, his pastor, to discuss what could be done to reach this goal. He was willing to spend some money on a study. I reasoned to myself, how good it would be if we could open an institution similar to Dordt College in Sioux Center, Iowa, and The King's College in Edmonton, Alberta, which hoped to open its doors in the near future. I thanked Andy and promised to think about his proposal and to stay in touch with him.

Andy's idea to establish a Christian college in Ontario immediately appealed to me. However, I was well aware that such an undertaking was no simple task and next to impossible. Private Christian post-secondary education would be expensive. If we wanted such an institution to be a Reformed Christian college, the money would have to come primarily from the recent immigrant communities across the province of Ontario.

For more than a century, Calvinists in the Netherlands had established Christian schools for the education of their children. Such education was rooted in the theology of the sixteenth century reformer, John Calvin. The migration of Dutch Calvinists to the U.S.A. in the mid to late nineteenth century had been the cause of the establishment of many Christian schools and a number of Christian colleges in that country.

Andy Langendoen.

But in addition to the theology of John Calvin, the recent immigrant communities in Canada had also been influenced by the neo-Calvinist theology and philosophy of the late nineteenth and early twentieth century, which bloomed in the Netherlands during the formative years of their generation. The neo-Calvinist theology had been developed by theologians such as Dr. Herman Bavinck and Dr. Abraham Kuyper. The latter also was the leader of a Reformed Christian political party and served a term as prime minister of the Netherlands.

In his inaugural address on his appointment as professor at the Free University of Amsterdam, Dr. Kuyper had introduced the concept of "Sphere Sovereignty" and the concept that there is not one square inch of creation over which Christ does not lay claim. He emphasised that this total creation must serve the King of Creation in harmony. Each institution in human existence, such as the family, the state, the church, the school and the business enterprise, had a primary responsibility for, and was *sovereign* in, its own area of operation. Institutions which operated primarily in other spheres should not interfere with the primary task of such an institution. At the same time, each institution was to recognise and respect the autonomy of the other spheres. In Dr. Kuyper's view, it was the primary task of the state to give the necessary room for each institution to carry out its task and to make certain that all the institutions could work in harmony.

On the theological side, the neo-Calvinist theologians in the Netherlands were well aware that we live in a broken and sinful world. They taught that the fall into sin and the consequent expulsion from Paradise had ruined the perfect and harmonious creation that God had made. However, they also firmly believed that Christ's redemption not only saved humankind from eternal damnation, but that His sacrifice on the cross of Calvary also reconciled creation to Christ's Lordship. They viewed it as the task of God's people to reclaim all of creation for Christ's service.

On the philosophical side, the post-World War II Dutch Reformed immigrants had been greatly influenced by the school of Christian philosophy developed by the brothers-in-law, Dr. Herman Dooyeweerd and Dr. D. H. Th. Vollenhoven. This philosophy came to be known as the "Philosophy of the Cosmonomic Idea." This philosophy also known as the "Philosophy of the Law Idea," became available in the English-speaking world through the translation of Dr. Dooyeweerd's four volume *A New Critique of Theoretical Thought*. In brief, this Christian philosophy attempted to explain all of creation in a systematic structure. This philosophy was very attractive to the common people of the Netherlands because it provided an explanation for much of what was observed in nature, while at the same time holding true to the biblical givens. Christians no longer needed to be apologetic about their faith. They discovered that they could fulfill their Christian calling in all vocations of life. They understood that they could be educated and trained to speak and work not just as lawyers, doctors, teachers and business people, who were at the same time Christians. Instead, they believed that they could become *Christian* lawyers, doctors, teachers and business people, provided that they would receive an education that properly prepared them.

These visions and insights drove the Dutch Reformed immigrants to establish their own privately funded Christian elementary and secondary schools within a few years after they arrived in Canada. They wanted their rich, theological and philosophical systems and principles developed and taught to their children in their newly adopted country. They wanted to teach these visions and principles not just to their own children, but they wanted to share them with all God's people in this new country. That is why they were firmly opposed to establishing church schools. They did not establish and operate Christian schools because of a dissatisfaction with the academic quality of education or discipline in the public system. They also did not want to create "greenhouses" to shield their children from the sinful world out there. Rather, they wanted to prepare and train the next generation of Christians on the basis of biblical principles developed in a respectable Christian philosophy so that they would be able to take up their calling in the world. They saw the purpose of each Christian's vocation in life as a call to reclaim a small portion of God's fallen creation for Christ. That vision and commitment required Christian schools.

As a result of their strong vision and commitment to Christian education, these Dutch Reformed immigrants were willing to sacrifice substantially to establish the local Christian elementary and secondary schools and to keep them operating. I believe that it was also that vision and commitment which had caused Andy to come to my office with his request. I knew that it would be that same vision and commitment that could bring about the establishment of a new Christian college of the arts and sciences in Ontario.

I also reflected on where we would be able to find a sufficient number of faculty members who would have had their formal education in the vision and principles that I have just described. Would we be able to find sufficient students who would be willing to study at a small infant institution? Already in the 1950's, some visionaries had tried to establish a teacher's college, but the Reformed Christian community was not ready for such an enterprise at that time. Would they be ready to embrace a Reformed Christian college now?

Furthermore, the Institute for Christian Studies in Toronto was already in existence at the graduate level, but it was difficult to finance even that small organisation. The very thought of another school for higher learning in addition to the Institute and the anticipated opening of The King's College in Edmonton, Alberta seemed ludicrous.

Yet, were all these questions not substantially the same when we started the Christian grade school and even more so when the first Christian high school was contemplated? Nevertheless, the impossible had become reality; one school after the other had been established and was operating. I reminded myself that the God who had brought many of us to this country also promised to lead us forward, if we would only trust in Him. That is the gospel I preached every Sunday. As God's Kingdom workers, we are asked to step forward in faith. I prayed for that faith and decided to consult my two colleagues in St. Catharines, the Reverends Jacob Kuntz and Ray Sikkema.

The Feasibility Study

Both men agreed to meet with me, and after I explained to them the purpose of the meeting, they agreed to participate. Even though there were some reservations, we decided to consult some business people in St. Catharines and ask for their input. We invited four or five people, and they in turn advised us to call a meeting of representatives from several areas of the province in order to obtain their opinion about conducting a feasibility study for the purpose of establishing a Reformed Christian college in Ontario. I do not remember exactly how many people accepted our invitation, but quite a number of representatives from many areas in the province arrived at the meeting. We discussed the different aspects of such a study for a long time, and finally we agreed to form a feasibility study group. Most of those present were willing to participate.

When we decided to study the feasibility to establish a Reformed Christian college in Ontario, various "classes" of the

Christian Reformed Church in Canada had begun to follow the practice of the denomination in the U.S.A. of appointing chaplains to work in the secular universities. (A "Classis" in the Christian Reformed denomination is a grouping of local churches within a geographic area similar to a district, diocese or presbytery of other denominations.) Classis Hamilton had also appointed a committee to look into the possibility of appointing a chaplain at McMaster University. When that committee reported to Classis, the question was raised whether a chaplain could adequately minister to our students at McMaster. *Had the time not come to start a college in Ontario?* some asked. Classis Hamilton expanded the mandate of the chaplain study committee and asked for a report that would answer the questions raised.

When I heard of this development, I approached Rev. John Zantingh, who chaired the chaplain study committee. I told him of our activities and proposed a merger of our two committees to avoid duplicating the work we had already started. John brought our proposal to Classis, and it decided instead to relieve the chaplain study committee of the mandate to investigate the possibility of a new college in Ontario. As a result, John agreed to join our group and his participation in our study proved to be of considerable value.

Where do you begin such a study? When I was a pastor in Calgary, Alberta, I had been involved in the study to begin The King's College in Edmonton. I remembered that Dr. Robert (Bob) Vander Vennen, who at the time of our study was an administrator at the Institute for Christian Studies in Toronto, had been asked to conduct the study for the Alberta Christian College Association. We approached Bob and asked him whether he was willing to conduct the study for us. He told us that he was employed by the Institute for Christian Studies and that he was unable to devote the necessary time to conduct such a study. However, he indicated that he was interested in our project and that, had he not been employed full time by the Institute, he would have been willing to accept our request.

As a result of Dr. Vander Vennen's response, we talked to the administration at the Institute and asked them to release Bob to us for half a year. We explained the importance of the study. The Institute gladly gave Bob a leave of absence to do the study. Since the funds to conduct the feasibility study had already been committed by Mr. Andy Langendoen, Bob accepted his appointment to study the feasibility of starting a Reformed Christian college in Ontario.

At the completion of his study, Dr. Vander Vennen presented the committee with a thorough and realistic report. The focus was on the Christian Reformed community. It had already demonstrated its support for Christian education; therefore it was important to know the reaction of the Christian Reformed people. The report noted that students ready to go to college were, by and large, interested in a Canadian education. Only a minority indicated that they preferred Calvin College, Trinity Christian College or Dordt College, all located in the U.S.A. Most of the students who were interviewed intended to go to a secular university in Canada. Even more disturbing was the fact that up to 80 percent of the students who attended a secular university had lost their faith or were lost for the church. (This percentage was confirmed by Rev. Aren Geisterfer, chaplain at McMaster University, in one of his reports to Classis Hamilton in the early 1990's.) The report indicated that it would be possible, with hard work, to recruit about fifty first year students to attend a new college in Ontario.

Bob recommended a junior college. This is how Dordt and Trinity Christian began. A junior college offers a one or a two-year program in the arts and sciences after which most students transfer to other institutions to complete their degree programs. If we established a junior college, it would undoubtedly be possible for students to transfer to the existing Christian colleges in the U.S.A. Another advantage was the fact that our Christian high schools educated their students only to Grade 12, while Grade 13 was the normal university entrance requirement in Ontario. As a result, university-bound Christian high school graduates either had to continue their high school studies at a secular high school, or apply for admission to a college in the U.S.A.

Among the Christian high schools in Ontario, only Toronto District Christian High offered the Grade 13 program. Therefore, a new junior college could be of help to students from most of our high schools by offering the equivalent of a Grade 13 program. Such a program would assure students that they would be admitted at any university as well as at the Christian colleges in the U.S.A.

Our committee received Bob's excellent report with gratitude. A lengthy discussion followed. Some were of the opinion to forget about the project, while others were stimulated to continue. Finally it was decided to present this report to the general public within the Reformed community, and seven areas throughout the province were chosen. Those who would come to the meetings would be asked for their opinion; more specifically, they would be asked whether or not we should form an association in order to start a college. These meetings were well attended. Many questions were raised, but in all areas the feasibility study committee was urged to continue and to establish an association, praying that, with the help of the Lord, we might have a Christian college in Ontario.

OCCA's Organization

On November 13, 1976, the feasibility study committee, consisting of: Dr. John Cook, Rev. Henry De Bolster, Dr. Leo Jonker, Rev. Jacob Kuntz, Dr. Tony Looy, Mr. Paul Senechal, Rev. Ray Sikkema, Dr. Henk Van Andel, Dr. Bob Vander Vennen, Dr. Jack Veenstra, Mr. Harry Voortman and Rev. John Zantingh, called a meeting at Conrad Grebel College in Waterloo. The agenda called for the organisation of an association to establish a Christian college in Ontario. At that meeting, the Ontario Christian College Association (OCCA) was born with a membership of 104 people. A board was elected with the mandate to draw up a constitution with bylaws and to work toward the establishment of a Christian college in Ontario.

The first task of the board was to draw up a constitution. It was not the first time that such a document was composed; hence there were many examples and models we could draw from. However, each organisation has its own unique needs. We needed to address the question as to what kind of organisation OCCA would be. Would it be a church-controlled association, or would it be a membership society? The organisational meeting in Waterloo had already answered that question; hence under the *gover-*

nance heading, the constitution stated that the College would be a free, nondenominational society.

The greater question concerned the basis of the College. Of course the basis was going to be the Word of God—the Bible—but how was that to be interpreted? A small committee was appointed, which dealt with the relationship of the church creeds and education. Should the College be based on the creeds of the Reformation, or should we compose an educational creed as the Institute for Christian Studies had done? Could we do justice to both? Finally the committee came with a Statement of Basis and Principles, which was adopted by the board and later by the membership. The statement read as follows:

> Our supreme standard is the Bible. These Scriptures, both Old Testament and New, reveal some basic principles relevant to education, which we affirm:
>
> *Scripture.* The Scriptures are the written and inspired Word of God, the infallible and authoritative rule of faith for the direction of the whole of life.
>
> *Creation.* God created and structured the universe in all its many ways by His Word. The meaning of creation is focussed in man, God's imagebearer, with whom He has established a special covenant relationship in Jesus Christ.
>
> *Sin.* Man's disobedience, which brought God's curse upon all mankind, alienated man from his Creator, himself, his fellow man, and the rest of creation; distorted his view of the meaning and purpose of life; and misdirected human culture and learning.
>
> *Redemption.* Christ, the Word of God incarnate, is the only Redeemer, the Renewer of our whole life. He restores man and the rest of creation to God and calls man back to his God-appointed task in the world.
>
> *Human life.* Man is by nature a religious being. All of human life, including educational work, must be understood as a response to

the one true God. Consequently, man serves either the Lord or a god of his own making.

Knowledge. True knowledge of God, ourselves, and the rest of creation is made possible only by means of a true faith in Jesus Christ, in whom are found all the treasures of wisdom and knowledge. True knowledge is attained only when the Holy Spirit enlightens men's hearts by the integrating Word of God and sets them in the truth. However, by God's gracious providence after the fall, those who reject the Word of God do provide many valuable insights into the structure of reality.

Teaching and Learning. In the context of their scholarship, the teachers of the college are called to lead students towards a deeper understanding of God's world and its history and to help them reach a cultural maturity grounded in Biblical faith. In order to carry out this calling, the teachers and students of the college should endeavour to discover God's laws and the structures of the creation so that the students may effectively take up their specific responsibilities and vocations in a way that will further the coming of the Lord's Kingdom.

We believe that this Statement of Basis and Principles is wholly in harmony not only with Scripture, but also with the historic creeds of the Reformation.

The committee wanted to maintain the Reformed character of the College, but concluded that the creeds do not say much, if anything, about education. The committee did not want to identify its Statement of Basis and Principles as a "creed," since that is a document identified with the church. However, we, the committee, and all those who would be involved in the organisation of the College, were members of the church and could not ignore the creeds when we worked outside the institutional church. Therefore, the Statement of Basis and Principles needed to be in conformity with the creeds of the Reformation.

This Statement, when read today, reveals the time in which it was drafted. The emphasis on "man" instead of "human" is embarrassing today, some twenty-five years after its composition. I remember that when we were admitted as members of the Association of Universities and Colleges in Canada, one female president from one of the universities in Nova Scotia reprimanded us for being chauvinistic. Shortly after that incident, Redeemer College put a note with the Statement saying that "man" and "he" should be read as "human" and "he/she." This incident demonstrated how quickly society had changed.

The second task of the board was to work toward the establishment of a Christian college in Ontario. That was easier said than done. First we needed to know exactly what the law of the province required in starting a post-secondary institution. Therefore, it would be necessary to visit the Ministry of Colleges and Universities, as well as the universities in Ontario. To accomplish this, OCCA appointed Dr. Theodore Plantinga as Director of College Development, on February 5, 1977. Later he became the Executive Director of OCCA.

Theodore contacted the government and met with a representative of the Ministry of Colleges and Universities. This man promptly informed Theodore that degree-granting colleges and universities could not be established without the permission of the

John Zantingh, Henry R. De Bolster and Theodore Plantinga.

Legislature of Ontario. Moreover, there was a standing policy, called the "Robarts Policy," which stated that "no new free-standing, secular, degree-granting institutions could be established in the province." The only way new degree-granting institutions could be formed was by way of affiliation with an existing university. At the time we were not too discouraged, since we expected to be able to affiliate with a university rather easily. Before Theodore turned to the universities in Ontario, he met with Dr. Tony Diekema, president of Calvin College. Theodore explained to him what we had in mind, and Dr. Diekema immediately promised him help and support in our efforts. However, he also said that since Calvin was the college of the Christian Reformed denomination, he would continue to raise funds and recruit students in Ontario. Calvin College has been true to its word. We received much support from Dr. Diekema and many others at Calvin College. Calvin College was willing to consider the affiliation of our two institutions. However, affiliating two institutions in two different countries proved to be too difficult.

With encouraging support from Calvin College, Theodore made appointments with the presidents of a number of Ontario universities. Even though he was cordially received, it quickly became clear that no university was interested in a possible affiliation. To our amazement, universities that had been Christian institutions, like McMaster and Wilfrid Laurier, were the least interested. While those doors closed, we at least were encouraged by Calvin College's promise to stand with us. We were also able to strengthen the ties with Dordt College. Right from the beginning, Rev. B. J. Haan, Dordt's founding president, gave us solid advice. He had experienced many of the challenges that an institution faces before it becomes established. I must say that the relationship with our American sister colleges was encouraging from the very beginning.

The OCCA board also requested Theodore to write a book which would promote the cause of Christian higher education. He wrote *Rationale For A Christian College* in a very short time. Theodore is also the person who must receive credit for the name of our college. Members of our board raised the question what the name of the future college would be. A number of names were put in the hopper. Some were deleted rather quickly, like Kuyper College, but others were discussed at length. One of these names,

Redeemer College, was suggested by Theodore. Name after name was eliminated so that, finally, Redeemer College was left. It took a while for that name to sink in, but slowly everyone became enthusiastic about it. Finally, it stuck and was chosen as the name of our college. The name truly indicates the reason for our existence: the redemptive work of Christ, which opened the reality of work and workers in God's Kingdom.

In November 1978, Theodore informed us that he was no longer able to work for OCCA on a part-time basis, because his employer, Paideia Press, needed him full time. It was very difficult to replace Theodore. The board looked for a full-time person who would function as the chief executive officer of OCCA, hoping that this person would also become the president when the College was established.

The board had four people in mind, and Rev. John Zantingh and I visited all four of them, asking them to join us. They were Dr. Gordon Spykman, Dr. Nicolas Woltersdorff, Dr. John Van Dyk and Dr. Robert Vander Vennen. All four declined. This brought the board back to square one. Fortunately, Theodore was elected to the board and did a lot of work as its secretary. When it was impossible to find a CEO, the board advertised for another person who could do Theodore's work. We found Dr. Vander Vennen willing to be a consultant to the board. His help was an answer to prayer. It helped us to accomplish some of the groundwork that needed to be done. But the work that was required became too much for a volunteer board. Dr. Theodore Plantinga informed us in November 1979, that he was able and willing to become our executive director again on a half-time basis. We gladly accepted his offer and regarded this, too, as an answer to prayer.

In 1980, Theodore accepted a position in the department of philosophy at Calvin College and started teaching there in the fall of that year. Fortunately, we were able to find two people who became worthy successors to Theodore. They were Mr. Justin Cooper, who took Theodore's place as part-time executive director, and Mr. Dick Kranendonk, who accepted the position of director of business and development on a half-time basis.

Affiliation Efforts

Even though the administrators at the universities did not encourage a possible affiliation, the OCCA board did not give up. An affiliation committee was appointed in 1977, consisting of Dr. Remkes Kooistra, Dr. Bob Vander Vennen and Dr. Jack Zeyl. All three persons were acquainted with the university scene. Dr. Zeyl was a professor at Wilfrid Laurier University in Waterloo.

The affiliation committee was able to get a hearing at a few of the universities. The most favourable contact was at the University of Waterloo. When Dr. Matthews, president of that university, thought he knew who we were, he showed interest in our proposal. He had experience with the presence of some church-related colleges on his campus, one of which was Conrad Grebel, a Mennonite college. We had held our first membership meeting at that college in 1976. Our affiliation committee met with some representatives of this university and the initial contacts appeared to hold some promise.

At the same time that these consultations took place, Dr. Theodore Plantinga and Dr. Bob Vander Vennen met with Dr. Earp, president of Brock University in St. Catharines. Brock had just concluded an affiliation agreement with an evangelical seminary and was discussing the possibility of an affiliation agreement with a Buddhist group. President Earp was willing to listen to what we had to say and seemed interested. He was of the opinion that some kind of cooperation could be possible. At least there appeared to be an open door, and this exceeded our expectation. Suddenly there were officials at two universities who were willing to talk to us: Brock and Waterloo. This new development made our next board meeting an exciting event.

The affiliation committee was given a mandate to come with concrete proposals as to what an affiliation agreement should include. This was a difficult mandate for the committee. We had no experience in this area, but we had a thousand questions. Our main question was whether or not it would be possible to start a Christian college as we had visualised. Who would set the standard of education? Who would have the authority in hiring the faculty?

Would the decisions of our board be subject to ratification by the university board? In other words, would we be able to maintain a sense of independence, or would we be part of the university with which we would affiliate?

The first university our committee visited again was the University of Waterloo. The discussions were very friendly and initially very hopeful. President Matthews was open to our ideas and suggested a possible affiliation. I considered that he had a lot of experience with the four church-related colleges on his campus, and possibly would not have serious objections to a Reformed college on campus, in addition to a Roman Catholic, an Anglican, a United and a Mennonite college.

At the outset, he told us of the restrictions the University imposed on the church related colleges. Two of these restrictions gave us serious concerns.

The first had to do with the admission policy of the University. The University would retain the right to set the admission standards and these standards would be exclusively academic in nature. If, for example, the University would set a 75 percent minimum for admission, then all students, including those at the affiliated colleges, would be required to have a 75 percent high school graduation average to be admitted. We saw potential problems. If, for example, John's father was a supporter of the College, but John only attained an average of 74 percent, the College would not be able to admit John.

The second condition concerned the religious perspective in accredited courses. Any course given by the College needed to be accredited by the University. The University would not accredit a course which it viewed as secular in nature, i.e. the general arts and sciences, if such a course would be taught by us from a religious perspective. But, locating our College close to the University, or perhaps even right on its campus, sharing the University facilities, cross-registration, and credit transfer to the University seemed very attractive. In addition, the College could count on the help of an experienced institution, while a fringe benefit would be the availability of government funding. Our affiliation committee was told that our faculty would need to be approved by the University senate. Assurances were given that as long as appointed faculty was academically qualified, the approval by the University would be a mere formality.

It became clear than an affiliation agreement with the University of Waterloo would severely limit the holistic Christian education based on the neo-Calvinist theological and philosophical perspective of the College. Yet the affiliation committee was encouraged to continue discussions. It wanted to make sure that the University would comprehend what we meant to accomplish with the establishment of a Christian college. After its meeting with the University of Waterloo, the committee visited Brock University. Brock did not wish to deal with the question of affiliation, because that seemed less attractive to them. However, the administration at Brock was friendly, although noncommittal, inviting, yet vague. When they were pressed about a formal institutional relationship, their answers were not any different from the ones we had heard at Waterloo.

We also visited the University of Guelph and McMaster University in Hamilton. Both visits were disappointing. Neither university gave us any hope for a working relationship on terms acceptable to our purpose and vision. Several visits were made to other universities, as well as to the existing affiliated colleges at some of the universities. The colleges at the University of Waterloo were very satisfied with their existing arrangements. All of them urged us to do what they had done. To our great surprise, none of these colleges saw any conflict in the decision of the university not to accredit "secular" courses with a religious perspective. Our affiliation committee decided to proceed carefully.

Important as the issue of affiliation was, it was not the only item on the board's agenda. We were mandated by the membership to prepare for the opening of a college in the not too distant future. Several committees were appointed by the board. When I look back, it amazes me that so many people, both members of the board and members of OCCA, were willing to give of their time and energy to get this college off the ground. Let me give you an overview of the various committees and their mandates. On November 19, 1977, the following resolution was passed by the board relating to the standing committees of OCCA.

1. **STANDING COMMITTEES:**

The Association shall have the following Standing Committees, whose job description and composition is set out below:

    1.1. ACADEMIC AFFAIRS COMMITTEE,

    1.2. BUSINESS AFFAIRS COMMITTEE,

    1.3. DEVELOPMENT COMMITTEE,

    1.4. STUDENT AFFAIRS COMMITTEE.

2. **ACADEMIC AFFAIRS COMMITTEE**

(1) The Academic Affairs Committee shall consist of four members of the Board of Governors who are knowledgeable about higher education, one of whom shall be appointed Chairman by the Board, and three members at large, not members of the Board of Governors, chosen by the Board of Governors, provided that they are Association members in regular standing and are not employed by the College as faculty or administrative staff.

(2) *Ex officio* members may be appointed from time to time as deemed necessary by the Board of Governors.

(3) Members at large shall be appointed for a term of three years and may serve a maximum of two consecutive terms. Retiring members-at-large will be eligible after one year for reappointment. Members from the Board of Governors and *ex officio* members shall be appointed annually.

(4) Frequency of meetings shall not be less than six times a year.

(5) A simple majority of the membership of the Academic Affairs Committee shall constitute a quorum.

(6) The Academic Affairs Committee, consistent with the policies of the Board of Governors and subject to its authority, shall have the following powers and duties:

    (a) to establish the educational policies of the College and to engage in academic planning,

    (b) to make recommendations to the Board of Governors regarding the operation of the College,

    (c) to consider and act on proposals relating to academic

matters made by the College faculty and administration,

(d) to determine: curricula; policies regarding the appointment, promotion and tenure of faculty; admissions policies; examination policies,

(e) to hear appeals regarding applications for admissions and examinations,

(f) to recommend to the Board of Governors the granting of degrees.

3. **BUSINESS AFFAIRS COMMITTEE:**

(1) The Business Affairs Committee shall consist of a Chairman who is the Treasurer of the Association and of four other members of the Board of Governors and of senior administrative staff of the College appointed by the Board of Governors who will serve as *ex officio* members.

(2) The Business Affairs Committee shall concern itself with the financial condition and management of the College and Association, including both the operational funds of the College, any of its endowments or other capital funds and all other property including buildings.

(3) Without limiting the generality of the foregoing, the specific responsibilities are as follows:

(a) The preparation of the annual budgets, which shall cover the estimated income and expenses of the Association for the next ensuing fiscal year, to be submitted to the Board of Governors;

(b) The preparation of periodic, interim financial statements with appropriate comparisons to the budget and prior accounting periods, for submission to the Board of Governors at its regular meetings;

(c) Arrangement for annual audits of all financial books and records by independent auditors; and

(d) The development of policies and plans, with respect to the financial affairs of the College for the operation and maintenance of physical resources of the College for recommendations to the Board of Governors.

4. <u>**DEVELOPMENT COMMITTEE:**</u>

(1) The Development Committee shall consist of at least eight members, including two staff members and six members of the Association, at least two of whom shall be members of the Board of Governors.

(2) The Development Committee, consistent with the policies of the Board of Governors and subject to its authority, shall be concerned with:

(a) community, church and public relations;

(b) all aspects of corporate development, including improvement and expansion of the College;

(c) fund raising; and

(d) student recruitment.

5. <u>**STUDENT AFFAIRS COMMITTEE:**</u>

The Student Affairs Committee shall consist of at least six members of the Association, including two members of the Board of Governors, one of who serves as Chairman, two students and two members of the staff. Other persons may from time to time be appointed by the Board of Governors. This Committee shall be concerned with all aspects of the life of students at the proposed College.

It stands to reason that all aspects of the committees' mandates could not be implemented immediately, but the framework was in place. It was also decided that the affiliation committee would be a subcommittee of the academic affairs committee, so that all proposals of that committee would be looked at by at least one other body before they would be presented to the board for approval.

The affiliation committee reported regularly to the academic affairs committee about the many visits that were made to the University of Waterloo and Brock University. Not much progress was made. The academic affairs committee proposed to the board guidelines for further meetings of the affiliation committee with

Waterloo and Brock. The board accepted these guidelines on October 7, 1978. They read as follows:

> Guidelines for academic criteria, which any affiliation agreement with a university must satisfy in order to be considered acceptable:
>
> 1) The university should accept course credits from our Grade 13 equivalent program as being the equivalent of comparable credits from a standard Grade 13 program.
> 2) Students who have successfully completed our first year (Grade 13 equivalent program) with an average which meets the usual university admission guideline should be admitted to the second year of our college program and therefore should also not fail to be admitted to the host university as first year students.
> 3) Credits from our foundational and liberal arts core courses should be recognized by the university as credits to be counted toward a degree.
> 4) Students enrolled in the second year of our program (which would be the first year of university) should be allowed to take all of their remaining core courses and at least 60 percent of their liberal arts core courses at the college. Normally this would mean a maximum of 1.5 courses could be taken at the host university. A student in our Grade 13 equivalent program would take all of his courses at the college.
> 5) Our college should be able to teach courses in all the basic areas of the arts, humanities, social sciences and natural sciences. It is understood that whatever courses are taught would meet proper academic standards.
> 6) Students (and staff) from our college should be free to engage in a process of guided interaction in connection with first year or upper level courses which our students are taking at the university.

On December 2, 1978, the affiliation committee proposed a move toward affiliation with the University of Waterloo. The board, however, was not satisfied with the committee report and sent it back with the request that the committee prepare a paper giving the pros and cons of affiliation versus independent status, as well as location at Brock University (St. Catharines) versus the University of Waterloo. This paper was to be ready before the next board meeting. To give each board member ample time to study and reflect on the proposals, the report was mailed out on a timely basis. It was to include an evaluation of operating as an independent college in Waterloo. All other committees were asked to look at these questions from the perspective of their committees. These committees were to give their evaluations of the options to the board at its next meeting. On February 3, 1979, the board discussed the report from the affiliation committee. It took a great part of the day to review the different options, but the board did not come to any conclusion. There were too many different opinions, and no consensus could be reached. The academic affairs committee, to which the affiliation committee had reported, asked for more time.

Dr. Albert Wolters had made a suggestion that we formulate some nonnegotiables in the discussion with the University of Waterloo. The board referred that matter to the academic affairs committee. On March 31, 1979, the academic affairs committee presented a report to the board entitled, "Academic Nonnegotiables." The committee proposed that these principles be used in our negotiations regarding affiliation. The board debated these nonnegotiables at length. At the end of the day, the following academic nonnegotiables were adopted:

1. <u>**ADMISSIONS**</u>
   a) Credits from our year five program must be considered the equivalent of Grade 13 credits and therefore be sufficient for admission to the university.
   b) An arrangement must be worked out, whereby students, who have satisfied our requirements for the year five program, will be able to continue the following year as first year university students in programs that are recognizable continuations of the work they have begun in the OCCA college on the year five (Grade 13) level. (This arrangement, i.e. probationary status, would apply to a few marginal students who might otherwise be

excluded if the university in a given year raised its admission standard by a point or two.)

Ground: The continuity of our students' academic program should not be subject to the year-to-year fluctuations of the university's admission policies. We cannot operate unless students, who adequately complete our year five program, can be assured of going on in first year university.

2) ACADEMIC PROGRAM

a) In each of the basic disciplines of the arts and sciences, our college must retain the right to offer a broad range of courses for credit in the various majors programs so that our students will be able to take 70-80 percent of the courses for their three year B.A. major within our college.

b) There must be sufficient latitude in the three year B.A. majors programs in each of the basic disciplines of the arts and sciences to allow students to satisfy our foundational and, as a rule, our liberal arts core requirements.

c) Our courses must be given academic recognition by the university in the discipline in which they are taught. For example, introductory and methodology courses in which a Christian perspective is especially evident should always be given credit and recognition in the discipline in question.

d) Students and staff of our college must be free to engage in guided interaction, whereby our students would be helped to discern the paradigmatic frameworks in terms of which courses taken in the university are taught.

Ground: It is essential to OCCA's purpose of establishing a college with a distinctively Reformed identity that we retain the ability to develop and maintain a full range of liberal arts courses, which are both informed throughout by a Reformed perspective and recognized as academically sound and worthy of credit.

3. FACULTY AND STAFF

Our college must retain the freedom to hire, supervise and dismiss academic faculty and staff without interference from the university administration, faculty association or staff union. It is understood that the people hired will have the requisite qualifications for the position in question.

4. <u>FACILITIES</u>

We must have access to library facilities and physical education facilities. In addition, the university must be willing to allow the use of laboratory space, which is essential if we are to be able to offer courses in the natural sciences.

It was clear to me that the affiliation committee was ready to make compromises in order to achieve affiliation. The OCCA board was not ready to move in that direction. Board members did not think alike on this matter of affiliation. If at all possible, we needed to come to a consensus. The executive committee proposed a meeting in a retreat setting. The board had done that once before, when we had difficulties agreeing on the Statement of Basis and Principles. That retreat had served the purpose of bringing the different views within the board together, and the executive hoped that the same thing would happen this time. The proposal was accepted, and April 28, 1979, was chosen as the date for the retreat. Dr. Vander Vennen and Dr. Plantinga were asked to prepare introductory statements to set the stage for the discussion at the conference retreat.

Mr. Paul Senechal, the treasurer of the board, worked at Dofasco. He was able to secure the boardroom of his company and on Saturday, April 28, fourteen of the eighteen board members met to listen to each other, to discuss this important matter of affiliation and to come to a consensus. In the morning, the board divided itself into three discussion groups, which reported after lunch to the plenary session. The reports indicated that we were very divided on the question before us. All members were asked to give their opinions with grounds so that we all would know exactly where we stood. The end result was that seven members expressed themselves for affiliation and seven members against. We were deadlocked. It is difficult to describe the feelings of all those who were present. We were disappointed, and yet we needed to carry on. The last half hour was spent in an official session of the board. During that time the following motions were passed:

1) The Board charges the Affiliation Committee, in consultation with the Academic Affairs Committee, to begin negotiations with the University of Waterloo on the basis of the academic nonnegotiables adopted at the March 31 meeting and whatever else is pertinent to the negotiations. The Board asks the Affiliation Committee to keep in mind the danger that the negotiations could go on endlessly and asks the committee to do everything in its power to bring the negotiations to a conclusion as quickly as possible.

2) The Board urges the other standing committees to look into the matter of affiliation as well. If those committees have anything pertinent to the negotiations that should be communicated to the Affiliation Committee, this ought to be done at once.

I was one of the seven who expressed myself against affiliation. I was very afraid that we would lose our independence and that the real purpose of starting a Christian college in Ontario would fall by the wayside. I went home after that meeting thinking that we had come to the end of our efforts to start a college. I prayed that God would show us the way, so that our planning would still be blessed and that our efforts would not have been in vain. I am sure that I was not the only one who felt downhearted. Nevertheless, our next board meeting was set and even the standing committees met despite the deadlock.

On June 28, the board met again. The affiliation committee had not been able to meet with President Matthews of Waterloo, but the committee did ask that details of the Grade 13 equivalent program be worked out as quickly as possible. The board agreed that this was important. At that same meeting, the development committee presented some of its own nonnegotiables which the board passed as "important considerations." The following are the "important considerations":

1) GOVERNANCE. The governance of the college, staff and program should be done by the Board of Governors, elected by the supporting community, and must not be controlled by the university.

2) GROWTH. The college should be free to expand its programs into other areas, such as a teacher training program for our Christian schools or a community education program. (University recognition would not be essential for these programs.)

3) CAMPUS. The college should have its own physical facilities (classrooms, lounge areas, dormitories), so that students may have a centre around which they may form a community.

4) FINANCES. The association must be free to finance its college without interference from the university (i.e. set membership fees, provide scholarships, administer endowments, etc.).

It is interesting to note that the development committee also wanted to safeguard our independence.

Even though the matter of affiliation remained on the agenda of each board meeting, the first time that something of significance was reported occurred at the meeting of the executive committee on December 11, 1979. Then Dr. Vander Vennen reported on the progress of the affiliation discussions with the University of Waterloo. He reported that the committee had been working with three models. Model A: an independent college. Model B: an affiliated college subject to our nonnegotiables, and Model C: a college offering both affiliated and non-affiliated courses. He reported that Model B was unacceptable to the University. He informed the board that the affiliation committee was already working tentatively with Model C. The executive committee decided that this matter had to be decided by the board and that the affiliation committee should provide the board with a report explaining the various features of the new model, which included four distinguishable types of courses.

On January 12, 1980, the board met to deal with the request of the affiliation committee. The committee explained why the discussions with Waterloo had changed. The University did not wish to enter into an agreement on the basis of the nonnegotiables. Therefore, to accomplish the goal of affiliation, Model C needed to be approved. During the discussion the following motion was presented:

...that the Board of Governors endorses in principle the affiliation plan which would also permit our college to offer a number of courses on an independent basis for transfer to the University, and mandates the Affiliation Committee to bring back to the Board details of how such a plan would function, on the basis of which the Board would make its decision whether or not to enter a formal agreement with the University of Waterloo.

The minutes of that meeting indicate that "the discussion on that motion was somewhat tense." The board accepted that motion, but at the same time a motion was passed to the effect that "the executive committee appoint a committee to investigate Model C with a post-secondary institution other than Waterloo." The members of the second committee were Mr. Justin Cooper, Dr. Theodore Plantinga and Mr. Albert Bakker, QC.

The last we heard of these two affiliation committees was at the April 18, 1980, board meeting. The first committee reported on its contacts with the church colleges on Waterloo's campus and the promise was made that these discussions would be completed by year's end. The second committee gave only a report without any particulars. The slow progress was in part due to the fact that on February 13, 1980, the government introduced legislation which would make the Robarts policy law. This legislation became known to us as the infamous Bill 4. It was this legislation which eventually led us to our own degree-granting charter. Looking back, it is clear to me that the Lord was at work in all this. He knew that it would become impossible to start a Christian college by means of affiliation with an Ontario university. All doors were closing, but God used the introduction of an infamous bill to show that He provides for his children and that work done in His Name would be blessed. Allow me to explain.

During the time of the affiliation negotiations, we continued our discussions with the government. We kept asking why we could not operate an independent college in Ontario. We pointed out that The King's College was operating in Alberta and that Trinity Western College was operating in British Columbia. Our sister colleges in the U.S.A., i.e. Calvin in Grand Rapids, Michigan; Trinity Christian in Palos Heights, Illinois; and Dordt in Sioux Center, Iowa, had been in existence for many years. All of these post-secondary institutions provided quality education in the arts and sciences without government funding. All our arguments appeared to be in vain. Repeatedly we were reminded of the Robarts policy, which was intended to preclude fly-by-night institutions from operating in Ontario; institutions that were regarded as "degree mills." Since we were not yet established, the government did not want to take a political risk by granting us a charter. It was a no-win situation. The government was willing to consider our request only if we were in existence, while it was unwilling to allow us to become established even as a junior college which would hold any degree-granting powers in abeyance until it had a proven academic record.

Still, the government provided us with an opportunity to explain the nature of our community and its purpose and vision for a Christian college of the arts and sciences to the officials of the Ministry of Colleges and Universities. We asked Mr. Wilson, the assistant deputy minister, to arrange a meeting with the Minister. Unfortunately, we were never invited to meet with the Honourable Betty Stephenson, the Minister of Education and Minister of Colleges and Universities. It became clear that she had no intention of giving us an audience or a listening ear, neither did she ever seriously consider granting us our request for a charter. It is ironic to note that much later, this same Ms. Betty Stephenson became the proponent of private universities in Ontario. During those, for us, dark days, acceptable terms of affiliation could not be negotiated with any of the Ontario universities and the government refused to grant us permission to operate as a privately-funded university college.

We continued solely because of our faith and our firm conviction that we were doing the will of the Lord. It must have been the Lord who, by His Spirit, gave us the courage to persevere, even though it felt as if we were regressing. Several times someone would come to me to render his or her resignation as a member of the OCCA board. It often took a lot of persuasion to convince people to withdraw their resignation. Some were so deflated that they left anyway. Others were encouraged and stayed on to continue the battle in the hope that, with the Lord's help, we would ultimately prevail.

Bill Pr 48: Our Charter

The future became darker, yet when the government introduced, as I mentioned previously, the infamous Bill 4, an *Act to Regulate the Granting of Degrees*, in the Legislature. We almost despaired. No free-standing secular degree-granting universities would be permitted to operate in Ontario, unless the Legislature would pass legislation to allow such a new institution to come into existence. The government made it very clear that it would not grant such a request, and so OCCA was in danger of collapsing. But when the situation looked totally hopeless, the Lord in His wisdom used that infamous bill to open a door for us.

When the government introduced Bill 4 early in 1980, it was in a minority position and needed the support of the Opposition to pass any Bill. The Opposition was willing to give its support to Bill 4 provided that religious schools, such as the Bible colleges in Ontario, would be allowed to apply for a charter from the Legislature. The government gave its assurance that the Bible colleges in Ontario who applied for a charter would be granted one. But OCCA was *not* a Bible college. Even though it was not yet in existence at that time, it would be a college offering the full range of courses in the arts and sciences.

A special committee was appointed to make representations to amend Bill 4. Mr. Albert Bakker, Mr. Justin Cooper, Mr. Adrian Guldemond and Dr. Theodore Plantinga were mandated: "to analyse the difficulties imposed by Bill 4; to consult with other affected organisations and institutions; to discuss the issues with government officials; and to prepare a report to the executive with concrete recommendations." However, the government was not to be moved from its announced position. Furthermore, the Opposition in the Legislature had no intention of introducing amendments to the Bill. When amendments to the Bill proved impossible, Mr. Bakker met privately with the deputy premier, the Honourable Robert Welch of St. Catharines, to explain our situation. Mr.

Bakker knew Mr. Welch personally and had met him several times in regard to other issues. Mr. Welch expressed an interest in our plight and promised to talk to the Minister about our dilemma. Mr. Welch was as good as his word. When we contacted the ministry again, we were welcomed and were told that the ministry was willing to work with us in the matter of granting a charter to establish a religious school.

Our discussions took place with Mr. Jamie McKay, who listened carefully. We finally had an opportunity to explain our vision for a Reformed Christian college of the arts and sciences to the ministry. When the time came to formulate the objects of the proposed college, the ministry was willing to permit us

> to provide, at the post secondary level,
> a) for the advancement of learning and dissemination of knowledge on the basis of the Reformed confessions, traditions and perspectives,
> b) degree, diploma and certificate programs and courses of study based on Biblical and theological studies in the foundations of Reformed Christian perspectives.

Then we were told that the ministry had reserved the name "Redeemer Bible College" for our institution. We were not displeased with the opening sentences of the objects clause, but we wanted more. But the name "Redeemer Bible College" was out of the question for us. When our arguments were not effective, we asked Mr. Bakker to speak with Mr. Welch once again. Mr. Welch urged the ministry to accommodate us and to bring our application for a charter to an acceptable conclusion. Once again, Justin Cooper, Dick Kranendonk and I went to meet with the ministry. This time, Mr. Wilson was present in person, and we met in an office next to that of the minister. Justin presented a document, which he and Dick had formulated with the help of Mr. Bakker. We told Mr. Wilson that we accepted the ministry's proposed objects, but we wished to add after the words "Reformed Christian perspectives," a comma, and then continue:

which programs and courses may include studies in the general arts, humanities and sciences, both natural and social, permeated by such scripturally-directed Reformed Christian perspectives, in accordance with the Statement of Basis and Principles as set out in the by-laws of the College.

To our amazement, our proposal was accepted by the ministry.

The only remaining obstacle was the name of the College. We suggested the name "Redeemer Christian College." This name would have been acceptable to the ministry if there had not been a Roman Catholic seminary by that same name. (This name was on the title page of our private members bill when it was first introduced in the Legislature. That name continued to cause confusion at the time of second and third reading in the Legislature.) The ministry then suggested the name "Redeemer Christian Reformed College," but we rejected that name as well, because it would make us sound like a college of a denomination. We wanted to be a Christian college that would be independent from the control of any denomination and our name should not suggest otherwise. I then suggested the name "Redeemer Reformed Christian College." The ministry officials asked to be excused for a moment to consider our proposed name with the minister. After a few minutes, they came back and announced that the name we suggested was acceptable, since Christian Reformed or Reformed Christian gave the same message for them. Hallelujah, praise the Lord, we were finally able to move forward!

We discussed the names of the degree-granting powers only briefly, because at that time we had no intention of granting degrees in the foreseeable future. At this stage we simply wanted to establish a junior college. Since a junior college only transfers students and does not confer its own degrees, we were quite willing to defer the degree issue until such time when we had achieved an academic track record.

Mr. Ashe, the MPP from the Bowmanville area, was willing to introduce a private members bill in the Legislature. Mr. Bakker sat down with the lawyers of the Legislature to draft the technical aspects of Bill Pr 48. Besides the objects and purposes, which had been agreed to by the Ministry, the main point was the identity of the degrees. We accepted that we would be restricted to granting the Bachelor of Christian Studies (BCS) and Bachelor of Christian Education (BCE) degrees. The final objects and purposes read as follows:

The objects and purposes of the College are to provide, at the post secondary level,

a) for the advancement of learning and dissemination of knowledge on the basis of the Reformed confessions, traditions and perspectives;

b) degree, diploma and certificate programs and courses of study based on Biblical and theological studies in the foundations of Reformed Christian perspectives, which programs and courses may include studies in the general arts, humanities and sciences, both natural and social, permeated by such Scripturally-directed Reformed Christian perspectives, in accordance with the Statement of Basis and Principles as set out in the by-laws of the College;

c) diploma and certificate programs and courses of study in the general arts, humanities and sciences, including both pure and applied natural and social sciences in accordance with the Statement of Basis and Principles as set out in the by-laws of the College;

d) degree programs and courses of study in the general arts, humanities and sciences, including both pure and applied natural and social sciences under the supervision of and pursuant to a written agreement with,

i) a university established under an Act of the Legislative Assembly,

ii) an educational institution established outside Ontario which has the authority to grant non-religious degrees and which the Minister of Colleges and Universities has determined is accredited in its jurisdiction of origin, or

iii) an educational institution not referred to in subclause i or ii with the written consent of the Minister of Colleges and Universities, and

e) diploma and certificate programs and courses of study sponsored jointly with other educational institutions, or with industry or commerce.

These objects and purposes gave us everything we wanted. None of these were changed when the College was given the right to grant the B.A. and the B.Sc. degrees. They remained the same, even when the Act was amended to change the name of the College to Redeemer University College. Thus, the objects and purposes have remained constant throughout our existence. At the time of our first charter, we possessed all the powers of a university, except for the nomenclature of the degrees. For this reason the graduates who had earned the BCS degree were able to exchange that degree for a B.A. or B.Sc. when we received the power to grant them. The programs and courses of study leading to the two types of degrees were the same.

Bill Pr 48 received first reading on November 21, 1980. After Legislative committee, which met the following week. We were invited to represent the College to the committee, and Bert Bakker had prepared a statement, which I read.

Within minutes, the committee accepted all the clauses. However, near the end of our presentation and the committee's discussion, an NDP member on the committee asked us whether or not our students would receive government loans and grants. I answered that we had not discussed this issue with the ministry, and so the ministry was asked for its opinion. Mr. Jamie McKay, who represented the ministry, responded by saying that if the committee would refer the legislation back to the ministry, it would look into the matter. We indicated that we would gladly leave this issue out of the legislation and the discussion, and that we would take this matter up with the appropriate ministry personnel at a future date. The committee approved the private members bill and sent it back to the Legislature.

On December 10, immediately following a question period, the Redeemer College Act was presented for second reading. Only a few members were present in the Legislature. Mr. Robert Nixon, the leader of the Opposition, asked whether the name of the Act was correct. He remembered a different name on an earlier printing. Mr. Ashe was not able to answer that question immediately, but fortunately several of our board and staff members were present and we were able to confirm the name "Redeemer Reformed Christian College." The amended legislation passed a second reading and immediately thereafter it passed third reading. We were elated and grateful to all who had helped to make this moment for the College a reality. Above all, we thanked the Lord for His blessing and for answering the many prayers that had been offered for this successful conclusion.

Mr. Welch congratulated us first. Photographs were taken and later published in *Calvinist Contact* (now *Christian Courier*), a Christian newspaper. It should be noted that, even though we were one of the last of the religious schools to apply for a charter, we were the first school to receive one.

Left to right: Sam Cureatz, chairman of the Legislative committee, Albert J. Bakker, Robert Welch, Dick L. Kranendonk, Henry R. De Bolster, Justin Cooper and Robert Ash.

Finally, we were officially recognised by the government of Ontario. It was the end of a lengthy struggle. Receiving our charter was nothing less than a miracle worked by our heavenly Father. We experienced that miracle intensely. It has always stayed with me. We went through difficult times, but God took away all the obstacles. The evil intent not to allow us to start a college had failed. It serves to remind us that the promises of God will go with us from day to day as long as we remain faithful to the basis of our charter. It is and always will remain my prayer that Redeemer University

College will keep the promises made at that incredible beginning by being faithful to God in giving instruction "on the basis of the Reformed confessions, traditions and perspectives." The miracle magnified when the Legislature was dissolved the day after our charter had received royal assent. A new election brought back a majority Conservative government.

After Bill Pr 48 became law, the board met once again in a retreat setting at the Crief Retreat Centre near Guelph. The board consisted of the following persons, who also signed the charter at that retreat: Rev. Henry R. De Bolster, chairman; Rev. John Zantingh, vice-chairman; Mr. Adrian Guldemond, secretary; Dr. Henry Aay; Mr. Albert J. Bakker; Dr. Philip C. Bom; Dr. Henry Brouwer; Mrs. May Drost; Dr. Remkes Kooistra; Rev. Raymond Sikkema; Dr. Henk Van Andel; Dr. Robert Vander Vennen; Mr. Gary Van Eyk; Mr. John Van Rooyen; Mr. John Vriend; Dr. Albert M. Wolters; and Dr. J. Zeyl. The advisors to the board and employees of OCCA were Mr. Justin Cooper and Mr. Dick Kranendonk. Their hard work and dedication contributed much to the milestone we had reached. I continue to be grateful to them.

We were unified and rejoiced. No longer did we talk about affiliation. We talked about the blessings of God, and John Zantingh offered a meditation. We prayed and gave thanks to God. At that retreat the board made a bold step in faith and decided to open Redeemer College in September 1982 D.V. and to appoint two committees, one to search for a suitable location, and one to commence the search for a president. The fulfillment of these two goals would make our dream a reality.

The board displaying the newly received provincial *Charter*. From left to right, front row: Gary Van Eyk, John Zantingh, Henry R. De Bolster, Adrian Guldemond; second row: Justin Cooper, Raymond Sikkema, May Drost, Jack Zeyl, Robert Vander Vennen, Dick L. Kranendonk; back row: John Vriend, Remkes Kooistra; Albert J. Bakker; Henry Brouwer, Henry Aay, Henk Van Andel, John Van Rooyen, Albert M. Wolters, and Philip C. Bom.

Two

Preparations
for Opening

The board appointed two committees, a staffing committee and a location committee, to search for a president and a suitable location.

The Appointment of the President and the Administrators

The staffing committee met on January 13, 1981. Even though the minutes indicate that I was present at that meeting, I recall that I was absent. I read in the minutes that the committee "reviewed discussions and specific names in discussions, two years ago. The committee also discussed the option of an academic appointment, a pastoral appointment or a combined appointment for the president's position." Several names including my own were recorded.

I remember Rev. John Zantingh phoning me after the meeting and informing me of the inclusion of my name on the list of persons to be considered for the presidency. My response was a good laugh. I felt I was not qualified to be president of an academic institution. I told John that the very thought of being considered was beyond my comprehension. He insisted that the committee was serious in having my name on the list. Some very qualified people had been proposed. Therefore, I thought that my name would soon disappear from the list of candidates. Hence, I did not insist that my name be taken off.

All the candidates were contacted and urged to let their names stand for the position of president of the new college. Several indicated that they were not able to consider the presidency. After lengthy discussions, the committee decided to interview three people. I was one of the three.

These interviews for president took place on Friday, March 27, 1981. The committee wanted to present its nominees to the board, which was scheduled to meet the next day. That Friday I was informed that the committee was going to present two nominees for the office of president to the board. To my utter amazement, these nominees were Dr. Henk Van Andel and myself.

I did not sleep well that night. I could hardly believe that the committee had included me to be a nominee for such an awesome position. I prayed a lot. Certainly, the Lord, who leads all things, must be telling me something very important. Could it be possible that He wanted me to be directly involved in the establishment of this college? Trusting that the Lord does not make mistakes, I released my thoughts and fears into the hands of the Lord. I reminded myself that the other candidate, Dr. Van Andel, had all the academic credentials, which I lacked. Moreover, the appointment had not yet been made. I was merely asked to come for an interview. Incredible as it may sound now, I found comfort in the fact that my interview did not have to result in an actual appointment.

On Saturday, March 28, 1981, the board met in the Dundas Christian Reformed Church. I was interviewed in the morning. I was very nervous, and in response to relatively basic questions, I drew blanks several times. My answers did not always come easily. Dr. Van Andel was interviewed in the afternoon. After the interviews, both Dr. Van Andel and I went to another room of the church and waited for the board's decision. We waited a very long time. The longer it took, the more convinced I became that Dr. Van Andel would be appointed. Finally, after approximately an hour and a half, Dr. Al Wolters called me to follow him to another room. There he informed me that I had been appointed by the board to be the first president of Redeemer College. I could not believe my ears. My emotions got the better of me. I broke down and cried.

The first official announcement of my appointment was made to the council of the Maranatha Christian Reformed Church in St. Catharines. I had served that congregation for almost ten years. The brothers were not surprised. They had expected me to get the appointment because of my involvement with the College from its very beginning. They were kind enough to say that they were sorry to see me go, but encouraged me to accept the appointment. My appointment as president was to be effective June 1, 1981, so I had a few months to say farewell to the congregation. I am sure that all ministers find it difficult to move away from a church where they had served with joy. It was indeed difficult for me because I had established some special relationships. Yet I regarded this appointment as a call in my ministry which I would accept, albeit with trepidation. I was convinced that the Lord would give me the strength to fulfill this awesome task. The words from 1 Thessalonians 5:24: "The one who calls is faithful and he will do it," gave me strength and comfort.

The staffing committee considered which positions, next to the president, needed to be filled first in order to implement the board's decision to open the College in September 1982. To that end it recommended opening two additional administrative positions: acting dean and director of development and business affairs. Of course, an executive secretary was needed as well. The board concurred and advertised for these positions.

The first appointment was director of development and business affairs. Several applications came in and after the normal procedure of interviews, the board appointed Mr. Dick Kranendonk. Dick had been working for the College on a part-time basis ever since Dr. Theodore Plantinga had accepted a teaching position at Calvin College in Grand Rapids in 1980. Dick's full-time work would start at the same time as the president would begin his duties on June 1, 1981. During the remainder of his part-time appointment, Dick visited the Christian high schools to speak to the graduating classes. Dick was well known in the Christian school community because he was also working part-time for the Ontario Alliance of Christian School Societies to assist the schools with their tuition receipting difficulties. His book *Christian Day Schools: Why and How* was also well known in the Christian school community. He encouraged the students who would be graduating in 1982 to apply for admission to a unique institution where they would forever be remembered as the pioneers. In addition to this initial recruiting work, Dick also worked hard at gain-ing new members for the College. These efforts were blessed so that we had about 2,000 members by the time of my inauguration. In 1982, Dick was relieved from the recruitment and fundraising functions when Mr. Arend Kersten was hired to look after these responsibilities for the College.

The position of acting dean was filled very quickly. Mr. Justin Cooper had been working for the College part-time and was willing to become the acting dean on a half-time basis, in addition to his appointment as assistant professor of political science. His new appointment would also begin on June 1. Later, Ms. Jeanette De Boer was hired as our executive secretary. By the middle of August, all three initial positions were filled.

The first staff in the Burlington office: left to right:
Dick L. Kranendonk, Henry R. De Bolster, Jeanette De Boer
and Arend Kersten.

The denominational office of the Christian Reformed Church in Canada was located in Burlington and had space available that suited our needs. We rented these facilities until we moved to the campus on Beach Boulevard in 1982.

Faculty Appointments

The academic affairs committee, which had been in existence during the OCCA years, was mandated by the board to compose a curriculum for the College and to advertise for a faculty. The board had decided to operate a two-year college; hence the committee worked on a two-year program for the years 1982 and 1983. The 1982 instructional program would consist of a pre-university year—the equivalent of Grade 13—and the 1983 program would consist of first year university. This program was accepted by the membership at its May 30, 1981 meeting.

This committee immediately involved itself with the hiring of the faculty. Advertisements appeared in some church related newspapers and magazines, and in *University Affairs*, the paper read by the university community. We received applications from professors at established educational institutions, as well as from some who were engaged in a profitable professional practice. We were amazed at the response we received, since Redeemer had not proven itself as either an academically or financially viable institution. These professors did not only apply, but accepted initial appointments. They were also stepping forward in faith because these pioneer faculty members gave up secure positions; they "burned their bridges behind them" as the saying goes, believing that the Lord called them to this exciting faith enterprise called: Redeemer College.

At the membership meeting of May 30, 1981, I could announce that the following men had accepted their appointments to the College: Mr. J. Bolt - theology; Mr. J. Cooper - political science; Dr. T. Plantinga - philosophy; Dr. H. Van Belle - psychology. Soon afterwards we received word from Drs. Harry Van Dyke - history, that he also accepted his appointment. That only left English in the arts division of the College. We asked Mr. Hugh Cook, who had been teaching at Dordt College for many years, to come over and help us. Again the Lord answered our prayers and Mr. Cook accepted the appointment. We attracted Mr. Peter Bulthuis, vice-principal of the Smithville District Christian High School, to teach geography on a part-time basis.

Appointments in the "arts" were now complete, but our college needed to be a broadly based academic institution in the arts and sciences, so we needed to make some appointments in the science division as well. Again we approached some well-established scholars, and we were very pleased when Dr. Wytse (Vince) Van Dyk, professor of physics at Dordt College, accepted the appointment as professor of physics and mathematics. The only vacancy left was in the area of biology and chemistry. Dr. Jitse Vander Meer, who was teaching at Purdue University in Lafayette, Indiana, came to our attention. He was a biologist, who was willing to consider a move to Canada. When we contacted him and had explained who we were and what we were trying to accomplish, he expressed his willingness to come for an interview. The interview went well and we asked him to join us at Redeemer College. However, he was a Dutch citizen and was teaching in the U.S.A., which made it next to impossible for him to gain entry into our country. The Immigration Department told us to hire a Canadian. We explained our unique situation: a Reformed Christian college, with a special charter. Then Immigration advised us to get permission from the Human Rights Commission to discriminate on the basis of religion. We applied and received that permission very quickly. That letter was kept on file and whenever necessary we would and could use it.

The next hurdle was to help Dr. Vander Meer who had already applied at the Canadian Consulate in Chicago to immigrate to Canada. There he met Mr. Bill Van Staalduinen, one of the consuls. Mr. van Staalduinen was a member of Redeemer College and was able to expedite Dr. Vander Meer's application. Very soon we received the news that Jitse had obtained a visa and that he would be able to start when the College would open its doors in September 1982. Today Mr. van Staalduinen is the vice-president of development at the College and the executive director of the Redeemer Foundation.

The Lord had provided in a remarkable way. Every professor who accepted his appointment was our first choice in his area of expertise. What a blessing! In our student recruitment we could assure prospective students that they would receive an education which would be second to none. The supporters of the College would also be pleased that the board decided to include as a condition for employment at the College that "all faculty and senior administrative staff from senior secretary and above must be active members in the Christian community and that this must be evident in regular church attendance and in support of and participation in Christian day school education at the elementary and secondary levels."

A Community College?

At the membership meeting on May 30, 1981, the question was raised whether a new liberal arts college was adequate. The concern was for those students not entering a B.A. program. A formal motion was made to keep those students in mind. The motion read:

> We affirm the preparatory work the College Board and Staff has done for laying the groundwork for Redeemer College. We would suggest the following advice and that it be resolved that the Board study and report to a future meeting of the membership, how those students who are not entering a full Liberal Arts B.A. Program will be attracted to Redeemer College. We especially encourage study in the following areas:
>
> a. Potential credit transfer to the Community Colleges
> b. The possibility of streaming the program to serve a larger segment of our youth
> c. The possibility of a Certificate program (to attract non-college, undecided, or pre-program students)
> d. The promotion of Redeemer to those students who are not geared for a Liberal Arts B.A.

This motion passed and the board asked me to study the matter and to report back. I appointed a committee of four people, who spent nearly a year studying the question of a one-year program for students who would later study at community colleges. It was a difficult assignment for the committee. When it reported to me, the recommendation was to ask the College to see what could be done for these students if they were to take professional courses in addition to a liberal arts program. I handed the report to the academic affairs committee, which urged extreme care not to depart from the original purpose of the College. After much discussion, it was decided to include a certificate program, which would assist the students mentioned in the resolution. This program would consist of core courses, including theology, philosophy, English and a science course and could easily be added to our curriculum, since our charter already spelled out a certificate program.

In this connection I felt it necessary to write a memo to the faculty members, in order to keep them up-to-date, and to ask them for their input in this and other important matters. This memo was written on March 29, 1982, and read as follows:

Plea for Some Aims and Objectives of Redeemer College

This is a first and humble attempt to make a beginning at formulating some of the aims and objectives of our College. I would like you to read them critically, to work them out, adding to them or subtracting from them as you see fit, and to send your response to me, so that we will have a better idea of what we have in mind when we begin our College.

One of the aims of our College is the matter of academic excellence. We wish to be second to none. That is why we searched far and wide for a qualified faculty, and, at least in that regard, the Lord has blessed us by sending you men to us.

Of course, the standards of our school will be determined to a large extent by other institutions of higher learning. I refer particularly to the Christian colleges in Alberta and the United States, but secondly, and not less important, to the secular universities around us. It will be very important how McMaster University judges the courses, the course outlines and the qualifications of our faculty. I hope that we will never compromise the academic quality of the instruction given at our College. It is indeed my hope, wish and prayer that our College will receive a reputation of excellence in the academic world. That will very much depend on how we work together as a faculty, and how willing we are to listen to each other, so that we will work as a team, rather than as individuals.

In the second place, I want Redeemer College to be a school that will meet the needs of the constituency. That, of course, is something new. Often times a college sets the goals, the courses and the program for the college, and not very often do we find a school which listens to the needs of its constituency.

When I discussed this matter with the other presidents of our Christian Colleges, I found a change in thinking. They agreed that, until recently, the colleges set the programs, which were always theoretical and abstract. A liberal arts college was a college where academic instruction was given to the students in order to prepare them for further study. The students would receive as broad and general an education as could possibly be given, but further study in graduate work was more or less expected at graduation. That is changing rapidly. The colleges in the US have already determined that the education should be much more practical and much more career oriented. That is why Calvin just added its nursing program; Dordt has its agricultural program and even a two-year program leading to an associate degree; and Trinity Christian has many applied arts programs.

Our concept of community colleges, it seems to me, is that the work has a strong practical concept while the programs in the States are very much academic. The student is still confronted with the questions of the "why," in addition to the "how." Only The King's College opposes this trend and wants to remain strictly a liberal arts College. I do not know how long The King's will be able to function that way.

When we were planning to open the College and visited different high schools, we asked the students why they studied, what their plans for the future were, etc. You can imagine how many different answers we received, and yet there were three programs which came through consistently. There were many students who wanted to become a teacher. Then, quite a few, especially in the rural areas, indicated their intent to be better farmers and were looking for a program of study in agriculture. A number of students were looking forward to go into business and were looking for courses dealing with business administration. I think all three areas are career oriented. Even teaching is not strictly liberal arts, but is an applied course of study.

We discussed this matter with the Ontario Alliance of Christian School Societies, and they asked us to set aside our Bachelor of Christian Education degree as the equivalent to the Bachelor of Education degree. The Christian Farmer's Federation pleaded with us to do something for the students, who go into farming. They asked us to pay particular attention to environmental studies. The business people asked us: "Can you please prepare some of our young people to become Christian business people, who are not only qualified, but who also know what it means to be in business from a Christian perspective?"

It seems to me that we must be open to the several possibilities before us. If we enter the discussion with an open mind, I am sure that we will be able to come up with a course of study that will be academically sound and meet the needs of the constituency. I believe that Dordt College could help us a great deal. I am referring to their publication "The Educational Task of Dordt College," which says among other things the following about the content of education:

Members of the body of Christ need the ability to distinguish sharply, to think critically and to judge wisely. In their daily lives they are continually confronted by the difficulties and problems of our age. National and international tensions enter their homes through the media; political and economic problems touch their everyday lives; and the power of technology and mass communications affects them all. In addition, Christians are surrounded by the subtle influences of the secular spirits of our century. Coping with these multi-dimensional problems requires an advanced level of insight. Furthermore, many vocations and occupations have been professionalized to the extent that broad knowledge and a wide range of skills frequently are prerequisites for one's career. Hence, as our civilization advances, more and more insight is needed, not only by leaders, but by every Christian as he seeks to do the Lord's bidding in our complex culture.

In this connection we are confronted with the request of the membership to look into the matter of community colleges. As you remember, we already discussed this request at our last faculty meeting, and I mailed the report of the committee to you, together with the recommendations of the academic affairs committee. I do not quite know what to do with these reports and I would like to receive your input. I wonder whether it would not be possible to advise the students who intend to go to community colleges: "Please invest one year of your life in receiving Christian instruction, in which the perspectives of life will open up for you and which will be very beneficial for you in your further studies."

Perhaps, we can spell out a core program, which these students could take. Perhaps, these courses should be the same as the courses taken by our own students. We could conceivably lighten the load by requiring four courses instead of six, and we should spell out the courses they should take. Right now I would be inclined to say that these students take Religion and Theology, Philosophy, History and English. But then again, this is only an initial response to a complex problem and I would appreciate your thinking and input. It would be great if I could come with a unified recommendation to the Board and to the membership, and make a principial decision in this matter.

Furthermore, I want the education at our College to be thoroughly Reformed. It is going to be of the utmost importance to share and discuss what we believe the Reformed perspective of the College to be. I want to share with you my fear that the Christian Reformed Church, from which we will receive the bulk of our students, is in danger of moving into the direction of, what I would call, a generally Christian Church. Both fundamentalism and liberalism are creeping in. In subtle ways this comes through from different pulpits. The conservative element in the church is not helpful either, and so, we will have to consolidate our resources and stick together as a faculty, convinced as we are of the Reformed principles.

I know that Kuyper already talked about Reformed principles, and even though attempts have been made to define what is meant, the Reformed community has not been very successful in doing so.

Nevertheless, I am convinced that we all know that we are talking about the sovereignty of God, the infallibility of the Scriptures; the creation of man in God's image and thus his calling to be God's officebearer to serve the Lord; sin, which is radical, and which has changed humans in the root of their existence. We must proclaim that sin is still a reality. Sometimes the impression is created that because Christ conquered, we have been fully restored. In principle we are restored, but sin is still very much with us and plays an important role in our behaviour and direction. I hope that this element will not be forgotten in the instruction. Of course, the centre of our instruction is the Lord Jesus Christ, whom we honour and glorify. He is the One who suffered, died, but arose from the dead and sits at the right hand of God, the Father. It is in Christ that we have received renewal.

We also want to emphasise the Biblical teaching of the covenant; that God established His covenant with the believers and their children, and that, therefore, we are not in the College, first of all, to convert young people, but to place before them the tremendous calling they have to respond to God as citizens of His Kingdom. Of course, the Kingdom of God must receive a central place, and that Kingdom is here and now. Let us make sure that the direction of the Kingdom and the behaviour in the Kingdom will be taught and lived. I hope that we as teachers will be examples to our students in the way we speak, behave and dress. Students need to know that education is life itself, not only while they are in school, but until they die. Hence the perspective of that education determines for whom they live. Life is religion.

These are just a few thoughts I wanted to share with you. I asked you at the beginning to give them some thought. Please do. As I already said, you may make changes, expand on it, cut from it, as long as the main message, which I tried to communicate remains true. May God richly bless you as you prepare to come to us. I can hardly wait until July rolls around. Then we will be able to sit down more often and discuss these very important matters. Thank you very much for listening, men. Thanks for your dedication, thanks for your faith. May God be with you and with us, as we prepare for the beginning of the instruction at our College.

> Sincerely yours,
> Henry R. De Bolster
> President

I only received positive comments from the faculty members in response to this communication.

Investiture and Ministerial Credentials of the President

The highlight in the early stages of the College was the investiture of the president. The board decided that the inauguration of the president should not wait until the official opening of the College, but that it would be good to install the president earlier. People needed to be convinced that we were serious about opening the College in 1982. Reformation Day, 1981, appealed to all. After all, Redeemer College wanted to be a college of the Reformation, hence, October 31 was chosen as the date of my installation.

The inauguration took place in the Centenary United Church in Hamilton. It was a beautiful, sunny day. All preparations were made. Guests arrived on time and the ceremony started at two o'clock in the afternoon. I make mention of these details because the installation almost did not take place. On Wednesday, October 28, I developed a pain in my left arm so severe that I went to see my doctor. Unfortunately, he was not in his office and I proceeded to the emergency department in the hospital. When I told the nurse at the desk of the pain in my arm, she immediately arranged for me to be seen by a doctor. I could not understand why I received this sudden attention, while the waiting room was full of patients. It became rather clear to me when the doctor told me that he was afraid that I had suffered, or would suffer a heart attack. I was admitted to the hospital and promptly wheeled into the intensive care unit overnight. That was a night I will not soon forget. All kinds of thoughts went through me. Is my heart bad? Can I be president? I prayed a lot that night and I found rest in the knowledge that I was safely in the hands of the Lord, and if the Lord wanted me to be president of Redeemer College, He would also take care that everything would fall in place.

The next morning I was examined again, x-rays were taken and by noon, I was diagnosed as having a pinched nerve in my neck, which caused the pain in my arm. The relief was exhilarating when I was told that I could go home. The cardiologist told me that he wanted to make sure that it was not my heart that was causing the problem, and so he insisted that I would take a stress test the following day. The stress test showed that my heart was not the problem, and the doctor gave his permission to go on with the installation the next day. You can imagine the anxiety and relief felt by the staff. We thanked the Lord and we asked Him to help us in the last preparations for the big event and to bless the ceremony itself.

Rev. John Zantingh was in charge and led the service. Many representatives of other institutions and organisations were present. Rev. Arie VanEek represented the Christian Reformed Church in North America. The Christian Reformed Church had decided in its classical assemblies in Ontario, that Redeemer College was its regional college and therefore eligible to receive financial support from the churches. Mr. John Stronks, education coordinator of the Ontario Alliance of Christian School Societies, represented the Christian school movement in Ontario. Dr. Bernard Zylstra, principal of the Institute for Christian Studies was there, as well as the presidents of our sister colleges: Dr. Anthony Diekema, Calvin College; Rev. Bernard J. Haan, Dordt College; Dr. Gerald Van Groningen, Trinity Christian College; and Dr. Sidney C.J. De Waal, The King's College.

The first faculty members. Left to right: Justin Cooper,
Harry Van Dyke, Hugh Cook, Henry R. De Bolster, John Bolt, Theodore Plantinga
and Harry Van Belle.

I was especially delighted that all the appointed faculty members were present at the installation. Even though they would not take up their employment with the College until the summer of 1982, it was a moment of great joy for me, and all those present, when I introduced them to the audience. They were: Mr. John Bolt, Mr. Hugh Cook, Mr. Justin Cooper, Dr. Theodore Plantinga, Dr. Harry Van Belle and Drs. Harry Van Dyke.

The program was well prepared. Mr. Harry Der Nederlanden composed a meaningful litany in which the greatness of God was honoured, the reality of sin confessed and the miracle of our calling in the service of the Kingdom of God masterfully presented. Rev. Zantingh conducted the investiture with the following words:

> "In the name of God, our Creator and Redeemer, to whom we totally belong, upon the authorization of the Board of Governors, and as a member of the body of Christ gathered here as witnesses, I do invest you, Henry R. De Bolster, with the office of President of Redeemer Reformed Christian College, and with all the rights, privileges and responsibilities of that office. May you, by the grace of God, dignify your office with wisdom, leadership, devotion and godliness. In token of this investiture, we clasp hands in confirmation and covenant."

The audience responded by saying:

> "As members and loyal friends of Redeemer College, we pledge you our praying hearts and supporting hands, that we all may live unto the glory of God, and for the coming of Christ's everlasting Kingdom through this academic institution."

Dr. Carl Kaiser, associate professor of music at Calvin College stirred all of us by singing several solos.

My inaugural address was entitled "The Witness and Foundation of Redeemer Reformed Christian College." I emphasised that Redeemer College was founded out of obedience to the Word of the Lord. In carrying out this obedience I pointed to the fact that God demands from his people a response. This response comes to expression not only in our confession and commitment (the "why" of the College), but also in our focus and direction (the "how" of the College).

The ceremony was moving. It impressed on me both the tremendous privilege as well as the awesome responsibility that rested on my shoulders. At the same time, I knew that the Lord would guide me and that the prayers of God's people would accompany me. During the reception, a few of my colleagues spoke to me personally and all of them indicated the same thing namely: "Remember this day for a long time and pray for similar highlights and experiences like this. You'll need them in days to come. It's a good thing that you do not exactly know what the future will bring." Ominous words, spoken from experience. They were right; our young institution was to face many challenges, disappointments, unfair criticisms, questions that could not be answered easily. But, through it all, the certain knowledge that I was doing the work of the Lord never disappeared.

I regarded my appointment as president to be a call from the Lord as a minister of the Word in the Christian Reformed Church. Since I moved from St. Catharines to Burlington, I approached the Burlington church and asked that church to call me as associate pastor to work as president at Redeemer College. My request was discussed at a council meeting of that church in July 1981. The minutes of that meeting tell us that the request was tabled until the August meeting, because a number of officebearers were on vacation. The brothers were urged to read the letter carefully, so that a decision could be made in August.

This careful study was initiated because Synod 1981 of the Christian Reformed Church in North America had decided that the function of a president of a Christian college was not ecclesiastical in nature. Therefore, a minister of the Word, who accepted the presidency of a college, would lose his ministerial status. That seemed to be a very clear decision by synod. It appeared to prevent the Burlington church from granting my request. However, another president of a church related Christian college had been permitted to retain his ministerial status. Consequently, there was a contradiction in practice. Moreover, even though the synod of the Christian Reformed Church had decided that the president in question could not retain his ministerial status, the classis where his credentials had been accepted had not yet made the decision to withdraw his ministerial credentials. On the contrary, that classis decided to appeal synod's decision to the synod of 1982. Hence the execution of synod's 1981 decision was postponed.

In August, the consistory of the Burlington church accepted the following motion:

> That the Burlington Christian Reformed Church become the calling church of Rev. De Bolster in accordance with article 12c of the Church Order. And that our consistory request Classis for permission to become the calling church for Rev. De Bolster.

Article 12c of the Church Order reads:

> A minister of the Word may also serve the church in other work which relates directly to his calling, but only after the calling church has demonstrated to the satisfaction of Classis, with the concurring advice of the synodical deputies, that said work is consistent with the calling of a minister.

One of the elders of that church disagreed with the decision of the Burlington church consistory, and appealed to the same classis meeting where Burlington's request was on the agenda. Classis Hamilton met on September 23, 1981, in the Rehoboth Christian Reformed Church in Niagara Falls. The synodical deputies, who represent synod, were present as well. They are the persons who make sure that the rules and decisions of synod are applied correctly. Both the requests of the Burlington Church and the appeal of the elder from Burlington were given in the hands of an advisory committee. The minutes of that classis meeting read as follows:

Re: Ministerial Status

Article 23

The appeals committee reports, Rev. Van Weelden reporting: The matter deals with an appeal by a member of the Burlington consistory in regards to the decision of this consistory to call Rev. De Bolster as Associate Pastor of the church:

1. The motion that the appeal was legally before us, CARRIED
2. The recommendation that Classis do not sustain the appellant in his appeal, after much discussion during which time the appeal was read, was CARRIED
3. The motion that Classis give permission to Burlington to call Rev. De Bolster as Associate Pastor as President of Redeemer College, for a term of two years, after which his ministerial status will be reviewed by Classis: ADOPTED—with the concurring advice of two Synodical Deputies, and the non-concurrence of one of them.

Classis was of the opinion that after two years this matter would be cleared up. Synod of 1982 discussed the appeal of the decision of synod 1981 and sustained the appeal. Synod, by that decision, allowed a minister of the Word to retain his ministerial status when he accepts the presidency of a Christian college.

Following the decision of synod of 1982, the Burlington Church addressed Classis Hamilton with the request to be permitted "to continue its relationship with Rev. De Bolster as its associate pastor to function as president of Redeemer Reformed Christian College." That permission was granted, and I could retain my ministerial status in the Christian Reformed Church.

The president, staff and faculty were in place, but we did not yet have students. In addition, we did not yet have the financial resources that would be needed. How were we going to finance a project like Redeemer College? Perhaps those in the feasibility study were right, when they made the point that we could not expect much more from a financially overburdened constituency. Yet that thought never occurred to me. I was convinced that we were doing the Lord's will and that He would provide. Of course the Lord answers prayer, but He expects us to work hard. It is still *Ora et Labora*. Both Dick and Justin were of the same opinion, and we sat down many times to consider how to secure the necessary funds and how to attract the students to make the College a viable institution.

Fundraising

At my inauguration, we had a membership of about 2,000. A very good beginning, but the funds that the membership fees brought in would not be enough to finance a college. We believed that Redeemer College should be the college of the entire Christian community. Hence we decided to make a beginning at expanding our base by visiting and communicating with the primary support community, the Christian Reformed Church congregations in Ontario. But it would be impossible to do all that work with the two-and-a-half people, and our secretary. Early in 1982, we heard that Mr. Arend Kersten would be available for fundraising and student recruitment. We hired Arend who did a good job of promoting the College. I dare say that his enthusiasm and determination brought our student enrollment for the first year far beyond our expectations. He was a tireless worker, visiting the Christian high schools and individual students many times. He was able to persuade students to give our young institution a try. We owe Arend a lot of thanks for the excellent student recruitment work he did.

In addition to the recruitment work, Arend was also our main fundraiser. The board instructed the staff to come with a workable fundraising plan. After many discussions between Arend, Dick and myself, Arend came with an idea, which we called "the seventeen-cents plan." The intent of the plan was to visit all the Christian Reformed churches in Ontario and to ask their members to contribute seventeen cents per day for the development of the College. It was to be something like "het VU busje" in Holland. Many of our older members who had immigrated from the Netherlands remember the Free University in Amsterdam. This university was supported by the "kleine luiden" (literally, the "little people"; the common folk in contrast to the rich and famous) who daily deposited their pennies in a little can (a piggy bank) for the development of the Free University. Arend suggested that we do something similar. The board gave its blessing to the plan and we looked for a church where we would introduce this fundraising idea.

The Woodstock and Ingersoll churches were chosen for our pilot project. We knew that it would be impossible to get 100 percent participation, but we estimated that if 25 to 30 percent of the people would participate, we would be able to collect between $7,000 and $11,000 in the Ingersoll/Woodstock area. If that goal could be reached, the seventeen-cent plan could be rolled out across the province. We were well received in Woodstock. Quite a few people in attendance encouraged us to go to the churches with this seventeen-cent plan. People pledged $11,000 that evening. How grateful we were, and following the Ingersoll/Woodstock experience, we mailed our plan to many Christian Reformed churches in Ontario.

In preparation for the province-wide fundraising drive, Arend and I visited many ministers. It was a good thing we did. In these face-to-face conversations, we heard, first-hand, the reactions of the congregations about the plan to open Redeemer College in 1982 and our fundraising plan to make that goal possible. We heard that most ministers and their congregations supported the establishment of the College. Only a few ministers were not in favour of starting a Christian college in Ontario. Some were of the opinion that we should not have opted for a "limited charter" as they called it. They believed that we should have either insisted on a charter with general-degree granting powers, including the B.A. and B.Sc. degrees, or not accept a charter at all. Some worried about the funds that the College would need as they were convinced that the burdens on God's people were too much already. They believed that another "seventeen-cent scheme" would turn people off. We listened carefully. We were of the opinion that if it were not possible to get the support of the ministers, it would be even more difficult to convince the members of the church to contribute to Redeemer College. We were reminded that a "piggy bank" plan was already in operation in many of the churches for the benefit of the local elementary Christian school and the area Christian high school.

Back to the drawing board we went and settled for different initiatives. As I mentioned earlier, we had approached the Christian Reformed Churches for "quota" support. Let me explain what that quota support was all about. Calvin College, an undergraduate college in Grand Rapids, Michigan, was effectively "owned and controlled" by the Christian Reformed Church in North America. The annual budget of Calvin had to be approved by the synod of the Christian Reformed denomination. It was, therefore, also the obligation of the denomination to finance that college. This financing was done by means of a quota, set annually by synod. The quota was the amount of money that each family within the denomination was expected to contribute for the work of the denomination and its agencies, including the denominational college.

In 1962, synod decided that area colleges, like Dordt College and Trinity Christian College, should also share in this quota system. These colleges were attended by students belonging to the Christian Reformed Church, many of whom would have gone to Calvin College, if these regional colleges had not been in existence. Churches that acknowledged a regional college were permitted to subtract an amount, set by synod, from the Calvin College quota and to give that money, saved from the Calvin quota, to the regional college. All area churches could determine through decisions made by their classes whether the college in their area would be their regional college. Because of this 1962 decision, Redeemer College approached the churches in Ontario and asked them to declare Redeemer College as their regional college. This would permit the churches to contribute the amount saved from the Calvin College quota to Redeemer College. Arend, Dick and I visited all the classes in Ontario and asked them to declare Redeemer College as their regional college. All the classes responded favourably, and every year until my retirement, I visited all these classes annually and presented the churches with an update on the College.

In 1982, we began to receive some of that quota money. In the beginning some of the churches did not quite know what to do and used the difference between the Calvin quota and the regional college quota to lower their quota payments. Other churches only gave the College a small portion of the designated amount. Yet I am very grateful to the churches for that initial support given to the College. The amount of church support increased every year and became a substantial amount as the years went by. The money from the churches was used for student support. These funds made it possible for many students to attend Redeemer College.

Next to the annual visits to the classes, I continued to visit individual churches. Both Arend and I were present at many congregational meetings. I continued to preach in many churches, and most of the time I was given the privilege to speak to the congregation about the work of the College after the services.

Obviously, we also contacted businesses owned and operated by members of the Christian Reformed community. Initially, Arend wrote 140 letters to the business people. Their responses were disappointing. In retrospect we were too idealistic. We were excited about the College, so we expected everybody else to be excited, too. In our own enthusiasm we made mistakes. We followed up the letters with phone calls, rather than with personal visits. Some negative responses actually helped us to communicate in a more meaningful way next time.

Fundraising is difficult. Not everyone is skilled at soliciting funds. When I first started this activity, I felt very uncomfortable. People would ask all kinds of questions about the College. Then, at the end of answering their questions, they would say, "Sorry, we have already decided where to give this year and you are not in the picture." At times I felt like a beggar, who, with cap in hand, was asking for a gift, and who, like so many beggars, was sent away empty-handed.

I learned fast. I reasoned, "I am not asking for myself, but I represent a cause in which I firmly believe." Moreover, even in the beginning and later on more often, someone would come through in a remarkable way. I have had people give me such large donations, that I left trembling, with tears in my eyes, thanking God for the love shown to this part of His Kingdom. It became a privilege for me to visit these people and to experience the joy with which these gifts were made. I have never seen anyone grumble who gave me a substantial donation. It was always a laugh or a tear. So often I heard donors say how privileged they felt to be able to give money which, according to their own testimony, was God's, given to them to manage for Him.

As we visited the churches, we also tried to gain members for the College. The fee was set at $10 per month or $120 per year. Seniors and students under the age of twenty-five were asked to pay $5 per month or $60 per year. This membership fee never changed. It has made it possible for many people, who could not give larger gifts, to be part of Redeemer College.

We needed money to pay for an actual campus as well. We might want to buy a suitable facility, or rent and do some renovating. I was convinced that it would not be possible to raise additional donations for that purpose. Hence, I suggested that we ask our members to lend us money which the College would pay back from an amount that would be included in the budget. We hoped that most of the loans would carry a low interest rate, or no interest at all. In March we sent out 2,300 small brochures explaining our goal, as well as a form, on which the member could indicate the amount of the loan he or she could afford to make. The emphasis was totally on loans, not on gifts. An advertising agency had told us that in a mailing of the size we had sent, we should be very happy if 5 percent responded. By June we had received 247 pledges, more than 10 percent of the mailing, for a total amount of $264,350. Included in this amount were donations totalling $30,000. What a blessing! What an encouragement! We had stepped forward in faith, and the Lord answered mightily.

The board agonised over the budget for the opening year 1982-1983. It appeared that we would need $1 million! We were shocked and convinced that such a budget could not be carried by students and constituency. We cut as much as we responsibly could, which included a voluntary cut in pay by the senior administrators, and the president. When everything was said and done, a budget of $800,000 was adopted by the board and accepted by the membership. Quite a challenge, but one which could be met with the Lord's help.

Student Recruitment

Student recruitment is always a priority in every college and university. How could one attract students to a new institution, which had only a few professors, no facilities, and where credit transfer was not assured in all circumstances. The sister Christian colleges in the U.S.A. promised to accept the credits earned by our students, but the universities in Ontario were only willing to look at our students if they would finish the Grade 13 equivalent year with good marks. Fortunately, there was a lot of enthusiasm for the new college, and most principals of the Christian high schools supported our efforts. Nevertheless, it was a very difficult task.

Our research indicated that most of the students who graduated from high school did not continue their studies. Of the small percentage that did go on, most attended secular universities and community colleges. Our first challenge would be to change the mind of those students who intended to enrol at secular universities. In our discussions with our sister colleges, we discovered that all of them were faced with the same dilemma. Why do students choose to go to secular schools when Christian education is available? Had the time not come for the college presidents to meet with pastors and high school principals, to discuss that trend? Should we, together, explore the question whether this trend could be reversed?

A conference was arranged for February 4 and 5, 1982, in Chicago. Arend and I went to represent the College. Mr. Ren Siebenga, principal of the Durham District Christian High School in Bowmanville, and Mr. Wayne Drost, principal of London District Christian High School, came with us as representatives of our region. Approximately thirty people met, and for two days we discussed the question: "Why do so many Christian Reformed young people attend secular universities, rather than our Christian colleges?"

The group was divided into small discussion groups and each group had representation from colleges, high schools and churches. Many different points of view were presented. Let me mention some of them.

It was acknowledged that students have a lot of choice. Many universities and colleges invite them to apply, very often with tempting promises of scholarships. Moreover, a liberal arts education was becoming less and less popular. Universities train for specific professions and students are encouraged to take courses in their particular field of interest, rather than in a wide variety of disciplines. Why should an engineering student, for example, take history or philosophy courses, it was argued. Cost was identified as another factor since private education is much more expensive than public education.

More important, we discussed where we as a Christian community fell short. How seriously did we take our covenant promises? Did the home, the church and the Christian schools still teach and proclaim obedience to the Lord? Was it more important to obtain an education where Christ is at the centre of learning rather than to go to an educational institution where Christ is negated and often ridiculed? It was noted that students often considered a degree from University X more beneficial for their future than a degree from Christian College Y. Whether that pleased the Lord did not occur to them. Did parents help these students with these life-altering decisions? Did the churches still proclaim these responsibilities to both parents and students? In other words: was Christian education a priority or an option? Did we regularly pray for our Christian schools? We came to the conclusion that the churches should be much more diligent in promoting Christian education from the pulpit and in praying for the Lord's blessing on Christian education. Some remarked that it was fairly rare to hear a sermon about Christian education in general, let alone a plea to choose Christian higher education.

Unfortunately, not much has changed since that conference. The indifference of many students, parents and churches toward Christian schools and colleges/universities continues. I pray to the Lord for renewal, so that Christian education at all levels will remain a covenantal necessity and not an option that can be taken or ignored. I applaud the many people who tirelessly work in and for our schools, and who do everything possible to help our students understand that this world belongs to God, and that we are privileged to live for our Lord.

The colleges were urged not to compete with each other as they had in the past. We were asked whether it would be possible for the five colleges to combine their advertising efforts and urge students, especially at young people's conventions, to choose a Christian college rather than urging students to disregard College A in order to study at College B. The colleges took that admonition to heart. For several years, advertisements appeared in which the five liberal arts colleges (Calvin, Dordt, Trinity Christian, The King's and Redeemer) unitedly promoted Christian higher education. I particularly remember the advertisement in the *Banner*, the official publication of the Christian Reformed Church, of the egg with the five yolks.

It was a worthwhile conference. We went home encouraged and determined to do our part in the promotion of Christian education. The trip back home was not very pleasant as we drove for eleven hours on snowy and slippery roads. We were thankful to be safely home again.

It would indeed be a challenge for the College to meet its target of fifty students as Dr. Vander Vennen had suggested in his feasibility study report. Initially, it had been primarily Dick Kranendonk's task to recruit students. He did most of the recruiting and occasionally I went with him or I went by myself. We were utterly amazed that we had 69 applicants by March 1982. However, at that time it was not certain that even one of those would attend Redeemer College, even though most of the 69 had indicated Redeemer College as their first choice.

When Mr. Arend Kersten joined us early in 1982, he had to inform all the applicants that they were not eligible for any financial assistance from the government, such as Canada Student Loans—that assistance became reality when we had been in existence for one year. Four years later, our students also became eligible for the grants and loans under the Ontario Student Assistance Plan. We made sure that the applicants knew that we would do our utmost to give them financial assistance. It had been decided to assist our students with the regional college quota savings funds that would come from the churches of the Christian Reformed denomination in Eastern Canada.

I am sure that it would have been helpful if we could have told our students where the College would be located, but that was not possible. We were able to tell the applicants that tuition and housing would be lower than at Calvin and Dordt. Later we heard from our students that both Calvin and Dordt promised to meet our cost, which made it even more miraculous that students even considered Redeemer. Yet by July 1, we had received 103 applications. When we contacted these students, 90 told us that they had decided to enrol at our college. Most of these applications came from students who were graduating from Christian high schools in Ontario, but some mature students and some Grade 13 students indicated their intention to come as well. We were especially surprised to hear that two students from the island of Dominica were going to join us. These two young men wanted to become pastors in the Methodist church in the Carribean. They were excited that someone was willing to support them to study at Redeemer. What a blessing and what a responsibility!

Even though we had not officially opened, that summer we taught courses in education for teachers in cooperation with Calvin College. It was a moving moment for me to be able to conduct the opening devotions for these summer courses on July 5, 1982. That same morning I welcomed our faculty. Our staff had made the necessary preparations for that moment. Together we read Scripture, thanked the Lord for the safe arrival of the faculty and prayed that He would give us his indispensable blessing on the work which was about to begin.

When Labour Day 1982 arrived, we welcomed not fifty, not seventy-five, but ninety-seven students, who were ready to begin their studies at an institution that could not promise much, except an excellent, scripturally-directed education. I praised God for those first students, who soon became known as the pioneer students at Redeemer College.

THREE

Selecting the Site

When the board appointed a location committee in December 1981, it gave the committee the following criteria in order of preference:

1. That the College be located off-campus, but in proximity of a provincial university. The word proximity is defined to include the following ideas:
   a. The College should have its own campus,
   b. the closer to the university the better,
   c. that participation in the larger academic community is a desirable and worthwhile objective,
   d. close in this case is thought to be between 20 and 30 minutes on foot, or by public transportation, but not further,
   e. it was agreed that accessibility was really a function of proximity.
2. That the College should have adequate facilities for a complete program and for the eventual growth of a distinct and independent academic community.
3. That the College should be accessible to the larger Christian community in terms of two concepts:
   a. in terms of the Province, it should be centrally located among the major centres,
   b. it should be accessible by public transportation.
4. That the College be located in a strong support community. A strong supporting community would be a Christian Reformed Church community, which had a proven record of financial and spiritual support for Christian education in all its facets and dimensions.

5. That the cost of the campus in terms of both capital outlay and maintenance be reasonable for the community.
6. That the location be such that prospects for good working relations with provincial universities not be jeopardized.
7. That the location be such that part-time staff be readily available.
8. That the campus location be such that special programs, which would require special facilities be available at the provincial universities, such as environmental studies, education and agriculture, and accessible to the students of Redeemer College.
9. That the location have good possibilities for regular student employment.
10. That the campus would accommodate ten years of potential growth to a student body of 1,000 students.
11. That the location be such that housing for staff and faculty be financially feasible to the average academic.

Where would we find such a location? Some of the board members wanted to locate in St. Catharines. Others preferred Waterloo. The board also visited a reform school in Bowmanville, a school which the government was vacating. But that location was far from any university, and after a visit to the school, we came to the conclusion that too many alterations were needed to make it suitable for our purposes.

We were helped in our selection by a meeting with Dr. Alvin A. Lee, president of McMaster University in Hamilton. Dr. Lee was introduced to the College by Dr. David Humphreys, a fine Christian academic, who was a dean and a professor of chemistry at McMaster. Dr. Humphreys had heard about our efforts to start a Christian college and became an enthusiastic supporter. He arranged a meeting of some staff and some board members with Dr. Lee. Dr. Bob Vander Vennen, who had been involved at Trinity Christian College in Palos Heights, told Dr. Lee how Trinity Christian started as a junior college with students transferring from Trinity Christian to other institutions after two years of study. He explained how Trinity Christian was financed and how it operated independently without affiliation with any other institution. Dr. Lee was impressed and showed a great deal of interest in our plans. He even suggested the possibility of renting a school close to the University.

After the meeting with Dr. Lee the same group met with the location committee and reported on a new location possibility for the College. The prospect of locating in Hamilton suddenly eliminated the discussion between the St. Catharines and Waterloo proponents. It only took a few moments for the committee to recommend to the boards "that the general area for locating the College be the Hamilton/Burlington area." This recommendation was adopted unanimously by the board and accepted by the membership on May 30, 1981. That membership meeting also decided "that the board be and is hereby authorised to set September 1982 as the opening date of the College on a full-time basis."

The Upper James Street Property

Two days after the membership meeting, I began my work as president of the College, together with Dick Kranendonk and Justin Cooper. One of the first things we did was to contact a number of real estate agents asking them to search for a suitable property to house our students as well as suitable facilities for our academic programs. These agents told us immediately that it would be very difficult to find such facilities. That proved to be true, because we received no proposals from any of them until September, even though I regularly reminded them of our needs.

In September one agent came to us who informed us of a suitable property on Upper James Street. It was not a large building, but we thought it would be able to house us for two or three years. Not ideal, but if this was the only building available after a three-month search we needed to take action. We made a conditional offer on the building, with the condition that the zoning would be for institutional use. A further condition was that the board and the membership would also need to approve the purchase. The board, however, rejected the purchase, and therefore we decided to cancel the membership meeting.

The owner of the building became very angry. He accused us of a breach of contract and threatened to sue us in court. Hence we reinstated the membership meeting immediately. We had cancelled the meeting on a Tuesday only to reinstate it the following Thursday. In the meantime, Dick and I visited the owner, who had accused us of dishonesty and deceit. We felt terrible. We were convinced that the real estate agent had not communicated well with his client. The executive committee of the board held a special meeting and instructed me to do whatever I could to avoid a court case. The College did not need a lawsuit at that early stage of its development.

Again we had arranged a meeting with the owner. This time Rev. John Zantingh, the chairman of the board, joined us. The owner had invited Rev. Ray Sikkema and the real estate agent to be present. Rev. Sikkema chaired the meeting. We met from 8 a.m. to 12 noon and failed to resolve the matter. The owner continued to accuse us of breaking a binding contract. He argued that the conditional offer was signed by the chairman of the board and the secretary, under the corporate seal of the College. It was his position that these signatures and the attachment of the corporate seal signified that all the conditions in the offer had been waived. Therefore, he argued, we had reneged on a binding contract. Even today, I have trouble understanding the owner's position, especially since he had personally been a real estate broker for many years. We went through an awful time.

A membership meeting was convened in the afternoon of November 14. In the morning, the board met to prepare for the meeting. Our solicitor informed us at that meeting that the current zoning of the property did not allow us to move into the building. This in itself was sufficient reason to declare the offer null and void. Yet the board decided to present the offer to the membership and to make mention of the fact that the zoning needed to be changed.

That Saturday the membership met. We did not inform the membership of the court threat, but we did inform them of the zoning problem. A motion was made to purchase the building, but that motion was soundly defeated by the membership. After the meeting, the owner was informed of the decision of the member-ship to reject the purchase. The owner informed us that he intended to continue his lawsuit.

Rev. Zantingh, our solicitor Mr. Bert Bakker, and I went to con-sult with a major law firm in Toronto. We wanted to be certain that we had dealt correctly with the offer to purchase. When we met with that Toronto lawyer, he was very surprised. His reaction was that there had to be more to the case than we indicated. When we showed him the contract, he could not believe that anyone would accuse us of wrongdoing. He said that our contract was "a normal way for any corporation to make a conditional offer for purchase."

A short time later, we were informed that the owner had dropped the lawsuit. However, he did not return the $1,000 deposit to us. Sometime later, we agreed that the $1,000 deposit would be donated to The Bible League of Canada. It was a great relief to put this episode behind us.

Following this debacle, the need to look for other suitable facilities became a pressing priority. We were only nine months away from opening the College. We had no idea where we would be located. Suddenly more buildings became available and we inspected them all. Having learned from the previous difficulty, we asked board members to accompany us. We evaluated the Hamilton Library Building; we visited the Jewish Community Centre; we looked at the Lido building, a commercial building close to McMaster University; we were intrigued by an old build-ing in Dundas, a Music Hall which had been closed for 15 years. Last but certainly not least, we were introduced to the Dundas District High School.

The Dundas District High School

The Dundas District High School was destined to be closed. We all agreed that, if we would be able to get that high school, we would have the necessary facilities for our college. But how to acquire that school? The first person we contacted was the mayor of Dundas, Mr. Joseph Bennett. The mayor received us cordially and told us how upset the town was that the high school was closing. A parent protest group was trying very hard to keep the school open, even by means of a private school. When told of our plans he promised his full cooperation.

Next we met with the chairman of the committee of the Hamilton-Wentworth Board of Education, which was responsible for the disposal of surplus buildings. Mr. Hewson confirmed that the Dundas High School would be closing and that the board intended to dispose of the building. He informed us what an interested party needed to do. With that information in hand, we wrote a letter to the Dundas Town Council. In it we asked the council to welcome us to Dundas and to help us find the needed facilities. We delivered the letter on January 4, 1982. It was well received and given into the hands of the administration and fire committee, which would meet on January 25.

Before the committee met, we met with Mr. Greenleaf, director of education of the Hamilton-Wentworth board, and Mr. Webb, business administrator. In great detail, these men explained the steps that needed to be taken to be able to dispose of a school building. We were surprised to hear of the many regulations that the Ministry of Education imposed. A surplus building must first be offered to agencies such as the Separate School Board, McMaster University, Mohawk College, the Region, the Town and some federal agencies before other offers could be considered. All the preferred agencies were to be allowed 90 days to respond. The board had already sent a letter to these agencies on December 16, so it could have taken till the middle of March before all the different groups would have responded. If none of these prescribed groups would indicate an interest in the property, the board would be permitted to request the ministry for permission to put the building on the market by way of public tender. Mr. Greenleaf and Mr. Webb expected that the permission of the ministry would come about 30 days after receiving the request. That process would have taken until the middle of April to complete. Public tendering would take another two months. Then, if nobody would have shown an interest it would be possible for the board to negotiate with a private party such as Redeemer College. That would have taken until the month of June at the earliest, a timeline that we could not agree to.

We asked whether it would be possible for one of the prescribed agencies to buy the property and then sell or lease it to us. They indicated that from their point of view such an approach might be possible. They emphasised, however, that their only concern was the sale of the building.

Armed with this information, we prepared two briefs for the Dundas Town Council. The first brief explained who we were, and the second dealt with the Dundas District High School. We indicated in detail the obstacles we faced should we be required to purchase the building on our own. We appeared before the planning committee on January 25. Immediately after that committee meeting, we met with the entire council and told them of our intention. We asked the council for their cooperation. We also told them that we had been in touch with the protest group of parents and had invited the chairman of that group, Mr. Charlie Gunn, to be present. Mr. Gunn told council of the group's desire to make arrangements with us to rent part of the facilities.

We were pleased that the planning committee was willing to present council with a motion including the three recommendations which we had placed before them, namely to:

1. Inform the Board of Education that you are interested in the High School;
2. Instruct your staff to negotiate a lease or purchase of the building together with us from the Wentworth School Board; and
3. Ask your staff to come with recommendations to the Council to remove the obstacles that are there.

Council passed these motions unanimously. We pointed out that we needed a firm contract by April 15. Council agreed that the time schedule was tight, but a promise of full cooperation was given to us. Already on February 1, council met to pass resolutions dealing with the zoning obstacle.

The zoning of the high school was "public use by public agencies." This zoning restriction originated forty years earlier when the land was donated with a restricted covenant clause. Fortunately, the town's solicitor, Mr. Johnson, and our solicitor, Mr. Bakker, agreed that the restricted covenant clause was no longer valid. Council referred the rezoning issue to the planning committee which promised to discuss a further plan with us regarding the exact rezoning of the property.

The school board and the College each commissioned an appraisal of the school. We hoped the report would be submitted in a short time frame because time was of the essence for us. Yet by the end of March, we still had not heard from the school board. Neither had we heard from our appraiser. We began to suspect that there was much more to the school property than had first met the eye. Our appraiser indicated that the reason for the delay was the difficulty in obtaining information from the escarpment commission and the Dundas fire department. He had been investigating the sale of similar schools to be able to come with a price that was reasonable. We reminded both our appraiser and the school board of our deadline, which was the middle of April.

On April 13, our appraiser presented the figures he had accumulated for us. He suggested, that a building like the Dundas District High School would be appraised from $10 to $20 per square foot. Since there were difficulties with the water coming down from the escarpment through a creek which was judged to be too narrow, since the fire alarm system needed to be changed, and since the building was an older one, he thought that the price would be in the neighbourhood of $10 per square foot. The building was 61,240 square feet, which meant that the building would be valued at $612,400. In addition, he estimated that the parking lot would cost $20,000 (half an acre at $40,000 an acre). An additional two acres of land required for parking were situated across the street from the school and would likely cost $50,000 per acre. Therefore, the cost of acquiring the two properties would be $734,400. He was of the opinion that the appraisal of the school board would come in at more than $1 million. We were stunned! Our expectations were dashed because the price was totally out of reach.

The whole business became more questionable, yet when we were made aware of an old report prepared by the conservation authority regarding the Spencer Creek that ran through the rear of the school property. We had requested the Reinders Engineering Company to do some investigating. They became acquainted with a 1979 report in which the conservation authorities told the school that the Spencer Creek was too narrow to swallow and absorb the water coming from the escarpment in an extreme storm, a "once-in-twenty year storm" they called it. In 1979 the estimated cost to repair this defect was $750.000. The escarpment commission had no power to enforce their findings on the School. However, with a new owner, someone would make sure that the long awaited repairs would be made. Undoubtedly, the new owner would have to pay for those expenses.

We went back to the Dundas Town Council and discussed the purchase of the school once more. We informed the council of the $1,500,000 appraisal report prepared for the school board, a copy of which we had received in the meantime, and the $500,000 appraisal report submitted by our appraiser. The Spencer Creek problem was also discussed. It was to our advantage that the Dundas Town Council did not want to see the high school closed, and so they were willing to listen. We proposed that they purchase the school, and lease it to us for a period of ten years. The council responded that they had no money to purchase; hence we offered the ten-year lease money up front. We had been told by Mr. Webb, when he presented us with the board's appraisal, that the school board had a track record of selling school properties for 70 percent of the appraised value. We offered council to pay the school board $300,000 which was 70 percent of our appraisal's $500,000 value and that the property would be owned by the Town of Dundas. The Dundas Town Council gave us permission to present this offer to the Hamilton-Wentworth Board of Education.

In May, the Hamilton-Wentworth Board of Education met to consider our offer. The delegation from Redeemer was asked to leave the room, while the school board deliberated. It took only fifteen to twenty minutes for a small committee of the school board to tell us that the board had rejected our proposal, but that the board was willing to continue negotiations with us. Since September was very close, we asked them to allow us the use of the school for one year, during which time we would try to reach a more permanent solution. Within a few minutes we were told that our proposal was denied. The committee gave us two reasons:

1. It is difficult to sell a school while it is rented,
2. Since we would be teaching Grade 13 courses, plus the fact that we had an understanding with Springhill Academy, a private school of parents who were upset by the closing of the school, we would be responsible for taking children out of the public school system.

We were astounded by the reasons that the school board gave to deny our offer. It was the middle of May and we did not know where we would begin our school year in September. Immediately we contacted the Jewish Community Centre, which had been offered for sale to us. The facility would only serve us for one year, perhaps two, but certainly not longer. We asked for a two-year lease, but they were not willing to look at a lease for less than five years. The Lido building was another possibility. It was large enough as we would be able to lease between 40,000 and 50,000 square feet. However, the asking price of $6 per square foot, and utilities, was too expensive for us.

The Bell Cairn Memorial School

In October 1981, we had heard that the Bell Cairn Memorial School on Beach Boulevard between Hamilton and Burlington was empty. We had not taken this information very seriously because of its location. First, the school was much further from McMaster University than any of the other facilities we had considered. Second, the smell from the steel mills, located across the bay, was very unpleasant at times. In addition, there would be the unbearable smell of the dead fish in the spring. By this time, however, we were in a crisis situation. We would look at anything, as long as it would be able to accommodate the space needs of the College. We opened the Bell Cairn Memorial School file once again and decided to do some real investigating.

First, we wanted to see the school. It is no use investigating the neighbourhood if the school is not suitable. The site visit convinced us that the facilities would be suitable and that only minor alterations would need to be made. We waited for a day when the wind would blow from the steel mills toward the school. Arend, Dick and I drove down Beach Boulevard with the windows open, sniffing to determine how severe the odour really was. It was noticeable, but not as bad as we had been told. Inside the school we could not detect any bad odour.

We also had been told that the neighbourhood was a slum area, and dangerous because of a high crime rate. We found the contrary to be true. Eighty-five percent of the residents were homeowners. Our observation of the neighbourhood was that the homeowners took good care of their properties. We talked to the proprietor of a small corner store across from the school about the crime rate. She was pleased to tell us that during the six years while she had operated the store, she had never been robbed.

We were warned that a motorcycle gang had made its home on the Beach Boulevard. A motorcycle club was situated about 300 metres from the school. The residents assured us that, though the club was noisy at times with loud music being played, the club had never been the cause of neighbours moving away. The police informed us that the crime rate on the Beach Boulevard was low in comparison to other areas of Hamilton. For example, in 1981 an average of 2,000 crimes took place in each precinct. The Beach Boulevard area only had 500 crimes, while in the area where the Hamilton District Christian High School and Immanuel Christian Reformed Church were located, the crime rate had been a little more than 2,100 over the same period.

When we had gathered all the information, we contacted the Hamilton Board of Education and asked them about the possibility of leasing the Bell Cairn school for one year. The school's size was a little more than 48,000 square feet. The board was kind enough to allow us to rent its facilities for one year. It also gave us the option to rent on a yearly basis after that for a total commitment of three years. However, we were required to make a firm commitment for just one year. Moreover, the board proposed to charge us for what they called useable space. They understood useable space to include classrooms and the auditorium, which amounted to 24,000 square feet. The other space like the hallways, storage and supply rooms, offices, and washrooms could be used free of charge. The rental rate would be $1.75 per square foot, which meant that the rent for our first year would only be $42,000.

I asked for a meeting of the executive committee of the board. The executive committee proposed to telephone all the board members and ask for their approval. We did not want to repeat the mistake we had made with the first property. Except for one board member, all agreed to present our proposal to rent the Bell Cairn Memorial School for one year at the annual meeting of the supporting members. The membership meeting had already been scheduled for the following week.

The location of the annual meeting was changed to the Bell Cairn school, so that everyone had an opportunity to see the facilities. The membership voted in favour of renting the school. By a spontaneous motion, the meeting also went on record urging the board to concentrate on purchasing our own permanent campus, to begin the planning for it, including dormitories, and to establish a building fund.

We signed the lease with the Hamilton Board of Education effective September 1, 1982, but we were allowed to occupy the building free of charge already on June 1, so that we would have sufficient time to do the necessary alterations and to prepare the school for rental occupancy in September. What a sigh of relief was uttered by all. The scheduled opening of Redeemer College in September had come so close that the lack of suitable facilities had given me many sleepless nights. But it is during such times that you multiply your prayers. I prayed a lot, and the Lord provided for our needs just on time.

The Lord provided in so many ways. We already had a faculty and staff. Dr. Harry Van Belle was willing to be the student affairs director on a half time basis. Mr. Arend Kersten would continue his involvement with the College as development director, while he would also assist in the student affairs department. We had classroom and office facilities, but we still needed student housing, equipment for our laboratories, and a library.

Student Housing

We thought that finding facilities to house the College was difficult, and it was, but to find housing for the students appeared to be next to impossible. The rental vacancy rate was less than one percent. When we revealed that we were looking for student housing, all doors closed. Who wants to rent to students when available space is at a premium? Mrs. Mary Verrips, one of our employees, was constantly scouting the area to find rooms for our students. She managed to secure some boarding places, for which we were very thankful. But since we anticipated nearly 100 students, it was impossible to find enough families who were willing and able to provide that many students with room and board. Again the Lord led us and surprised us.

Mrs. Susan Vander Vaart from Burlington joined us as a volunteer to help Mary in her inspection of the homes that were willing to welcome our students. She located townhouses which had suddenly become available. These townhouses were quadruplexes—four units under one roof. Each unit was large enough to house up to ten students—not ideal, but possible. I hoped and prayed that the students would still be friends at the end of the school year. Area rents had increased dramatically, because interest rates had soared astronomically from 10 percent to 18 percent percent. When the leases on the townhouse units expired, the tenants had been informed that the rent would increase from $450 to $650 per month. Heating and utilities were extra. Many occupants could not afford the higher rent and vacated their units. We approached the owners and told them of our predicament. One of the owners was very sympathetic, but the other was afraid that our students would be too noisy. At least they were willing to consider our proposal. A week later, after more discussions, we rented enough apartments to house all the students who still needed housing. We promised the owners that proper supervision would be exercised. One of our prospective students,

Mr. Jim Berry, was willing to become the residence director. Jim was a mature student, married with a family. He was a youth elder in one of the Sarnia churches. He wanted to enter the pre-seminary program at the College, because he intended to become an ordained minister. Jim was willing to live in one of the apartments with his family and some students. We would appoint a resident assistant in each unit, and Jim would supervise all of them. The students would live as a family unit, do their own cooking, cleaning and devotions.

At long last, we also had found sufficient housing that would be needed to house our students. What a relief! We thanked the Lord for the miraculous way in which He took care of us. Once again, He provided beyond our expectations.

Laboratory Equipment

One of our board members, Dr. Henry Brouwer, was a chemistry teacher at London District Christian High School. He often managed to get used laboratory equipment for his high school from the universities. He promised his utmost to do the same for Redeemer College. He contacted McMaster University and he was successful in obtaining equipment for our laboratories which McMaster no longer used. It was still in very good condition and quite useable for our purposes.

Library

"A college without a library is like a horse without a rider," someone once remarked. A very true statement indeed. It was, therefore, necessary for us to appoint a librarian, who would be able to structure and organise a library professionally. The person we appointed was Mr. Dan Savage, a qualified and experienced librarian. We had accumulated about 6,000 volumes by the time he joined the staff. He could begin his work of cataloguing those volumes immediately.

Prior to Dan's appointment, we had also asked Atticus Bookstore in Toronto to advertise for a liberal arts library. Dick Kranendonk had a Master of Library Science degree and, therefore, was well acquainted with books and libraries. He took the initiative to follow up on offers that came in response to our advertisement.

The first response came from a library in Philadelphia, Pennsylvania. A representative of Atticus Bookstore went to Philadelphia to advise us. Atticus Bookstores dealt exclusively with books from colleges and universities. The library consisted of about 15,000 volumes, of which only 1,300 books would be of use to us. We bought the 1,300 volumes at $4 a piece. Most of these books were reference works. Then another library became available in Sault St Marie. We were particularly interested in that library, because it was located in Canada. However, only about 4,000 volumes would be of use to us. Again, we bought the 4,000 books and paid $1 per volume. The books arrived quickly. Our librarian had sufficient time to catalogue and shelve these books in time for the September opening of Redeemer College.

One of the responses to our advertisement came from a Mr. Jim Stitzinger, a librarian of a Baptist seminary in the USA. He informed us of the sale of a library in Troy, New York, at a Franciscan monastery, used by the School of Philosophy of the Franciscan brothers in their preparation of students for the priesthood. Mr. Dick Kranendonk, Mr. Dan Savage and I, together with Mr. Donald Smith of Atticus Bookstore, made the trip to Troy to view the library. We were amazed at what we saw. Mr. Smith indicated that he had not seen a library of that calibre for many years. Every book had been purchased for the purpose of accreditation. The library consisted of 50,000 volumes and many more works on microfilm. The microfilms included all the works of the church fathers. The asking price of the complete library was $175,000 U.S. On the way out the business manager whispered in our ears that he was of the opinion that we might be able to purchase the library for $150,000 U.S.

We wanted to buy this library immediately, but we did not have the money. The budget only included $50,000 Canadian. for the library, and we had already spent some of that money. Only one option was open to us and that was to somehow raise the money. I went out fundraising. Economically, times were difficult. Interest rates were at an all time high: hence there were not very many business people who were able to donate money for a library in an as yet nonexistent institution. Fundraising was tough. I received some small donations. Some donors promised to give, but had to withdraw their pledges due to the difficult economic situations. I prayed frequently. I was convinced that the Lord wanted us to have the best. I prayed that the Lord would open hearts and pocketbooks to allow us to purchase this extraordinary library. My report to the executive committee of the board of August 9, 1982, makes mention that I received a total amount of $67,000. With that amount in hand, plus the money in the budget, the executive committee gave me permission to make an offer. It was one more step in faith.

I wrote a letter to the Franciscan Brothers, in which I explained who we were. The books would be used in a college setting once again, and the library would remain intact, I reasoned. I also let them know that we did not have much money and that the best we could do was to make an offer of $125,000 US. We made the offer in faith, and left it in the Lord's hands. We had asked the Brothers to give us their decision by August 9th. On that date we received the news that our offer had been accepted. However, part of their reference library, which consisted of about 2,000 volumes, would not be included. Later we purchased those books as well. The Lord performed another miracle.

Early in September, Mr. Savage and ten students, went to Troy. They packed the library, loaded the tractor-trailer and shipped it to the College. One of our donors promised to ship the library free of charge and had provided a tractor-trailer. When the truck arrived at the border in Buffalo, the truck appeared to be overloaded by 17,000 lbs. The books alone weighed some 66,000 lbs. or 33 tons. The truck was not allowed to cross the Peace Bridge. The driver then proceeded carefully over Highway I-190 to Lewiston. The man in the booth who had weighed the truck could easily have notified other stations that our truck would try to cross the border elsewhere, but he did not do that.

When the truck came to Lewiston, the driver drove by the scales at 30 miles an hour. Nobody stopped him. Arriving at the Canadian side, he did not have the proper documents. The truck was held up for an hour-and-a-half. Our librarian and the driver tried to convince customs that the freight was legitimate, but that the papers were wrong. The customs officers finally believed them, ripped up the papers and let them go. By that time it was 5:30 in the morning. How happy we were when we saw the truck filled with the books in front of the College.

Finally, we were ready to welcome the students. The Lord had performed miraculous deeds, hence we were able to rejoice and be glad. He had promised in His Word to give His blessings to those who trust in Him, and who believe in His Word. We had stepped forward in faith and experienced the truth of God's promises. The College was ready to open its doors and begin the wonderful task of educating students in the fear of the Lord.

Board and senior staff members at the time of opening. From left to right, front row: John De Jong, Stiny De Jong, Adrian Guldemond, Nick Van Duyvendyk, Albert J. Bakker, Henry R. De Bolster, Henry Aay, James Vreugdenhil; back row: Arend Kersten, Leo Smit, May Drost, Ineke Bezuyen, Dick L. Kranendonk, Joop De Voest, Cheri Buiter, John Cook, William Barneveld and Justin D. Cooper.

A student viewing the collection of library books
that had been acquired by the time of the
official opening of the College.

FOUR

On the Beach Boulevard

The vision with which Mr. Andy Langendoen had approached me eight years earlier, to establish a Christian college of the arts and sciences in Ontario, was about to come to fruition. Everything was ready for Redeemer College to open its doors and to enrol students into programs of higher learning. Praise the Lord! What an incredible miracle! When the first three full-time employees started working for the College on June 1, 1981, there was next to nothing available: no faculty, no students, no facilities, and very little money. Yet the Lord had blessed the works of our hands up to that point. The delivery of His blessings had at times been contrary to our dreams and efforts, for example, in the search for suitable facilities.

The Lord must, at times, have chuckled about our dreams and efforts. He demonstrated in very concrete ways that He had better things in store for us. I learned not to speak abstractly–as we often do—about trusting the Lord. Trusting the Lord must become real in our daily lives. There is a plaque hanging on the wall of my study that quotes Psalm 37: 5: "Commit thy way unto the Lord; trust also in Him; and He shall bring it to pass." This plaque has special meaning and memories for me, because it was a gift from the first student couple at the College whom I was privileged to unite in marriage. I experienced the truth of the text on that plaque on the day of the first convocation of Redeemer College, the official opening on September 6, 1982.

Opening Convocation

The festive occasion was held at Centenary United Church in Hamilton. Approximately 1,400 people crowded the church. Every nook and cranny was filled when our pioneer students, faculty and guests were led to their seats for this historic ceremony. Rev. John Zantingh, chairman of the board, was in charge. It was an inspiring afternoon. Mr. Harry Der Nederlanden had composed a fitting convocation litany. Dr. Joel Nederhood, director of ministries at the Back to God Hour, addressed us on the subject "Christian Education and the Reigning Orthodoxies." Greetings were brought by Dr. Alvin A. Lee, president of McMaster University, on behalf of the University, by Dr. John Hulst, president of Dordt College, on behalf of the Christian educational institutions, and by Rev. Lammert Slofstra, chairman of the interim committee of the Council of Christian Reformed Churches in Canada, on behalf of the churches. Mr. Joseph Bennett, mayor of Dundas, and Mr. William Powell, mayor of Hamilton, were also present. I left the church with a feeling of awe and thanksgiving. What a good and inspiring beginning!

Opening convocation. From left to right, Henry R. De Bolster, Joel Nederhoed and John Hulst.

Coat of Arms

An important part of this impressive ceremony was the presentation of the coat of arms. Not long after my inauguration, Mr. Albert Bakker suggested that we should have our own coat of arms similar to other universities. He had been in touch with Rev. Ralph Spence, an Anglican priest and a member of the Heraldic Society in Canada. We discussed this suggestion with faculty, staff and the board. The board agreed to investigate this possibility as long as it would not involve any costs. We talked with Rev. Spence, and found him to be an enthusiastic person. He was willing to help design an appropriate coat of arms for the College. He suggested that the arms portion contain an open book, symbolizing the academic institution, inscribed with the Greek letters α (*alpha*) and Ω (*omega*). It expressed an education directed by Scripture with the central message: the redeeming work of Christ. Above the book, he proposed a cross-crosslet, four Latin crosses set foot to foot making a Greek cross. That cross would represent the worldwide missionary spirit of Christianity, a spirit that had come to expression during the Reformation—the tradition from which the College had developed. The cross would be flanked by two trilliums. The trilliums are an emblem of the province of Ontario, and the threefold flowers would remind us of the Trinity. He suggested a tree or an animal as the crest. The development of a motto was left up to us. The colours would be red and gold—colours of the Reformation. We liked the imagery, except for the idea of a crest containing a tree or an animal.

This matter was temporarily set aside, since there were other, more urgent matters on our minds. When we placed the coat of arms on our agenda again, I suggested that the crest might contain the victorious Paschal Lamb above a wreath, expressing the Lordship of the risen Christ over all creation. I had also given the motto some thought, and asked Dr. Jack Zeyl, professor of classical languages at Wilfred Laurier University, for his advice. My proposal was *Agnus Dei, Rex Omnium* (Lamb of God, King over All). He thought that it would be an appropriate motto; however, a more elegant way to express this in Latin would be *Agnus Dei, Omnium Rex*. I recommended the Paschal Lamb and the motto to the board. Both recommendations were accepted.

We asked Rev. Spence to complete the coat of arms, and to present it at our first convocation. He gladly obliged, but informed us that the coat of arms would be unofficial since there was no Canadian Heraldic Authority. If we wanted our coat of arms officially registered, we would have to ask the Scottish heraldry to do so, which would involve extra cost. We were happy to accept the unregistered coat of arms that Rev. Spence presented to us at the convocation.

Seven years later, a Canadian Heraldic Authority was established. We contacted the heraldry, through Rev. Spence, and applied to have our coat of arms registered. The Canadian heraldry looked at our coat of arms and made a few changes to it. One change was the addition of two palm branches around the Paschal Lamb, bringing out the victory of Christ even better. On August 28, 1989, we received the official documents, indicating the registration of our coat of arms, which will be ours "forever." Part of the document read:

On May 31, 1989, the Deputy Herald Chancellor of the Canadian Heraldic Authority, Lieutenant-General François Richard, authorized the granting to Redeemer College of such armorial bearings as are fitting and appropriate....
NOW KNOW YOU, that pursuant to the authority vested in her Excellency, the Right Honourable Jeanne Sauvé to exercise the armorial prerogative of Her Majesty, Queen Elizabeth II, and the terms of my Commission of Office, I, the Chief Herald do by these Presents grant and assign to Redeemer College the following: (and then follows the description as above).

The document was signed by Chief Herald, Mr. Robert D. Watt, Herald Chancellor, Mr. Leopold Henri Amyot, and Deputy Herald Chancellor, Mr. François Richard. The coat of arms accurately reflects who we are. The original is permanently located in the board room and we proudly display it on special occasions.

The Work Begins

The real work of instructing students began after the convocation. Our final tally of students showed an enrollment of 97 full-time and 31 part-time students—far beyond our highest hopes. The first year was very busy and full of unexpected happenings. For example,

The official Coat of Arms

the students had to adjust to university education. When midterm exams and the deadlines for papers approached, they were convinced that the course of study was too difficult and that they would not succeed. It was especially difficult for these pioneer students, because there were no senior students who could encourage them. The encouragement of faculty members did not help, because they were perceived as the people who caused the difficulties. Of course, the faculty did not give in to these complaints, and the students not only survived, but they did very well. When the unpopular month of November had passed, the atmosphere at Redeemer College improved considerably.

It is interesting to note that the month of November remained a difficult month, especially for first year students. I always kept that in mind when I led chapel during that month. I would encourage them and tell them not to forget that God is their helper, and that He does not forsake them.

Our first students earned my admiration because of their perseverance. At the same time, the instruction they received was excellent because of the low student/faculty ratio. It gave these students constant access to their professors. The classes were never larger than forty-five students, and everyone knew each other. I want to share a letter I received at the end of that first year. It was dated June 14, 1983:

Dear Rev. De Bolster,

It is a quiet summer evening and a good time to enjoy the cool breeze, and have some time for thought. It is a treat to be able to have some quiet time without worrying about a paper to write or an exam! Actually, what it comes right down to is that I miss Redeemer and all the aspects of student life that went with it. 467 Beach Blvd. is a part of my heart forever.

I wanted to write and share a few of my thoughts with you, especially since I won't be coming back in the fall. When I decided to go to Redeemer, it was a last minute decision, which had to be made quickly, and I wasn't at all sure what the year would be like. (I guess no one did!) All I knew for sure was that

that was the place God wanted me to be. And now as I am busy with work this summer, I find that many times my thoughts and prayers are for the friends I made at Redeemer. Redeemer changed my life. Perhaps you smile as you read that, but I believe it to be true, not only for myself, but for many persons who were there. Since I went to a public high school, it was an opening of many doors to be instructed about certain areas and about life by Christian teachers—and by such excellent teachers. I think about things differently and more deeply than before. Above all I feel closer to God. I can feel so uncertain about the future sometimes, but the close fellowship I felt at Redeemer is something I cherish and still learn from. We all had that renewed when we went to the Open House for Art. I guess as students, our experiences at Redeemer were much different from someone like yourself, who has worked hard and long to see the doors open for the first time. But despite some mistakes and failures I hear from Redeemer students, I am sure, that the general movement of Redeemer College is positive! I was proud to be part of the "pioneer" student body and I hope that this year was as special for you as it was for us.

These are just a few of my thoughts. I am learning new things about myself all the time, and I am sure there will be a life-time of learning ahead. My prayers are with you and I ask your prayers for those of us heading in new directions.

Shalom,
Wilma Brus

What a precious letter. It did not hide some of our shortcomings, but it showed that Redeemer College had been an instrument used by God that first year.

Direction and Structures

Keep in mind that when you start from scratch, everything must be discussed and decided. True, much work had been done in the previous year-and-a-half, but now the faculty had arrived and needed to be involved in streamlining the plans we had made. The structures of the College had to be put on paper. Moreover, the faculty members had come from different institutions and needed time to become a faculty with a united view of Reformed Christian education. I remember the many discussions we had. Professors are strong-willed people. I was surprised how they expressed their disagreements with each other. They did not beat around the bush. You always knew their position. In my ears their critique was sometimes harsh, but through it all, they were friends, they respected each other and learned from each other.

We could not always come to a consensus, but when decisions were made, all would abide by them. In the beginning I felt intimidated by the faculty. After all, they were learned people and I felt inferior to them. That changed when I discovered that, even though they were highly educated people, their scholarship pertained to their specific discipline, which was usually narrowly focussed. When faculty members began to tell me how I should run the College, I soon found out that they knew no more about matters outside of their discipline than those with a general education.

I recall the lengthy discussion about the philosophical direction of the College. Should we only allow "Dooyeweerdian" sympathisers to teach at the College, or should we allow for a broader Christian approach? A heated discussion ensued. One of the professors wrote a discussion paper, which was entitled: "Was ist los in the Foundations Division?" We took our time to discuss these principles, but I don't think there was unanimous agreement when we decided to go with the broader Christian perspective.

Once, when there was a serious disagreement in a division, I invited the faculty of that division to my house. During dinner we were able to discuss the disagreement calmly. There was a genuine attempt to understand each other. One thing was certain: all wanted to be Reformed Christians. All had the best of the College at heart. I admired the intensity with which they showed their love for Redeemer College.

The question of authority was a subject of debate. Who would be responsible where? Does the faculty, by majority vote, make binding decisions? Is the president the final authority? These questions had been discussed by the board at the beginning of the establishment of the College. We could choose from several models, most of which made the president the final authority, who would be responsible to the board for the actions of the institution. But there was one noticeable exception. One school for higher learning had decided that the faculty in its meetings would make the final decisions. The board had decided against that model. Therefore, I proposed that there be a "College council" as an advisory body, consisting of all full-time faculty and administrators, where all important matters pertaining to the College would be discussed. The decisions taken by the council would be forwarded to the president as the council's recommendations. I have always listened carefully to the decisions of the council. During my tenure, there were only a handful of decisions made by me which were contrary to the recommendations of the College council.

In addition to the College council, I was greatly assisted by the administrative council. That council consisted of the dean, finance director, development director, student life director, and myself. The College council met monthly; the administrative council weekly. At the administrative council each division of the College would report and when there were questions or difficulties, the council would advise how to go about answering the questions or solving the difficulties. I have only the best memories about the meetings of the administrative council. The members involved were willing to listen, to advise and to support. What a wonderful group of people! I owe them my gratitude.

Mr. Dick Kranendonk and Mr. Justin Cooper had been busy preparing the *Policy Handbook*, the *Faculty Handbook*, the *Student Handbook* and the *Calendar*. That was a tremendous job. Those documents needed to be accurate. In order to make sure they were, the drafts were also studied by the College council before they were recommended to the board for its approval. When I think back about what was done that first year, and how many documents were prepared for long-term use, I can only thank the Lord for giving the necessary strength, insight and health to everyone involved. In addition to the normal work load, many hours were spent by all faculty and staff, and especially by Justin and Dick, to accomplish this task.

That first year we were not able to find a dean. Justin started teaching and, therefore, could not continue to be acting dean all by himself. Hence that position needed to be assigned to more than one faculty member. I was grateful that three of my senior faculty members were willing to share the deanship, and to divide the tasks among themselves. I appointed Dr. Wytse (Vince) Van Dyk, as the chairman of the triumvirate, and he would carry the title of dean. The second person was Dr. Theodore Plantinga, who would be the registrar, and the third person was Mr. Justin Cooper, who would be the curriculum coordinator. All faculty members were happy with that interim arrangement.

One of the questions the board had raised during my interview for the presidency of the College was: "What will you do if disagreements arise regarding the purpose and calling of the College?" The clarifying question of the interviewer was: "What will you do if one or more of the faculty members come to you with ideas which might or might not be sound or good for the College?" I responded that I would appoint a "purpose committee" to advise me on complex issues. Rev. B. J. Haan of Dordt College had told me, during one of my visits with him, that he had such a committee and that his purpose committee had helped him on several occasions. I decided that it would be wise for me to appoint such a committee. Of course, I wanted to appoint the best available persons, and since we had just accepted the triumvirate in the deanship, I appointed those three men to form the purpose committee. I hoped that I would never have to make use of this committee. But just in case there would be a need, I wanted everybody to know of its existence. During my tenure, I called upon this committee twice.

Expansion

The first student body consisted of Grade 12 graduates, Grade 13 graduates, mature students, and transfer students. Therefore, it was necessary to revisit the curriculum we offered. We did not teach just Grade 13 equivalent courses. We were immediately involved in first-year university courses and even some second-year courses. It did not take very long for all of us to realise that the Grade 13 equivalent program needed to disappear. We were a university college, and the sooner we would get rid of the high school image, the better it would be. Unfortunately, we had already created that image with McMaster University. It would take us years to have that University change its mind regarding our program. The first few years we continued to give courses with a zero as the first numeral, i.e. History 091, (Grade 13 equivalent), but later we eliminated all Grade 13 equivalent courses and only taught first year university level courses. Students who came to us from high schools, which did not have the required Ontario academic credits for admission to university, had to take some additional first-year courses. That made it necessary for us to upgrade the second year level courses at the College. These became second-year university courses.

When I read the reports written in that first and second year, I am amazed at the daring decisions we made. Many of these decisions were possible because of a much larger student body than expected. The second year we welcomed 167 full-time and 59 part-time students, and the outlook for the third year was a possible enrollment of 210 full-time students. Hence, the board was faced with the question whether to stay with a two-year program, or to immediately strive to become a four-year degree granting institution. After much discussion, both within the College, and by the board, it was decided to take a further step in faith and expand the instruction beyond the two-year college level. I even asked the board to declare six vacancies for the 1983-1984 academic year based on an enrollment of 210 students.

Another reason for program expansion was the news from the government that our students qualified for government loans, with a good possibility that our students would qualify for grants as well. This happened a few years later, when we were admitted into membership of the Association of Universities and Colleges of Canada.

In the second year we had difficulty finding a part-time French teacher. I approached Dr. Lee, with whom I had developed an excellent relationship. He was always ready to give me advice. I asked him whether it would be possible to have a McMaster French course taught on Redeemer's campus. He was willing to refer my request to the appropriate department at McMaster. A short time later, I was informed that the request had been approved. We then had a McMaster professor teach French to our students on our campus. We were able to appoint our own French professor the following year.

Term Appointment

It was one thing to declare six vacancies, but it was quite another thing to hire six new professors. Where would we find them? Would we be able to appoint scholars, who shared our faith and perspective? The future of the College depended on the kind of faculty we could recruit. For that reason, I wrote the following memorandum to the faculty and directors of the College. It was dated March 2, 1983:

It has become very clear to me that it is necessary to sit down together in order to define what we actually mean when it comes to appointing a full-time member to the faculty. The timing is crucial. Whatever we are going to do now will set a precedent for our future course. I've done a lot of thinking the last week and the following remarks are the result of that thought.

We have tried to say something about the qualifications of our faculty members in our Policy Handbook. Let me just quote from section 361:

Qualifications
Candidates for appointment to any position in the College must be committed Christians who:

361.1 Submit themselves to Christ's call to discipleship in all areas of life and acknowledge the radical nature of His Lordship over all College affairs, and demonstrate this commitment in word and deed especially through participation in the church and as it relates to Christian education at the elementary and secondary levels;

361.2 Have developed personal and professional views and lifestyles that are Scripturally-directed and consistent with Reformed Christian confessions and perspectives;

Our charter also says in its Objects and Purposes:

The objects and purposes of the College are to provide, at the post-secondary level:

a) for the advancement of learning and dissemination of knowledge on the basis of the Reformed confessions, traditions and perspectives;

This matter of Reformed Christian perspectives comes back again a little later under the same heading of Objects and Purposes in the Charter as well.

When I delivered my inaugural address, I pledged myself to work for, and to help maintain, a Reformed Christian College. According to my view, only those people who know and agree with the Calvinistic world-and-life view fall in the category of being Reformed. I am also convinced that everyone who joins our faculty as a full-time member, with all the privileges and responsibilities that go with that faculty membership, must hold to that view.

The history of many universities, and of many colleges in the United States, shows us that it is very easy to depart from that goal, and therefore we need to hold strictly to our position in order to be sure that the objects and purposes of the College will be fulfilled.

I regard our present faculty to be the nucleus. Each faculty member knows where the other stands. That stand, which I regard to be thoroughly Reformed, must be continued. Therefore, I strongly believe that only those who can convince us that they share our convictions, our commitments,and our world-and-life view, are allowed to join that nucleus.

I want to proceed carefully that we look for people who are academically qualified. Of equal importance, those who can wholeheartedly subscribe to the qualifications we have set for ourselves as described in the Charter in the objects and purposes of the College.

In other words, we need people who are acquainted with the Calvinistic world-and-life view, who agree with it, people who confess the Reformed confessions, and who hold to Reformed traditions and perspectives. Only those people should be allowed to join the nucleus of faculty we have at the moment.

It might not always be possible to find such a person. We might find someone who is, again, academically highly qualified, and who has a good Christian perspective, but who does not have that perspective rooted in the Reformed confessions and traditions. It seems to me, that we certainly ought to make use of such a candidate and help that person to develop. However, such a candidate is not qualified to join the faculty nucleus. Therefore, I suggest that we identify three different types of full-time faculty appointments, rather than the two we have at the moment.

We have the initial two-year appointment, with the understanding that this is, what we call, a tenure track or regular appointment. All things being equal, that person will be reappointed after the first two years for a further appointment. Next to that we have the terminal appointment. An appointment for one or two years, which then will be terminated, at least that is the way I interpret that particular appointment.

We ought to add a third category—the term appointment for two years. This appointment will be given to those who have a Christian perspective, but who do not know Calvinism as we interpret that to be. Such an appointment is either renewable or not, depending on the development of the faculty member. Such a person would receive limited faculty status as it is expressed under 362.2, and I would suggest changing this paragraph to read as follows:

Limited faculty status, which includes the right to attend, speak and vote at faculty meetings, except in executive sessions, and other meetings designated for regular faculty members, is granted to the librarian and to those appointed to a term, terminal or visiting appointment of any rank as defined in the Policy Handbook.

I believe that we ought to make that decision now, so that we can clearly set the direction for the future.

As I mentioned earlier, it is easier to depart from the goals that we have set, than to stay the course. It will need a continued examination of what we are doing. I would very much like you to discuss this matter at our next faculty meeting.

The faculty debated this matter at its next meeting and accepted the third category of faculty appointments. We used the term appointment several times and with promising results.

Since the board decided to expand our program, we were suddenly aware of our degree designation. The BCS degree was a misnomer, and unknown in the academic world. Hence we approached the government to ask for a change to our charter. In a separate chapter I will write about the dealings with the government; suffice it to say that this was the beginning of a long and frustrating process.

AUCC Membership

We looked for ways to change the position of the Ministry of Colleges and Universities. One focus was to be recognised by the university community. Dr. Wytse Van Dyk, our dean, informed us of the existence of the Association of Universities and Colleges of Canada (AUCC), an organisation of the presidents of Canadian universities and colleges, representing their institutions. Wytse had read its bylaws and was convinced that we qualified for provisional membership. The only questionable requirement was the number of students an institution must have to be admitted as a member. The bylaws stated that an institution should have 200 students for three consecutive years prior to admission as an ordinary member. A new institution could apply for provisional membership for a maximum of five years. After five years, an institution must qualify for ordinary membership or cease to be a member. No one at that time could guarantee that we would have 200 students for three consecutive years. We were convinced that we would, but would the AUCC share our belief? At that time, we had not yet achieved an enrollment of 200 students even for one year.

We asked for and received information and application material from the AUCC in September 1983. The board was happy with this development and encouraged me to apply for provisional membership. The application was completed, discussed with the faculty and directors, and given to our solicitor for his advice. When all the details were in place, we mailed it to the AUCC at the end of 1983. I am convinced that the board of directors of the AUCC questioned our application, especially since most universities were not even aware of Redeemer College's existence. Nevertheless, a visiting committee was appointed to evaluate our application and to report its findings to its board of directors. We received notice that the committee would visit on October 30 and 31, 1984.

The AUCC has a rule that members of the visiting committees must be presidents of universities from another province than where the applicant institution is located. The visiting committee consisted of: Dr. W.G. Saywell (chairman of the committee), president of Simon Fraser University, BC.; Mr. M.C. Hamel, rector of Université de Sherbrooke, PQ; Rev. G.A. MacKinnon, president of St. Francis Xavier University, NS; Dr. A.M. Kristjanson, director of research and analysis AUCC secretariat.

The AUCC evaluation committee. Left to right: G.A. MacKinnon,
A. M. Kristjanson, Henry R. De Bolster, Justin Cooper, W. G. Saywell,
M. C. Hamel, Dick L. Kranendonk and Wytse Van Dyk.

The committee stayed at the Holiday Inn in Burlington, and I met them at the hotel early on the morning of October 30th. They first met with me in my office to get acquainted and to find out who we were. I had the impression that these men were not very excited about Redeemer College. Later, Dr. Saywell confided in me that, when he arrived at the Bell Cairn Memorial School, he was convinced that we were a "mickey mouse" outfit. He even told his fellow members that it would not be necessary to stay both days. He thought that the committee could leave again around noon on the first day. His attitude changed when he met with the faculty and the librarian. He could not believe that such a young and different type of institution had been able to attract such high calibre scholars. Of course, he did not convey his impressions at that time. But I was grateful when he gave me his personal impressions later. During their visit, we did our best to let them know what we had done, who we were and what we believed our future to be.

The committee met with the administrators, students, including the president of the student council, and the academic council. In the evening, several board members and supporting members of the College met with them over dinner at the Holiday Inn. The next day, they inspected our facilities and paid particular attention to the library and the laboratories. They ended their visit by meeting with me once again. I drove them back to the airport and saw them off. On our way to the airport, I asked whether they had enjoyed their stay. The only reply I received was: "We will tell you in due time." Still we were encouraged by our own assessment of the visit. We anxiously awaited the committee's report.

We received a copy of the report, which was addressed to the board of directors of the AUCC, on January 3, 1985. It was a positive report. The committee had listened carefully and reported their findings accurately. They gave a summary of the history and philosophy of the College, and reported on the programs, the facilities, the governance and administration. Special attention was given to the finances, library and laboratories. They observed in detail the Policy Handbook's description of the hiring, terms of employment, sabbatical leaves, and time for research of the faculty.

Some concerns were expressed. For example, sabbatical leaves were not yet in place, even though some money had been set aside for those leaves. We were urged to declare a policy and to implement that policy as soon as possible. A concern was expressed that Redeemer College had insufficient computer facilities to support a business program, or courses in computer science. Another concern was that the enrollment requirements for ordinary membership within five years would not be met. On the whole, the report was very complimentary. The committee stated "that the courses constituting the Bachelor of Christian Studies program are comparable to courses leading to a Bachelor of Arts in Canadian universities." The report ended by saying:

> In summary, the visiting committee was impressed with the quality of the faculty, the competence of the administrative staff and the attention paid to good planning and development of their academic programs. We were particularly impressed with the commitment of all sectors of the college, students, faculty, support staff, administrative staff, and the supporting broader community to the idea of developing their own higher education institution of high academic quality.
>
> The visiting committee recommends to the Board of Directors that Redeemer Reformed Christian College be admitted to provisional membership in AUCC.

The board of the AUCC met on March 6, 1985, and accepted the committee's recommendations. The following day, the members met. The membership meets twice a year, once in Ottawa, and once in another university community. This time the meeting was held in Ottawa. I was invited to be present and to answer possible questions.

When our request for membership came up, Dr. Saywell reported. He gave a sympathetic account of the accomplishments of the College in such a short time. No questions were raised as to whether Redeemer was a credible and viable institution of higher learning. Apparently everyone seemed to agree that we were. The questions that were raised centred around academic freedom. A few presidents insisted that academic freedom and an institution of higher learning based on a faith commitment were mutually exclusive. This same discussion had taken place a year before, when Trinity Western University applied for membership in the AUCC. That request was tabled, because Trinity Western had a faith statement to which all university employees and students had to subscribe. Two meetings were spent dealing with Trinity Western's request, and finally the university was accepted. That decision paved the way for us to be admitted as well.

One female president had serious objections to our Statement of Basis and Principles. She accused us, as I mentioned earlier, of male chauvinism, and even of gender discrimination. Yet the motion to admit Redeemer College to provisional membership passed with an overwhelming majority. We thanked the Lord for His care, and for allowing us to make another step toward final recognition by all universities, especially in Ontario, and by the Ontario government.

In September 1985, we enrolled 242 students. That number of students exceeded AUCC's requirements of 200 students when we applied for ordinary membership a few years later.

Three Unforgettable Events

The year 1984 was a year I will never forget. Three events took place which stand out in my mind. The first, the evaluation of my presidency was not earthshaking, but it caused me some anxieties. Was my work satisfactory? More important, would the board want a non-academic at the helm of the College now that the College was off to a good start and running well? Many people were interviewed: staff, faculty, administrators, board members, members of the academic council, members of the support community and even Dr. Diekema, president of Calvin College and Dr. Lee, president of McMaster University. I do not know the details of the deliberations, but after a period of time the board reappointed me for another four years.

I felt humbled by the confidence expressed by the board in its decision. Who was I that I should be the person to continue such important work in the Kingdom of God? I was delighted at the same time, for I had hoped to be president a while longer. With the help of so many dedicated people around me, and above all, with the help of God, I trusted that I would be able to carry on with my work.

The second event was much more serious. One of our students, Art Vander Stelt, became very ill and was diagnosed as having a brain tumour, which proved to be malignant. Art underwent surgery, and for a while, he was able to continue his studies. Slowly he had to reduce his course load until finally he was no longer able to attend classes. Art was a very courageous young man, who was strong in his faith and an example to many. When he died, I could not attend his funeral, because I was very ill and hospitalised. Art will be remembered because he was the first one from the Redeemer College community whom the Lord took home. Since we were so small, the entire student body, together with staff and faculty, mourned the loss of Art and attended his funeral. In his memory, we established the Art Vander Stelt Memorial Scholarship, which is presented annually to a deserving student.

The third event was also very serious. I had not been feeling well, but I regarded the feelings as symptoms of the flu. After all, it was the flu season. During late January/early February, I had not allowed my not-feeling-well to take me from my duties at the College. I was convinced that I would soon feel better. Both my wife and I attended the inauguration of Dr. James de Jong, the new president of Calvin Theological Seminary, in Grand Rapids, Michigan, in February 1984. On the way home I felt so sick that I had a hard time driving home. The next day I phoned the doctor, who also diagnosed my illness as a severe flu attack. I stayed in bed a few days, but the illness worsened as time went by. I decided to go to the emergency department at Joseph Brant Hospital in Burlington, where I was immediately admitted.

After a thorough examination by a specialist, he told me that my disease was ulcerative colitis, a bowel infection. Since the bowel was severely swollen, the doctor decided to give rest to my bowel by intravenously feeding through my neck and chest for close to four weeks. Instead of getting better I became still more ill. Pneumonia, and a blood clot endangered my life. To top it off, my heartbeat became very irregular and so fast that my heart had to be shocked electrically in order to normalise the heartbeat. At that time the doctors, at the request of my son Len (who was a senior student at the medical school in Toronto), decided to send me to Western Hospital in Toronto. On Sunday morning I made the trip to Toronto by ambulance, with a nurse attending me during the trip.

That Sunday, a team of doctors examined me and conferred. Apparently, there was a difference of opinion. One of the doctors remarked that I was too ill to undergo surgery, while another doctor strongly felt that if an operation was not performed, my bowel would burst within 24 hours, with fatal results. Dr. Stone, the surgeon, made the final decision and scheduled an operation for the next day, March 20, the birthday of one of my grandsons. Many people and many churches were praying for me, and on the day of my operation, a special prayer service was held at the College. When I entered the operating room, I felt a peace that I find difficult to describe. I felt carried by the prayers of God's people. God would take care of me, and I knew that I was safely in His hand, no matter how serious my condition was.

That feeling of peace was not always present during my illness. I remember March 6, 1984, when I was still in Joseph Brant Hospital. That day I thought I would die, and I was not ready to meet my Lord. The reasons my thoughts were occupied with dying were closely connected with my family history. I had only one brother, who died during World War II on March 8. My mother died a number of years later on March 7, and my father died on March 9. Hence, when March 6 rolled around, I was convinced that it was my time to die and I was scared and struggled all day. My pastor, Rev. Jerry Hoytema, was with me, and encouraged me with words from Scripture, praying that I would receive peace. And God, who hears all prayers, granted me that peace later that evening.

The operation was a lengthy one, lasting five hours. The doctors took the major part of my bowel. Inside the bowel the doctors found a cancerous tumour. Surely, the Lord had driven the doctors to perform surgery, in spite of my serious condition, because the cancer needed to be removed. Clearly, the Lord was in charge: He still had a job for me to do, and so He spared my life. That operation was not the end of the trauma. The cancer was gone, but the little piece of bowel that was left did not want to heal. I was told that to prevent a recurrence of the cancer, the rest of the bowel had to be removed as well. On November 2, two days after the visit of the AUCC visiting committee, I went back to the hospital, and underwent successful surgery. No trace of cancer was found, thank God, and I was able to resume my duties at the College on January 1, 1985. My life has never been the same. I never take a day for granted. Each day is a gift from God, which I thankfully experience. Miracles do happen!

My thanks multiply for my co-workers at the College. During my absence Dr. Vince van Dyk, Dr. Dick Kranendonk and Mr. Arend Kersten took over from me together with the help of my assistant Mrs. Margaret Buma, who had been with us for only a few months. As a team, they did a wonderful job.

In response to my illness, the following policy was adopted by the board:

Policy for the Decision-Making Structure in the Absence of the President
1. Under the current management model, the President has two groups of primary advisors. These are:
   a. The College Council which is made up of all full-time faculty, the Librarian, the Directors and the Dean, and
   b. The Administrative Council which is made up of the Dean and the Directors.
In addition to advising the President, the College Council also advises the Dean and the Directors regarding internal policy. The Administrative Council deals primarily with matters of implementing College policies which have been approved by the Board of Governors. The President chairs all meetings of the College Council and the Administrative Council and the Dean is the Vice-Chairman.
2. To have the least disruptive process in the absence of the President, the Dean will act as chairman of the two Councils. The

Dean is the primary contact person and decision-maker, but in consultation with either one of the two Councils depending on the issue when a non-routine matter is involved. Routine business matters should be handled by the Director who is already responsible for the area.

3. Recommendations on non-routine matters should be discussed with the Chairman of the Board of Governors or his designate indicating the level of support for the recommendation. The Chairman of the Board or his designate (which may include the Executive Committee) shall then advise the Dean regarding the disposition of the matter. Such advice may include referring the matter back to either Council for further discussion.

4. The Dean is authorized to sign and attach the Academic Seal to any document either in the normal course of business or in business which has been approved in accordance with 2. and 3. above. Any documents requiring the President's signature and the Corporate Seal will be signed by the Dean after approval in accordance with 3. above.

We hoped and prayed that it would not be necessary to use this policy in the near future. But it was wise of the board to make arrangements in case of an emergency.

Tuition Fees

During the first few years, we had a hard time establishing a tuition fee that related to the cost of education. It was impossible to collect a tuition fee that would cover all the costs at the College. That was not necessary either, because we received donations from churches, individuals and businesses to help cover the cost. The tuition charged the first year was calculated as comparable to Calvin College. We needed to charge a lower tuition than charged by Calvin College to be able to attract students to our new institution. However, we could not maintain that level of tuition and pay the bills. Therefore, we needed to devise ways and means to balance the books, and not raise tuition for the students too much. Dick Kranendonk, who was a creative thinker, came up with some innovative ideas. Dick's plan was to raise the tuition, but ask parents with a higher income than the average parent to make donations to a scholarship fund. The revenue of that fund would be allocated in such a way that net tuition would be less for all students. Parents who donated to the scholarship fund would receive a tax receipt. Hence everybody would win.

We presented this plan at several meetings with the parents. Some were so excited about it that Dick, who presented the plan, got a spontaneous, warm applause at one of those meetings.

On the other hand, many parents informed us that they were no longer involved with helping their children who were in college. Those parents indicated that they had paid for Christian education during the grade school and high school years. Their children would have to take care of post-secondary costs themselves if they continued their studies. Still, other parents did not understand the plan. I received a few angry letters from parents, some accusing us of dishonesty. Even though we made use of this tuition schedule for a few years, we eventually reverted to the old way of charging tuition. Yet this plan was the forerunner of the "Forgivable Loan Program" of the Redeemer Foundation, which has helped many students at the College. The primary difference between the tuition plan and the Foundation's forgivable loan plan was that the first was considered coercive, while the latter was completely voluntary.

Facilities

The facilities at Bell Cairn Memorial School served us well. However, when the board made the decision to expand our program beyond two years, the staff was faced with a space problem. Bell Cairn school could handle a maximum of 250 students, and even then there were many limitations. We had only one laboratory, the library facility was getting too small, and there was not sufficient office space for faculty and staff. The request to place portable classrooms on the sports field was denied because the septic bed was located under the sports field. We had no choice but to look for other facilities. We approached the Hamilton Board of Education and asked them for help in our search.

The Hamilton Board of Education told us of two planned school closings: one in 1984 and another in 1985. One was a large high school on the Hamilton mountain which was occupied by two independent administrative units. One unit would close down, but the other would continue to operate. For all kinds of reasons, we came to the unanimous conclusion that it would not be viable for us to move into that high school, while it would continue to be occupied by a technical/special school. The other school was the Agnes MacPhail High School, a commercial high school located along Highway 403, across from the Roman Catholic cathedral. We became very interested in that facility for it could serve between 400 - 500 students, and it was not too far away from our dormitories and McMaster University. The same surplus school disposal policies were in effect for the Hamilton Board of Education as we had learned from the Hamilton-Wentworth Board of Education at the time of the Dundas District High School discussions. A surplus school must be made available to a list of public agencies specified in the *Education Act*.

I contacted the facilities committee of the College's board and asked the committee for a meeting to discuss the various options. The committee met on January 6, 1984, and made the following decisions pertaining to the possibilities before them:

4. The Committee recommends that the President and Business Director be authorized to negotiate the final option year of our current lease agreement with the Hamilton Board of Education.

5. The Committee recommends that an attempt be made in the lease under 4. a clause to the effect that we will be able to swap the Bell Cairn school for the Agnes MacPhail school beginning in July 1985 for a five-year lease period.

6. The Committee recommends that should it not be possible to include a clause as described in 5. above, that, as a fallback position, a further three-year annually renewable option be included in our current lease. It is to be clear that this final possibility will not be disclosed to the Hamilton Board until it is absolutely clear that a swap will not be possible.

7. The Committee further recommends that a Long-Range Facilities Planning Committee for a permanent campus be appointed consisting of Nick Van Duyvendyk, Sid Harkema, Fred Reinders, Jake Heeringa, Wytse Van Dyk, Hugh Cook, Arend Kersten and Dick Kranendonk.

A lease was ready to be signed as stipulated under number 4. above, but then the Hamilton Board of Education changed its mind about the closing of the Agnes MacPhail school. It was time for the long-range planning committee to get busy and begin planning for a permanent campus. In the next chapter I will relate the work of the committee, the building and the financing of the new campus.

The work of the committee was greatly invigorated when in July 1984 I welcomed a visitor to my office who had some wonderful news. He was a partner of an accounting firm in Hamilton and informed me that he came on behalf of one of his clients, who, according to him, had a very warm heart for the College. The accountant wanted to know who we were, what we were doing and how we had managed as a private institution without government aid. I explained everything as well as I could and inquired of him why he was asking all these questions. To my great surprise, he told me that his client wanted to donate $1 million to us for the development of a new campus. His client wanted to remain anonymous, and the accountant wanted to assure himself of the legitimacy of our cause. I almost rolled off my chair when he told me of that enormous gift. He told me that the money would not be available immediately, but that, in the meantime, we would receive interest on that money, which we could use as we saw fit. What an answer to prayer. For me it was as if the Lord was saying "Go ahead, build the campus, I will be with you."

Pipe Organ

In May 1985, the music department asked for permission to plan the purchase of a pipe organ for the new campus. A committee was formed consisting of Dr. Bert Polman (convenor), Mr. Paul Grimwood, director of music at Central Presbyterian Church in

Hamilton, Dr. Dick Kranendonk, Mr. Jan Overduin, professor of music at Wilfrid Laurier University in Waterloo and Mr. Christiaan Teeuwsen. The committee's mandate was "to study and make recommendations on all matters relating to the design and purchase of an organ for the chapel/auditorium for the new campus of Redeemer College." The committee solicited proposals from five organ builders; three in Canada, and two in The Netherlands. The choice was made to ask J. Reil Orgelmakers, Heerde, The Netherlands to build a new pipe organ for the Redeemer campus. Reil was chosen, because, according to the committee, "Reil had the best instrument at the best price." The executive committee of the board agreed and decided to have the president sign the contract for an amount of Fl.420,800. ($200,000). The rationale of the committee for buying the Reil organ was as follows:

Facts:
1. A pipe organ is needed for the educational program of the music department in the same way that a microscope is needed by a biologist.
2. Redeemer College has ordered a high quality pipe organ which will attract many serious students and performers to the campus so that in this area as well, we will be known for high standards.
3. The financing of the pipe organ is totally outside of the budget, and funds are contributed for this project by people who are convinced of its need.
4. At this time, about half of the cost of the organ has already been received in cash donations.

It took a while before the contract was finally signed. The distance and the unfamiliarity of the organ builder with the layout of the auditorium did not help. Many conference calls were made. Some of our people, including myself, who were in The Netherlands for other purposes, visited with the Reil brothers, and one of the representatives of the Reil firm visited us as well. The Reil people were very concerned about the acoustics in the building. If we had agreed to all of their proposals, we would have built our auditorium around the organ. It demonstrated that the Reil brothers put their heart in their work, as was also evident in the following quote from their letter:

> An organ has been developed from of old to support the human voice, the most beautiful of all instruments given by our Creator is that human voice. Following that example we build our organs. That's why we believe it to be our duty to do this as beautifully and well as possible.

The order placed on March 12, 1986, read as follows:

> We hereby order for delivery and placement at the Redeemer College campus in Ancaster, Ontario
>   1 only two-keyboard tracker organ with concave radiating AGO-Style pedal board and one straight pedal board.

The organ would consist of "Hoofdwerk," "Bovenwerk," and "Pedaal," with 23 voices. The entire organ would be enclosed in a cabinet of oak, cut from one tree. The pipes would be constructed of one batch of lead and tin. The weight of the organ was 4,600 kg. The material was selected by the builder at the time of the order. Actual construction began November 5, 1986. The organ was built in The Netherlands, dismantled and shipped in a container by boat to Canada.

The boat arrived in Toronto around the middle of September 1987. The crews for installation and intonation came on September 21, and the organ, which was installed on a moveable platform, was ready to be played on November 1, 1987. It was the first Reil organ in Canada. We were very pleased with the workmanship, the service, but above all, with the sound of the organ. When Chris Teeuwsen, music professor, played the organ, it gave me the shivers, and I thanked God that we were in the possession of such a beautiful instrument. My prayer is that, for many years to come, many of our students may learn to play on that instrument to the honour and glory of God.

The first staff of *The Crown*, 1983. From left to right:
John Noordhof, Rick Van Holst, Harry Zantingh,
Sylvia Keesmaat, Tony Boer, and Wilma Jonkman.

Telford Matthews, a student from Dominica.

Albert M. Wolters and Henry R De Bolster listening
attentively to a speaker at our first academic conference.

Picture of the Beach Blvd. campus.

FIVE

The New Campus

The greatest challenge we faced during my presidency was the planning for and the building of the new campus. As I mentioned in the previous chapter, a facilities planning committee had been appointed by the board, and on March 24, 1984, during my hospitalization, the committee was given the following mandate:

1. To present to the board by the 1st of September, 1984, a complete system for the orderly development of a campus for Redeemer College in the greater Hamilton area as outlined in board policy. The system should consider all aspects of the whole process and should break down the development process into development phases and each development phase into its simplest task component.
2. Each development phase and each task component should be described carefully. The description of each task component should include:
   a. who performs it;
   b. what information the person or group needs in order to perform the task;
   c. what task precedes the task being described;
   d. what task follows the task being described;
   e. who or which group of persons gives the authorization to perform the task.
3. The complete system will organize the phases and tasks within each phase into a logical pattern so that the whole development process flows naturally from its inception of this particular mandate, to the final completion of the campus. In addition, the system will include a check- plan with critical dates, target start-

ing dates, and target completion dates, together with a proper flow chart. In developing the system, the board of governors would like the committee to consider the following:

a. allowing related Christian agencies the opportunity of locating on campus;

b. providing the college with adequate classroom space, dormitory space, and administration space for the summer of 1986.

The board's executive committee during the campus development.
Left to right, front row: John Zantingh, Henry R. De Bolster,
Nick Van Duyvendyk, Ineke Bezuyen; back row: Kees Vreugdenhil,
Bruce Dykstra, William Smouter and John Vriend.

On April 2, the committee met and divided the many tasks system among the committee members and asked for regular progress reports and to come with recommendations to the board by September 1. Dick Kranendonk was the coordinator. He would stay in touch with the members of the committee and assist them as much as possible. He hoped to have a preliminary report ready by the middle of May.

Earlier I mentioned that the committee first looked at existing facilities that could be used for another couple of years. But since none were available, the committee began to focus all of its attention on planning for a new campus.

On May 15, F.J. Reinders and Associates presented its report called "The Planning and Design Process for Redeemer College." This was a thorough report dealing with questions of land and buildings and how the plans could be realised. It was pointed out that in order to deal with land and buildings, we must prepare a long-term curriculum plan. Special attention should be given to the social and financial viability of each course or program in the plan. The report raised the question: "What are your enrollment projections for the next five to ten years?" Based on the answer to this question it would be necessary to project building requirements, like: administrative, academic classrooms, academic labs, academic support (library, faculty offices, audio and video storage and control, study areas, etc.), athletic facilities, student services, circulation, building services and residential. The above would determine size and property location. I gave this report to Dick Kranendonk with the request to find answers to the many questions resulting from the single question in the Reinders report.

When the Reinders report came in, we were informed that a piece of land was available in Ancaster, on Highway 53 close to the proposed site of the Ancaster Christian Reformed Church, near Fiddlers Green Road. The land was owned by Mr. Peter Turkstra and some partners, which we referred to as the Turkstra property. I met with Mr. Turkstra, who had become an enthusiastic supporter of the College. When he heard that we were interested in buying the land, he offered it to us at a very reasonable price. However, the land was zoned "agriculture" and there was uncertainty whether a residential college could be built on that site. As part of the investigation, I met with Ms. Ann Sloat, the mayor of Ancaster. She believed that it might be possible to build a college on that property but that residences could be a problem. She promised to inquire with the Ministry of Agriculture. She was willing to support our plans and do her best on our behalf. The Ancaster News Journal of October 3, 1984 mentioned the mayor saying: "The college would be great for the community," adding, "it's certainly to our advantage to welcome you to our borders."

As a result of the Reinders report and the availability of the Turkstra property, the facilities planning committee and the executive committee met at the end of May and decided to accept the Reinders report as "our planning mode up to the construction phase," to use the decision of the board that Redeemer College would offer a complete degree program as the starting point for our discussions, and to place an option to purchase on the Turkstra property. It was also decided to retain F.J. Reinders and Associates Ltd. as our project manager to carry out the functions of the "Planning and Design Process."

Our first priority was to study enrollment projections to be able to estimate the total space that would be required. All faculty members were requested to provide an estimate of the space needed to teach their courses. As a result of these studies, the committee proposed "that the campus be developed to accommodate 500 students, using a "modular" construction mode, thereby allowing easy expansion to accommodate 1,000 students." Very rough estimates projected academic and administrative space requirements of 130,000 to 150,000 square feet and an immediate need for 48,000 square feet of residential space. When this report was submitted to the board, the committee noted that it had completed its mandate and asked to be discharged by the board. The board discharged the committee in September and agreed that the president should appoint a campus development committee which would report to him. I agreed to report the deliberations and activities of the committee to the board on a regular basis. I appointed the same people who had served on the facilities planning committee, with the exception of Mr. Fred Reinders, who had an obvious conflict of interest. All remaining members accepted their new appointments.

We soon found out that there would be serious difficulties in obtaining a zoning amendment for the Turkstra property. Both the Ministry of Agriculture and the regional government were opposed to a zoning change. If we wanted to continue our efforts to change the zoning, we would have to make an official request. Roland Jonker, who was assigned by F.J. Reinders and Associates to be our project manager, informed us that in all probability our application would be denied. The next step would be to appeal the local decision to the Ontario Municipal Board, which would not likely grant our request because of the official government policy with respect to agricultural land in the area. The delays and appeals would make occupying a campus by September 1986 impossible.

We informed Mr. Turkstra of our dilemma. He agreed that we would not likely be able to overcome the obstacles before us on time, and he graciously suggested that we look for another parcel of land which could be zoned for institutional use. We abandoned the offer to purchase with the concurrence of Mr. Turkstra and his partners. We were back to square one. Where would we find a suitable and affordable property? We wanted to locate in the general Ancaster area because it was so centrally located. Early October the town council had also given us a warm welcome. Not only the mayor, but the whole council was eager to have our college locate in Ancaster.

The Lord provided. We had experienced the Lord's timely intervention so many times during the College's short history. After our visit with Mr. Turkstra, we met in my office, together with Roland Jonker and Clare Riepma of F.J. Reinders and Associates, to consider our next step. We asked Roland and Clare to find other property that might be available in the general area of the Turkstra property. After our meeting, we brought this matter before the Lord in prayer and asked Him to open a way for us to acquire the necessary land. When Roland and Clare left, we committed them into the hands of the Lord, believing that He would provide.

The next day Roland and Clare visited a developer, Alarco Co., which owned land in the east Ancaster area on Highway 53, now Garner Road. To their astonishment, this developer told them that at a meeting the night before the company had decided to sell land that they would not be able to develop in the next ten years. Hence 50 acres of land along Highway 53 would be available. The land was zoned for agriculture, but the zoning could be changed to institutional use since the property was within the urban development area. The property miracle became even greater when they discussed the price. Land in that vicinity was selling for $7,000 to $12,000 per acre, but the developer was willing to sell the property for $3,500 per acre, the same price he had paid in 1967. The Lord had heard our prayers. It was a confirmation for me that our planning was being blessed by Him.

There was an old farmhouse on the property which had recently been partly destroyed by fire. In that house lived a bachelor farmer, Mr. Vivian Whaley, whose mother was the previous owner of the 50 acres. He personally still owned 26 acres of land adjoining the 50 acre parcel. We contacted Mr. Whaley and told him that we were interested in purchasing the 50 acres and that, if we did, he would have to move off the property. We offered to buy his 26 acres of land for the same price per acre as we would be paying for the 50 acres. At first he was not interested, but when we promised him that he could continue to live on the property, do some farming, and that we would provide a mobile home for him, he was ready to make a deal with us. Mr. Whaley lived on our campus until he died in 1995, shortly after I retired. He was a good neighbour. Even though his roosters would wake the students early in the morning, he was a unique presence on campus.

The executive committee of the board met to discuss this unexpected turn of events. It was clear to all that once again the Lord had worked in wondrous ways. The executive committee gladly approved the offer to buy the two parcels of land. The conditions were that the board and membership approve the purchase, that the zoning be changed, and that all the normal conditions, which are part of a commercial real estate transaction, be met. We made sure that all the conditions were clearly spelled out. We did not wish to be involved in another potential legal action because of procedural misunderstandings. The board approved the offer in January 1985, and instructed me to have our project managers continue the preparations for construction.

I informed the new mayor, Mr. Robert (Bob) Wade, of our plans and asked him to meet with our project managers. Mr. Wade was enthusiastic about our plans and promised to do what he could. Roland Jonker met with the town staff and was told that he could count on their full cooperation. On February 25, a public meeting of the Town Council was held. Many neighbours were present to hear about that new college. Many questions were raised. It was clear that several people did not understand what it meant to have a Reformed college in their neighbourhood. They heard the word "reform," instead of "Reformed," and were afraid that they would get juvenile delinquents in their backyard who were just released from prison. There were no objections to building a college, even though some of these same people later met with Roland and Dick about the erection of a six foot fence, to keep these "reform students" out of their property. This matter was resolved amicably. Once they understood the true nature of the College, our neighbours agreed that a four foot fence was sufficient.

After the public meeting, the council met to consider two important matters. The first one was the matter of re-zoning. The Council needed to amend the zoning by-law to designate our property for institutional use. This by-law was passed in three readings that same evening.

The second matter was more difficult. It dealt with the impost fee. An impost fee is a special tax the municipalities raise when new land is to be developed. It is charged for infrastructure development costs that municipalities provide because of the new developments. The town council could charge one. The town council staff had done their homework and reported that municipalities often waive that fee when an educational institution is involved. The mayor asked for a motion to waive the impost fee. The motion was made, but there was no immediate seconder. The mayor looked left and right to find someone to second the motion. When he was almost ready to declare that there was no support, one alderman said: "All right, I will second the motion." Since there were only five council members present, including the mayor, and since two members had already expressed themselves in favour, it only took a few minutes to pass the motion. That was a major victory for us, because the impost fee could have been as high as $100,000. What an exciting evening it was! We were able to report that two hurdles had been successfully overcome. Thanks be to God!

We had a property big enough to build a campus for 1,000 students, and to include the offices of the Ontario Alliance of Christian School Societies. But what would the buildings look like? We gave Roland the space estimates received from faculty and staff for classrooms and offices. We were anxious to know the proposed shape and form of the academic building. We had already discussed that we would like to have all facilities under one roof so that the students, once they were in the building, would not have to go outside to move from class to class. That idea came from Rev. B.J. Haan of Dordt College. He told me that he had one regret about the structure of the Dordt campus, namely that the students had to move from building to building to go to their classes. "If I had to do it again," he said, "I would build a tower."

Our students requested that we build townhouses for dormitories, instead of the usual university housing. They liked their present living arrangements and wanted to continue that lifestyle, provided the number of students in each home be restricted. They requested that we build homes that would house no more than eight students.

After tendering, and on the recommendation of Roland Jonker, we selected Mr. John Knibb of Roth-Knibb Architects to be our architect. It did not take him long to present some sketches. Mr. Knibb had visited Calvin College and studied the history of the Reformation. He wanted to create physical space which would bring the purpose of the College to expression. I remember that, when I saw those first sketches, I was overwhelmed and could not believe that we would ever build something so beautiful and yet so functional.

We were very busy running a college and making plans for a new campus. How were we to pay for both? It was wonderful to have great plans and to be moved by the possibility of a new campus, but we would need funds before our plans could become a reality.

Financing the New Campus

The board had witnessed rapid growth of the College and had made the decision to make campus development and construction a high priority. For that reason, we were not able to plan and execute a formal fundraising campaign. There were only so many hours in a day. With the approval of the board and the membership, it was decided to have a limited capital campaign. We needed more money than the one million dollar donation. That amount was not sufficient to build a campus. The board asked us to look for ways and means to borrow funds, but cautioned that the debt had to be manageable. Already on May 30, 1984, two financing plans had been presented to the board.

The first plan was to issue deep discount mortgage bonds to the constituency. These bonds would give a greater tax benefit to the purchaser than regular bonds. Interest on ordinary bonds would be subject to 100 percent income inclusion, while deep discount bonds would result in capital gains for the investor which would be subject to 50 percent income inclusion. The second plan was to set up a separate for-profit corporation which would own the campus and lease it back to the College. The board referred these plans back to the staff and asked us to involve Mr. Bert Bakker, our solicitor and Mr. Ronald C. Knechtel of Clarkson, Gordon & Co., our auditors, for further study.

A revised financing plan was presented to the executive committee on October 24, 1984. It was a variation of the deep discount mortgage bond plan, but with exciting new possibilities. Mr. Knechtel suggested that the College issue unitised mortgage bonds which would be eligible for self-directed RRSP investments. Ron informed us that such a plan had been used by some churches in their building program, and he gave us the documentation of a similar plan developed for the Sheridan Park Alliance Church. All regulatory approvals for such a plan had been obtained by Mr. Knechtel from the Pension and Profit Sharing Plans Section of the Department of National Revenue, Taxation in Ottawa. Our solicitor was positive about the plan, and advised adoption. Mr. Bakker's comments were:

a. The plan is simple and understandable
b. previous experience convinced him it works well
c. this plan does not require a prospectus under Ontario Securities legislation
d. the plan should be OK in light of Clarkson, Gordon & Co.'s experience and involvement.

The executive committee approved working out the details of such a plan and to contact a trust company which the College would be able to appoint as trustee of the mortgage bonds as well as the group RRSP.

At the same meeting, Mr. Nick Van Duyvendyk, chairman of the board, presented a letter he had received from Mr. Dick Van Dyke of Ottawa in which he outlined a "price level adjusted" bond instrument that had been successfully used in the United Kingdom and some other jurisdictions. The letter was given to Dick Kranendonk, who would further investigate this instrument to determine whether it would be compatible with the unitised mortgage bond structure.

By November 13, 1984, a report was submitted by the administrative council to the executive committee. This report was presented during my second absence from the College for further surgery. The report approved by the executive committee confirmed that the price level adjusted mortgage bond plan was indeed compatible with our bond structure, that the plan had been completed and that our solicitors were drafting the final documents.

Dick Kranendonk had developed the plan in consultation with legal and accounting professionals. The following explains the principles on which the price level adjusted RRSP eligible unitised mortgage bond plan and the overall campus financing had been based.

a. The bond investment costs were based on two factors:
   1. The rate of inflation
   2. the real interest payment of 4 percent
Only the interest portion of the investment costs was to be paid out to the bondholders on each June 30 and December 31.
The inflation portion was to be calculated semi-annually and added to the principal of each bond.
b. The real interest payments were not to be the cause for an increase in the tuition fees for the students at any time during the thirty years of the mortgage bond plan.
c. The principal and the accumulated inflation adjustments were to be repaid out of the following:
   1. net room and board fees

2. net ancillary services revenues
3. donations made specifically to retire the mortgage bond debt by investors who would donate their mortgage bonds or RRSP funds to the college
d. Bridge financing should be obtained from a financial institution, without the requirement of personal guarantees, at the prime lending rate or less to finance the difference between the available funds and the construction costs of the campus until the bonds would be placed with the supporting community. The bridge financing would be secured by the college's property.
e. The initial mortgage amount of $8.2 million (assuming a constant inflation rate of 4 percent and a steady increase of twenty students per year to 500 students by 1996) was projected to increase to about $11 million by 1999, because of the addition of the inflation amount to the principal of the mortgage bonds. If there would be no further construction, the mortgage indebtedness would begin to decrease in 1999.

The financing principles and structure was approved by the board on January 26, 1985. A mortgage trust deed for up to $25 million in constant 1985 dollars was drafted and approved as well as the immediate authorization to issue $8 million in 4 percent real interest bonds. All these plans were approved by the membership at the annual meeting held on April 13, 1985. That meeting also approved the campus construction plans. These approvals made it possible to begin selling the mortgage bonds and to apply for bridge financing.

We applied at two banks: the Canadian Imperial Bank of Commerce (CIBC) and the Bank of Montreal. The application was for bridge financing in the amount of $7 million for 1985 to be increased to $9.2 million in 1986. We asked for the prime lending rate or less, with a first mortgage as the sole security. To our great delight, the CIBC accepted our proposal, and charged us a rate of one-half percent below its prime lending rate. The only thing they asked for was a letter of comfort from the Council of Christian Reformed Churches in Canada. Rev. Jack Vos, chairman of the interim committee of the council, wrote a letter confirming the relationship between the Christian Reformed Church and Redeemer College. He also stated that the members of this denomination never abandoned a project to which they were communally committed. Two senior bankers, who were closely associated with the College, could not believe their eyes when they saw the agreement we made with the CIBC. Once again, the Lord inclined hearts and minds and made the impossible a reality.

Arend Kersten and I went into the community to solicit donations for campus development and to promote the mortgage bonds for direct and RRSP investments. Once more, we went to Woodstock and St. Catharines for our pilot project. On June 22, 1985, I could report to the executive committee that we had received a total of $2.5 million in donations, bond purchases and loans.

The price level adjusted mortgage bond plan was something new in the financial world and was consequently questioned by many people, especially by our business people.

We wrote the following to our business community:

> Redeemer College is approaching you as a member of our business community with a request to assist Redeemer College by providing the necessary bridge financing for developing the new campus. Bridge financing is also sometimes referred to as interim financing and covers the period between the time construction starts and committed funds are received. In Redeemer College's case this bridge financing is needed to cover the period between the time pledges are made by our members and supporters and the time these pledges are actually collected. The pledges consist of both donations and future RRSP investments.
>
> We are, therefore, not asking you, the members of our business community for a donation, but rather that you purchase Redeemer College bonds or RRSP's or provide us with loans. Clarkson, Gordon has informed us that the increase in value of the Bonds will be considered as capital gains and not as income. This consideration means that the return to the investor will be equal to or better than current investments in Guaranteed Investment

Certificates (GIC's) available from banks and trust companies.

Even though your return on investment will be equal to or better than GIC's, Redeemer College will save about 66 percent of what it would cost for a conventional mortgage. The benefit of the type of mortgage offered by Redeemer College is shown in an article which appeared in the April 6, 1985 issue of the *Financial Post*, which is attached.

Your investments in Redeemer College are secured by a First Mortgage Trust Deed between Redeemer College and Canada Trust.

Redeemer College will not commit contracts which it is not able to cover out of donations, bonds, RRSP's, loans and line of credit by its banker, the Canadian Imperial Bank of Commerce.

The article in the *Financial Post* read in part as follows:

New Bond Could Shake up Investment World

A new breed of bond is about to surface in Canada—possibly this month. One of its architects estimates it could account for more than $10 billion in pension fund assets in the short term. And, before too long, individuals might also be able to get in on the action.

The Post has learned that several provincial governments, Ottawa, and some corporations are studying the feasibility of issuing what they call "index-linked securities". These are long term bonds, which would guarantee investors a "real" rate of return after inflation as measured by the Consumer Price Index.

Return on the bonds would comprise a fixed portion (say 3-1/2 to 4-1/2 percent), plus the inflation rate for the preceding year. This would be compounded, effectively indexing principal and interest.

I am grateful that our business community responded so generously each time we approached them. The response to our request for bridge financing was such that we never needed more than $5.3 million from the bank for bridge financing, and because of our continued effort in asking RRSP contributions from our support community, we were able to eliminate our entire bank-debt in the early 1990's.

The finance committee of the board met at least once a month to determine which contracts could be awarded. Early in this process, Mr. Nick Van Duyvendyk, chairman of the board, made sure that the committee would be careful and remember its responsibilities towards the support community. Therefore he insisted on discussing the "worst case scenario," as he called it, each time a new contract was to be awarded. The committee monitored the campus construction by monthly up-to-date financial reports on cash flow. Contracts were reviewed on a monthly basis so that construction could be terminated on short notice in the event serious cash flow difficulties should arise.

We never awarded a contract without having the finances in place. Dick Kranendonk and Roland Jonker were the first to make sure that we could afford the next step in the construction process; next the committee looked at the proposals, and only when all agreed that the funds were in place were the contracts awarded. I have nothing but praise and gratitude for all who diligently met, monitored the progress and made responsible decisions, always asking the Lord to bless us and to allow us to step forward in faith.

The scale model of the new campus. Left to right;
Roland Jonker, Dick L. Kranendonk, Henry R. De Bolster,
Wytse Van Dyk and Hugh Cook.

Groundbreaking Ceremony

On June 22, 1985, the groundbreaking ceremony took place. Representatives from the provincial and federal governments, Mr. Bob Wade, the mayor of Ancaster, Dr. Lee, president of McMaster University, and representatives from the Christian school movement, including the Ontario Alliance of Christian School Societies were present. We were permitted to use the parking lots at the Ancaster Fair Grounds, almost adjacent to our property. A shuttle bus would take the guests to the place of the ceremony. However, on June 22nd, it rained hard. We could not even enter the property because the grounds were soaked. Peter Hoogendam, our maintenance director, brought a wheelbarrow with grass and top soil into the Merritt Hall on the Ancaster Fair Grounds, put the sods in a bushel and the groundbreaking ceremony took place inside the building. Holding the shovel were Mr. Nick Van Duyvendyk, chairman of the board, Mr. Chris Ward, our MPP, and Mr. John Luth, the president of the student council. I gave a short meditation on Psalm 127: l: "Unless the Lord builds the house, its builders labour in vain" (the text is engraved on the cornerstone of the academic building), welcomed everybody present and shared the joy of that incredible moment. In spite of the rain it was a memorable occasion, very unique considering the circumstances.

The Construction

The actual construction commenced in September 1985. The tenders kept coming in on, or below budget. Even though we experienced heavy rain in the fall of 1985, the work progressed. Roland Jonker kept assuring us that we would be able to move to our new campus by September 1, l986.

Arend Kersten and I were on the road most of the time to raise funds for our new campus, as well as for the regular operating expenses of the College. It was difficult to raise the budgeted donations for campus construction as many people were already giving for the College's operating needs. We organised host and hostess suppers in many communities. We wanted Redeemer College to be a grassroots organisation. The College belonged to God's people, and we wanted God's people to be very involved in this work. The people in the communities where we organised these host and hostess suppers were enthused with us, but apparently we had given the impression that these meetings were for public relations purposes only. Hence the donations we received at these meetings were minimal. Yet, the RRSP bonds sold well and helped us with our cash flow needs.

I was amazed then, and still am today, that we never lacked funds. There were times when we did not know where the money would come from to pay our bills and pay the salaries of our staff and faculty. It always came, because the Lord took care of us. Many times I was reminded that we were dealing with a project of faith and that it would only succeed if we kept our eyes fixed on the Lord and truly believed that He would take care of us. We were reminded that the Lord sent us people for our administration, committees, and board, who were not only qualified, but who depended on the Lord in all they did. For them, too, it was a labour of love. They performed their duties with joy and dedication, knowing that even though we stayed within budget, the money to a large extent had to come from donations.

During this time, Arend Kersten tendered his resignation to become the executive director of the Reformed Christian Business Professional Association. We owe Arend a lot for the work he tirelessly did for the College. We wished him well in his new position.

Six months later, Mr. William (Bill) Smouter joined us to assist Dick Kranendonk and to take over some of Arend's work. Bill resigned as a member of the board to become a staff member. He took early retirement from the Bank of Montreal to join our staff. Bill did a great job for the College the many years he served with me.

We also hired Dr. James (Jim) Payton to become the academic dean at the College. Jim served in that position for about two years, after which he became one of our history professors. Justin Cooper, who had successfully defended his doctoral dissertation, became dean in Jim's place. Justin had administrative experience since he had been one of our academic administrators at the beginning.

In January 1986, the board decided to bring the positions of dean and that of the business and finance director in line with the positions at other educational institutions. The board changed the nomenclature of these two positions to vice-president (academic), and vice-president (administration and finance).

In February, Mr. Nick Van Duyvendyk, board chairman, underwent serious surgery. We feared for his life, but he recuperated fully and was able to continue his work as chairman of the board. We thanked the Lord. Nick was a great help to me during the many years he served on the board. He was cautious, yet determined, always available and ready to lend a listening ear, even though he was a busy man as assistant deputy minister in the federal Ministry of Transport. While he had to travel all the way from Ottawa, he faithfully attended the meetings of the finance committee, of the executive committee, and of the board.

The Lord always provides the right people in building the Kingdom of God. We experienced that in the appointments of our faculty members. We were only a small—and in the eyes of the university community—an insignificant institution. Yet we had a faculty that was equal to, if not better than, the faculty of many larger institutions.

During the construction, several proposals were made to add to the academic building or to the campus. Some were good suggestions but out of reach for budgetary reasons. There were two items which were discussed at length. The first one was a proposal from some faculty members to install a stained glass window. The board was enthused about a special window in the College. Yet the proposal was rejected, not only for lack of funds, but also because the sketches of the proposed window were somewhat disappointing to the members of the board. Perhaps sometime in the future someone might be found willing to donate a stained glass window.

The other item was the question of a president's residence on campus. Many universities and colleges have a residence for the president. The board decided that such a dwelling was not in the budget and was not a priority item. Unknown to me, someone came forward and committed to cover more than half the construction cost if the house was built at the same time as the campus. The projected cost of the house was $100,000, which was far below market value. The board looked at the offer and decided to go ahead with the construction of a president's house, and gave the following ground for doing so:

> The net cash investment of the college to build the president's residence now is $40,000. The net savings to the college on an annual basis is projected to be in the order of $10,000 per year, on lower salary to the president, on campus entertainment of dignitaries, and on campus lodging of presidential guests.

The campus was finally completed in January 1987 at a cost of $13.3 million. A total of about $4 million had been received in donations, consisting of both cash and gifts in kind. The gifts in kind consisted of gifts like the grand piano in the auditorium, the back-up generator, and the amounts saved as a result of the low bids from contractors in the support community. Therefore, the total campus construction debt-load taken on by the College consisted of $9.3 million made up of $4 million invested by the support community in bonds and loans and the remaining $5.3 million in bank bridge financing. This meant that a total of about $8 million had been received from the support community for campus development between July 1984 and January 1987. What an incredible amount of money! It expressed the love and confidence of our community in the Christian higher education that is offered at Redeemer College.

The completed campus.

The price level adjusted bonds were designed to capitalise the inflation portion. We understood that our outstanding debt would increase for the first twelve years. Additional housing construction would generate more rental income and, therefore, would help to repay this debt. The amount paid for residence rent per student at the Frances Road location was $1,525 and for the academic building at Beach Boulevard it was $475. These amounts were to be allocated to the capital cost in constant 1984 dollars. This debt and repayment structure should have put everyone at ease when the financial statements began to show a deficit. However, the opposite became a reality.

The deficits increased when the rental equivalent of the tuition our students paid was used for the operating fund instead. This redirection of funds was understandable because we needed to expand our programs as well as hire new faculty. We knew that in these beginning stages we needed to concentrate on student enrollment to become a viable institution. To become a viable institution, we needed programs that would attract more students, as well as new faculty. That expansion program made the student/faculty ratio very advantageous to the students, but very expensive for the College. Nevertheless, it was the only way for the College to grow and to earn its credibility in the academic world.

During later years, when the full effect of the operating deficits as a result of the expansion of the academic program became greater, concern was more and more focussed on the campus construction and bond indebtedness because the inflation portion was not being paid out. It is good to remember that the construction of the campus was necessary for Redeemer to become a viable institution. The financing of the campus was well planned, and even the rapid expansion of the academic program did not alter the planned deficits. The mortgage deed of $25 million was the visionary decision made by the board so that the debt could increase to that amount. Accepting the projections that the student/faculty ratio would eventually reach 17 to 1, the board approved additional residence construction in later years. Even with that added expansion, the debt was not projected to increase beyond the year 2004. We were of the opinion that a reduction in the overall debt would begin as soon as the College would have an enrollment of 500 students. In my fundraising journeys, I always used the example of a transport company which, with one big truck, needed a full load to make ends meet. Similarly, we would accomplish the goal of a "full load" when the 500 student number would be reached.

The Move to the New Campus

On August 11, 1986, the day came to move from Beach Boulevard to the new campus. A moving company owned by a Christian was able to move us at a very reasonable cost in one day. The academic building was not quite finished, but it was possible for us to move in. Many volunteers helped us move everything into the gymnasium. At the time, the gym had only a cement floor, so the furniture and the many boxes did not damage anything. It took us a while to move everything into place. To make sure that we would be ready by September 1, we had asked all staff to take their vacations in July. After much hard work by everyone involved, we were indeed ready to register the students at the new campus when they came in early September. The residences were livable, even though the finishing touches still took some time to complete. The students cooperated wonderfully. It was a time of excitement, also of anxieties, but above all, a time filled with gratitude to God. All of us were overjoyed with our own incredible facilities.

Dedication and First Graduation

It was time to formally dedicate our campus to the glory of God. We wanted to have a ceremony where we could celebrate as well as give thanks. Already on May 27, 1985, I appointed a campus dedication/graduation committee to look into the many aspects of the opening ceremonies. I wrote in my memo:

> Though the official opening of the campus is still a long time off, nevertheless I believe that we are going to need a lot of time to get a good program together for the opening of the campus. Since I would like to consider the possibility of having our first graduation

exercises at the same time, may I ask you to be kind enough to form an official committee for these functions.

The committee consisted of Arend Kersten, Bert Polman, Jim Payton, Ineke Bezuyen, John Luth and Sylvia Keesmaat-De Jong. These people deserve a lot of praise. They met often. They included the staff, the faculty, the students and the community. The wishes and desires of all these groups were considered in the planning process.

At first the students were very divided about whether their graduation would take place in the month of May, or at the time of the official opening. I wanted the pioneer students to be part of the new campus, so that they would always remember that they were the first graduates both from Redeemer College as well as the new campus. After much debate, they agreed to go along with my suggestion and the graduating class became a very important part of the opening exercises. Another question raised was the role of the valedictorian. Should the valedictorian speak at the breakfast when graduands and faculty would be together, or at the ceremony in the afternoon? We were not sure, since we had never heard of a valedictorian speaking at an official graduation ceremony of other colleges and universities. The graduands were persistent and wanted their speaker to address the audience in the afternoon. Finally we decided that, because we were different, it would be special to have one of the graduands speak at the opening ceremonies. Sylvia De Bruyne-Taekema was chosen by the graduands to be their representative. She did such a wonderful job that ever since that first graduation one of the graduands speaks at the annual convocation. Here follows her speech in its entirety:

It is with a sense of great honour and even greater joy that I can bring, this afternoon, warm greetings and hearty congratulations to the College and its community on behalf of the pioneer students and first graduating class. Speaking here on behalf of my classmates, I find it rather fitting that I am graduating today with a major in history; for, we as graduates now represent, in part, the history of

Redeemer College. I also find somewhat appropriate the date of this occasion, centred as it is in the harvest time and the season of thanksgiving. History and harvest time. To many or most of us, these suggest something is at an end. Yet today we come together to celebrate "new beginnings." Do the two go together at all?

I have been taught and have myself adopted the view that history is not something dry and dusty, dead and gone, but something directed, living and purposeful. The present is and can only be a response to its past, be it a continuation of, or a radical turning away from it. And from my growing up years on a Southwestern Ontario farm, I have learned not only to celebrate the fullness of the harvest time, but also that the judging of methods and the hopes and plans drawn for next year are largely based on the success of the crop just taken in. Today, the 8th of November, 1986, we as graduates and as a college community take stock of yesterday's efforts and plan for tomorrow accordingly. I believe our past has proved a solid foundation for the present and we need not, we dare not, turn away from it. Coming together to celebrate new beginnings, we celebrate also the vision, the faith, the foundation, the labour which has brought us through the past to this present joyful day.

As students, we came to the College in September of 1982, uncertain of just what we were looking for, uncertain of just what we might find. Our reasons for coming were varied. Admittedly, many of us came because we simply did not know yet what else to do with ourselves. If we did not know the particulars, however, we did come seeking one thing, an education. And, thank the Lord, we graduate today having received one.

But why come to this college for our education? Surely there were many more schools to choose from. Why choose this one— indeed, many may wonder. Many more may shrug their shoulders but allow our decision in the name of individual freedom, including, I suppose, the freedom to make mistakes. There may be some who smile and dub our Christian focus nice, but not necessary. Indeed there are others who would suggest we came here seeking shelter from a reality with which we could not cope and who charge that the education we receive, with all its emphasis on the Bible and time "lost" on developing a "Christian mind," was not a real education at all, nor the degrees we receive today real degrees.

Redeemer College is no shelter from the so-called "real" world, and I deny the charge that in coming here we have somehow missed out on a real education. Rather, I submit that in coming here we have come further in discovering the reality of our existence and have been educated in the most real and valuable way possible.

For the reality of our world, be it confessed or denied, is that it exists as God's creation, and ours a true education that has taught us that we must respond to it as caretakers and stewards. The reality of our world is that all men are brothers in Christ, and ours a true education that has taught us we must relate under His law of love and respond with justice. The reality of our world is that progress and wealth are trusts, gifts, blessings that command humility, thanksgiving and responsibility.

The theme and point of it all is SERVICE. Life is, first of all, service to our God and to our neighbour. At Redeemer College, the confession remains that "learning is for serving." We worked hard at filling all our requirements in philosophy, languages, history, literature, the sciences, but with a confessed Christian perspective. Through all our learning our education aimed at preparing us to answer, "Speak, Lord, for your servant hears," and opened our ears to the command to "cast your bread on the waters." What good are the tools, quite plainly, if one does not know how to use them? Our task in learning and serving is a return to reality, to a recognition and accountability before the God of creation, the Lord of life, the King over *all*, and to test the spirits and challenge the lie being lived and promoted as truth.

As students we came to Redeemer College in the autumn of 1982. As for the various committee members, members of the administration, faculty and staff who came before us, our coming and commitment to the College was a response in faith. Now faith, according to Hebrews 11, is being "sure of what we hope for and certain of what we do not see." Some things have not to be seen to be believed, but *believed* to be seen. And that September we saw come into existence the college we had hoped for and were committed to.

We and the College began together. That is why we feel a special closeness to it. We experienced growing pains and bursts of energy together, tiredness and triumphs. Yes, there were questions and conflicts; yes, there were doubts and temptations; yes, there were sins and shortcomings. But there is no barrier to our cause for celebration today. The seeds sown in Christian college education in our lives have reached fruit-bearing age... And you reap what you sow.

I am awestruck by the steps, perhaps I should say leaps, the College has taken in so short a time. Beach Boulevard—how you have grown! Like the Lord's servant Job we can only lay a finger to our mouths and confess in our hearts the power and blessing of a mighty and loving God. I trust too that I, that we all, will be awestruck by the steps in service these graduates take, responding to the challenge of their education.

Our confession today as graduates is, as we take part in this dedication service: "Up to here the Lord has helped us." Here we set a stone and call it Ebenezer. This too must be the confession of Redeemer College as it celebrates the harvest time and, we pray, may continue to be its direction as it embarks on "new beginnings." We thank the College and its community and praise the Lord for your faith and commitment to real education in the past. We congratulate you and give thanks with you for the present. And we challenge and encourage you, as you have us, to continue into the future holding fast to your commitment. May the Lord bless you!

In addition to the date of graduation and the opening festivities, the committee had to look after the program, the litany, the speaker, the gowns and the style of hoods for the graduands, the gowns for faculty, and for the president. Where do we purchase these gowns and hoods? How about graduation rings? The question was raised whether we should commission a hymn concertato. Should we have a special dinner and evening for our invited guests? Of course, our graduands should have a central place in all these festivities. How and when? A hundred-and-one things had to be organised. And the committee did it well.

Mrs. J. Bos, one of our supporters and a seamstress, offered to make the gowns and hoods. What a beautiful job she did! We were proud to display her creations. It was decided to have a special banquet on Friday evening November 7th, and to open the banquet for special guests: representatives from other Christian post-secondary institutions, members of our own governing bodies, faculty, staff and student council. There would be an opportunity for those present to speak. Many people came that evening; many made use of the opportunity to share their joy with us and to marvel about the miracles we had experienced at the College.

The next morning, we celebrated our first graduation in an intimate setting with the graduands, the faculty and the administration. Several faculty members spoke, reminisced and took time to congratulate these fine, courageous young people. Some students told stories about the years they spent at Redeemer and I was privileged to address them and to bring them before the face of God in a prayer of thanksgiving.

That afternoon at two o'clock was the great event. It took place in the auditorium. But the auditorium had only 1000 seats and there were many more people coming to this celebration. We had opened the gymnasium as an overflow, where the audience would be able to follow the activities on closed-circuit TV. The procession went through the gymnasium before entering the auditorium, so that people in the gym would be part of the program. Both the graduands and the participants in the academic procession were led by the marshall, Jim Payton.

Fifty-five people walked in the procession, most of them robed, which was a spectacular sight. The program explained the reason why these gowns were worn:

> The special academic gown, hood and cap worn on this occasion carry a rich traditional and symbolic significance, even as a bride's elaborate white dress does for a wedding. While this is the

first graduation exercise for Redeemer College, graduation exercises for universities have been taking place for several hundred years. Universities as we know them date back to the middle ages in Western Europe. At that time students and faculty members wore gowns, hoods and caps like these as regular daily attire. Through the subsequent centuries, universities have mandated the wearing of such clothing at special occasions, especially at graduation exercises, as symbolic of their continuity with those early universities in the pursuit of study and learning...

Our graduating students wear traditional bachelor's gowns. In the medieval universities, these gowns served the students as their coats. Today's graduates will have the bachelor's hoods placed over their heads for the first time, as a symbol of their achievement of the baccalaureate degree. Originally, these hoods served as head coverings for protection against the weather, as the equivalent of today's student knapsacks for carrying of writing instruments and books, and as identification—indicating by their colours the nation from which the student came. In recent centuries the colours have come to be used to indicate the institution at which the student studied. Our bachelor's hood contains the colours of Redeemer College—the red symbolizes Christ's blood shed to redeem us, the gold the purity of faith tried by fire.

Henry R. De Bolster, assisted by dean of students and registrar,
Cornelius Kors, awarding one of the first B.C.S. degrees.

In addition to the special regalia, which I, as president wore, I also wore, for the first time, the presidential seal or medallion, indicating my office. The medallion was created by Mr. W. Dykstra, an art major under the supervision of art professor Mary Leigh Morbey. Let me again quote from the program:

> This presidential medallion at Redeemer College, presents, in its centre, the cross, deeply imprinted, as representing the salvation of Christ which is foundational to our life and service as His people. In bold relief appears, at the top of the medallion, a crown with the Alpha and Omega superimposed upon it, as representing the Kingship of Christ over all things. The open book and the hands offering the bowl symbolize the College's motto, "learning is for serving," and the maple leaf superimposed upon the relief of the Americas indicates our service in and to Canada and from this nation to the whole world, in Christ's name. The enclosure of the medallion in a rounded triangular shape reflects our commitment to the Triune God, Whose Name we bear as his servants and children.

The Presidential Medallion.

The ceremony began with an opening prayer by Kees Vreugdenhil, treasurer of the board, followed by song and the National Anthem. Next Nick Van Duyvendyk, chairman of the board, and

Ineke Bezuyen, the secretary of the board led the litany of dedication, which was composed by Bert Polman. Part of the litany was the presentation of the key by Roland Jonker, vice-president of F.J. Reinders & Associates, to the chairman of the board.

We listened to and confessed the Word of God's grace in a responsive reading, led by both chairman, Nick Van Duyvendyk, and vice-chairman, John Zantingh. We were congratulated by Tony Diekema, of Calvin College and Alvin Lee, of McMaster University. Sylvia DeBruyne-Taekema gave her valedictorian address. The responsive reading was composed by Jim Payton.

The main address was given by John Hulst, president of Dordt College who inspired us and encouraged us by speaking on the subject: "An Enduring Perspective." Since our organ had not yet arrived, we were privileged to be accompanied in our singing by Marian Van Til on the piano and the Crowning Brass Ensemble.

As part of the dedication, we had commissioned Dale Grotenhuis, music professor at Dordt College, to arrange a concertato for this occasion on the hymn "If You But Trust in God to Guide You." This hymn had become the theme song of the College. The concertato had been studied by our choir under the direction of Marian Van Til. For this special occasion we had invited Dale Grotenhuis to come and direct the Redeemer College choir in singing his arrangement of the hymn. To me, this was a very moving moment and reminded me of the faithfulness of God over my life and over Redeemer College. I received the necessary strength and determination to live the vision of the College in the fear of the Lord, and each time we sang that hymn in our college events, I was strengthened by it.

We received greetings and congratulation from Jerry Herbert, representative of the Christian College Coalition, Geoff Scott, MP, Chris Ward, MPP and Bob Wade, mayor of Ancaster. All other dignitaries walked by to greet me and extend their congratulations on behalf of their institutions.

The most important part of the ceremony took place when I, for the first time, conferred degrees on our graduands. Forty-one young people received their bachelor's degree. What a wonderful moment in the lives of these students and the life of the Redeemer College! I was very happy that we had decided to have them participate in the opening festivities. Right after the graduation, Sylvia De Bruyne-Taekema presented the gift of the graduating class with these words: "The graduates would like to present a gift to Redeemer College, a painting of our old campus, recalling not merely the building, for the College was and is certainly more than its facilities, but as a reminder of our foundation and the challenge to continue in the way." This painting found a place of honour by the entrance of the auditorium, where we are reminded of our beginnings. Our Convocation was closed with a prayer by Henk Van Andel, president of The King's College.

And so we said goodbye to the first phase of our existence—the exciting years on Beach Boulevard where the Lord had blessed us graciously. The time had come to take another step in faith. A new campus, more students, more programs, more faculty and more staff. Would we be able to manage? We had calculated, but we were totally dependent on the Lord to open hearts, minds and pocketbooks for Redeemer College to do its work. After the festivities were over, John Hulst wrote me a letter how thankful he was that he could participate in the events of November 8. At the end of his letter he said:

> And now we wish you God's blessing for the future. Carl F.H. Henry recently observed: 'It is one thing to begin a Christian institution; it is quite another thing to maintain a Christian institution.' God give you strength to maintain the Reformed, Christian direction of Redeemer College.

The same encouragement was expressed by Dale Grotenhuis who called the ceremonies "heartwarming, inspiring and God glorifying!" He, too, expressed the wish that "God may bless you and Redeemer College in the years ahead. How mightily God is using you!"

A "new beginning," indeed, and what a wonderful way to start! Everything went well and according to plan. It was also my prayer that God bless us on our new campus, and that He would find us faithful. To God be the glory!

The Reil pipe organ.

Six

On the
New Campus

Suddenly we had a lot of space. We did not have to cramp everything into a small area. Our offices were more than adequate; our students had study space in the library; our athletic program could expand with the availability of a new weight room and a beautiful double gymnasium. It took a while to finish the auditorium, but when it was completed with the organ installed, we were filled with awe. What a wonderful place for worship, for concerts, for theatre arts productions, for conferences, and for teaching large classes.

There was a great sense of gratitude among all those who helped us through the difficult challenges we had experienced. It took much longer for everything to be finished than we had anticipated. Student housing created particular challenges in that some of the rooms lacked proper heating, and some basements flooded during the spring runoff. The academic building also had some leaking roof areas during rainstorms. Once water pipes burst causing severe water-damage to many of one professor's books. But on the whole, there were few complaints. At the end of the first year I wrote the following letter to the Editor of the *Crown*, the students' newspaper:

Dear Mr. Editor:

Even though you did not include administration in your request for comments about our first year in Ancaster, I'm sure you will not mind if I give some off-the-cuff remarks.

Needless to say, we are very happy with the new facilities. There is no comparison with what we had at Beach Boulevard. I'm sure that we all agree on that point.

What stands out in my mind this year is the way we

blended. This first year on our new campus was not easy for anyone, including students, faculty, staff, and administration. Nevertheless, the cooperation has been overwhelming. The staff practically had to start from scratch. An almost new organization had to be set up and yet we did not only survive, we did our work well.

For faculty too it was a whole new experience. In the beginning the classrooms were not quite ready and even now classes are given in areas which are not suitable for lectures. I'm thinking of the music department in particular. It is difficult to teach while piano practices are taking place in one of the small rooms.

What adjustments our students have had to make! Many things were not ready when you arrived in September. You had to wait almost a whole semester before most deficiencies were taken care of and even now there are things which are not quite in order. Yet the complaints have been minimal.

If I may make an observation for this year then what stands out in my mind is a year of cooperation, understanding, growing love for Redeemer College, and a genuine sympathy for one another.

I'm sure that Steve's illness has helped to blend us together as well. Illness always brings home to us the importance of living close to the Lord. If we accomplished this then we had a good year.

We thank the Lord for guidance, encouragement and hope.

It will come as no surprise to anyone when I say that all the years of my presidency were formative years for the College. That started even before we opened the doors in 1982, but it continued the first years at Beach Boulevard. It did not change very much after we moved to the new campus. New policies had to be set and old ones had to be updated and changed whenever necessary.

Regular Appointment with Conditions

In chapter 4, I related the discussion about term appointments and the decision to make sure that the College would remain Reformed. But the effect of the term appointment proved to be negative for the appointees. Several times, the academic council discussed that issue. It decided to review the term appointment and to consider a more suitable procedure without compromising the Reformed character of the College. Let me quote from the report to the academic council and to the board:

Assessment

A number of negative factors have emerged. First of all, there is no doubt that without exception those who have been given a term appointment have felt less than full faculty members at the college. This has been the case for two reasons. When the appointment is made the designation and the explanation of the appointment give a clear message that they have not quite made the grade. It becomes an especially painful situation when academically well qualified persons with experience at recognized universities, are afforded this status.

Furthermore in practice the distinction between a term appointment and an initial regular appointment is not that clear and one is often faced with paradoxical situations. To "measure" satisfactory understanding and commitment to the Reformed Christian perspective is very difficult, if not impossible. Regular appointments are given to persons who come from the reformed community but whose perspective is weak but the stigma of a term appointment prevents such an appointment to be made even though that might be more appropriate. Often the college needs to attract a particular faculty member. In a case like that a term appointment is not very appealing.

The designation, term appointment, can also be misunderstood because it is used differently at different institutions. For example at Mount Allison University an appointment to replace a faculty member on sabbatical is called a term appointment. It clearly is what at Redeemer would be a *terminal* appointment.

A final difficulty is the length of the term appointment. Since a two-year appointment is reviewed after one year, insufficient time may be given to meet fully the specified conditions. However, given the need to decide within the two-year period, conclusions may be forced or reached prematurely.

A New Approach

It is possible to achieve the goals of the term appointment and more by adopting the following suggestion. We ought to abolish the term appointment and retain only the regular and terminal appointments. Furthermore a person receiving a regular appointment may have conditions attached which need to be satisfied before a reappointment can be considered. Such conditions may take on the same form of the term appointment in the past or may be of a different nature. In this way any uncertainties, large or small, on the part of the college with respect to the development of a faculty member can be discussed and developmental goals can be agreed upon.

These conditions could of course not become public knowledge; only the Vice-President (Academic), academic council, and the board would be aware of them, so that there be no need for the faculty member to feel that he/she is a second rate faculty member. Regardless of the attached conditions the faculty member would be eligible for membership on any committee or body open to the faculty. The committee membership is determined by the President and the Vice-President (Academic) so that they are able to ensure that on key committees the membership consists mainly of persons who are known to have a good understanding of the basis of the college and a strong commitment to it. To have one or two persons who are new to the college and new to Reformed Christian higher education can be of benefit to both the college and to the individual(s). In the past the persons who would stand to benefit most in terms of learning what the college is about (the term appointees) were excluded from deliberations which involved the principles of Christian higher education, for example, from discussions with regard to the appointability of certain faculty members.

Recommendations

Therefore it is recommended that any conditions attached to an appointment be understood as conditions attached to a regular appointment, which may extend into the first reappointment period if not satisfied within two years. Specifically it is recommended that:

a) the term appointment be eliminated;
b) the term appointment be redefined as an initial regular appointment with conditions;
c) where appropriate, the conditions attached to an initial regular appointment be extended to and normally satisfied in the first reappointment period of three years.

These recommendations were accepted by the board and the resulting change worked well. We were able to attract faculty members who otherwise would not have come to Redeemer. The stigma was taken away, the conditions were up-front and usually very much appreciated by the new faculty member. It was a joy to see these faculty members grow, while those who did not fit into the pattern of the college decided to leave on their own accord.

Reformed

With the rapid growth and the consequent additional faculty appointments, the question of the basis of the College and especially the question "what do we mean by being Reformed" was raised many times. I appointed a committee with the mandate to amplify and explain what we meant to say in our section 3a of our charter where it refers to "the advancement of learning and dissemination of knowledge on the basis of the Reformed confessions, traditions, and perspectives." The committee consisted of faculty, staff, administration and members of the board. The committee met regularly for about a year. It circulated its writings to faculty members, staff members, and supporters of the College, to make sure that they were speaking principally— expressing the faith of the College community. It did a fine job. The report was clear, precise and answered the question about the foundation of Redeemer College. After much discussion and several drafts, the board accepted the report and the contents became the official interpretation of the College's purpose as it was expressed in the objects of our charter. Here follows that important report in its entirety. It is entitled "Contours of a Reformed Identity":

WHERE WE STAND
<u>A Reformed Christian College</u>

Redeemer College, a Christian college of the arts, humanities, and sciences, values the Reformed tradition in which it stands. The provincial charter which it received in 1980 states explicitly that it aims to fulfill its academic task "on the basis of the Reformed confessions, traditions and perspectives" Article 3a).

<u>Our Roots</u>

As the Redeemer College community we find our roots and identity in the history of God's mighty acts of redemption, recorded in the Scriptures of the Old and New Testament, and culminating in Jesus Christ. Within the broader orbit of orthodox Christendom, we find our more immediate historical roots in the Calvinistic Reformation of the sixteenth century, and the renewal of Calvinism which took place in The Netherlands in the nineteenth century. It is by this broad historical rootedness that we define the distinctive mission of the college as a Reformed institution.

<u>Scripture</u>

In the tradition of historic Christian orthodoxy, we affirm that the Scriptures are invested with the authority of God Himself, that they are completely trustworthy, and that they find their centre in Jesus Christ (Hebr. 1:1-2).

Moreover, we stake our institutional identity on their authoritative relevance to the enduring issues of all human life, including the life of academic inquiry and teaching. They are like a lamp shining in a dark place (2 Pet.1: 9).

<u>The Calvinist Reformation</u>

As heirs of the Reformation, we appropriate for ourselves its rediscovery of the biblical teachings concerning sin and grace, faith and justification, priesthood and sanctification. More particularly, we identify ourselves with the confessions which came out of the Calvinist wing of the Reformation, both in the sixteenth century and thereafter. These include the French *Belgic Confession* (1561) [B.C.], the German *Heidelberg Catechism* (1562) [H.C.], the English *Westminster Confession* (1646) [W.C.], and the Latin *Canons of Dort* [C.D.] adopted at the international Reformed synod in

1619. Despite differences in emphasis and detail, these creedal statements, together with other confessions of a Calvinist stamp which have been drawn up in different times and places, belong to an identifiable group of Reformed confessions.

Among the distinctive biblical themes and emphases of the Calvinistic Reformation which find expression in these creeds are the following:

God is sovereign, both as Creator and Redeemer; His rights and claims to human life are universal and absolute (Ps. 99; Acts 17:22-31; Tim. 6:15-16; H.C., Lord's Day [L.D]. 8, Q. & A. 24 and L.D. 9; B.C. Art. 12, 13 and 26; W.C. II and III).

Human sin is so radical and pervasive that no aspect of human life is immune to it (Rom. 3:9-18; Eph. 2:1-3; Rom. 8:20-23; H.C., L.D. 3, Q & A. 8; B.C. Art. 14-15; C.D. III-IV, 3-4; W.C. VI).

A single covenant of grace binds together the Old and New Testament (Gen. 17:7; Jer. 31:31-34; Hebr. 8:6-13; C.D. I, 17; W.C. VII).

Divine salvation is so radical and pervasive that no aspect of human life of the believers is unaffected by it (Rom. 8:21; Col. 1:16-20; 1 Thess. 5:23; H.C., L.D. 6 Q. & A. 18; B.C. Art. 20-21; C.D. II 2-3; W.C. X-XI, XIII, XV).

Humans are called to be responsible stewards of God's gifts, both in their private and public life. All of life is to be lived to the glory of God (Ps. 8; Rom. 12:4-8; Hebr. 13:20-21; H.C., L.D. 33 Q. & A. 90-91; B.C., Art. 24-25; C.D. III-IV, 11-12; W.C. XIII, XVI, XIX-XX).

The Holy Spirit is the Author of life in all of God's creation, as well as the Renewer of sinful humans who are justified because of Christ's righteousness through faith (Gen. 1:2; Ps. 104:30; Rom. 8:1-17; gal. 5:22-25; H.C., L.D. 23, 32 Q. & A. 86; B.C. Art. 24; Nicene Creed; W.C. IV, X-XI, XIII, XVI).

The gospel does not abolish God's law, but reinstates it as the rule for our thanksgiving (Mat. 5:17-18; Rom. 3:31; Rom. 12:1-2; H.C., L.D. 33 Q. & A. 91; B.C. Art. 24-25; W.C. XVI, XIX-XX).

Salvation is reconciliation, re-creation, the restoration by God to His original creative purpose (Mat. 5:5; 2 Cor. 5:17; Eph. 2:10;

H.C., L.D. 5-6; B.C. Art. 18, 20; C.D. II, 3; W.C. VIII, XII-XIII, XIX-XX).

God's good creation was not abolished by human sin nor will it be annihilated, but rather purified, by divine judgement (2 Pet. 3:8-13; Rev. 21:1,26; W.C. V).

These themes and emphases we explicitly reaffirm in seeking to make fruitful for today the insights of the Calvinist Reformation.

The Revival of Calvinism

The Calvinist tradition in The Netherlands, after a long period of decline marked by dead orthodoxy and rationalistic modernism, came to new life in the nineteenth century, particularly in the vigorous movement known as Neo-Calvinism. This movement represented a return to the earlier Reformed confessions and a re-articulation of Calvinism as a coherent world and life view in the context of the modern world.

Such a biblically informed world and life view, which provides an alternative to the ideologies of modern secularism and a positive framework of reference for Christian thought and action, includes the following affirmations:

By virtue of the ordinances of God, creation everywhere displays an underlying order which is constant and reliable.

All of reality, including human society and culture, is subject to the God-ordained order which holds for it.

In response to God's mandate, human beings must responsibly develop the possibilities latent in creation to the glory of God.

All of human life, including such cultural pursuits as education and scholarship, is inescapably religious—that is, involved in the spiritual antithesis between obedience and disobedience to God's Word and creation ordinances.

Being citizens of the Kingdom of God, Christians have a vocation in every part of life to obey God's commandments and to discern and honour his creational order.

Humans, in pursuit of their historical task to unfold God's handiwork, may legitimately identify or demonstrate creational reality in cultural developments such as urbanization or the rise of modern science, even when they are distorted because of their apostasy. To oppose that distortion is not to reject the creational dimension, but rather to affirm and foster it.

Such affirmations spell out dimensions of the central biblical emphasis on the goodness and purpose of creation, the depth of the fall and the scope of redemption.

IMPLICATIONS FOR THE ACADEMIC ENTERPRISE
Scholarly Vocation

Education and academic inquiry are part of the mandated cultural task of the Christian community. Our collective religious vocation in the modern world includes the responsibility to be engaged in higher learning, not only to oppose the distortions of secularism, but also and especially to cultivate this sector of creational life as a positive area of service in its own right.

Neutrality Excluded

Human rationality and scientific research are not religiously neutral, but are part of the spiritual contest which pervades all human affairs. Underlying the selection of evidence, the marshalling of facts, the recognition of cogency, as well as the constructing of theories, there are necessarily assumptions of a metaphysical and ultimately religious nature.

Nevertheless, being bound to the created order, science does not imply subjectivism. There are given states of affairs which every one must take into account no matter how these givens are construed or interpreted. Scholarship cannot hope to be neutral but it must strive to be rigorous.

Academic Freedom and Responsibility

The responsibility and privilege of academic freedom apply to scholars doing their academic work within the institution, as well as to the institution itself in safeguarding such freedom and responsibility. The meaning of such freedom, and implication for both scholars and institution are adequately expressed in the *Faculty Handbook* and in the statement adopted by the Board of Governors in the May 21, 1986 letter from the college to the Association of Universities and Colleges of Canada committee dealing with AUCC membership criteria.

Reformation of Scholarship

High on the agenda of a Christian academic community must be the task of doing thoroughly Christian scholarship which can counter the effects of academic secularism and offer much-needed theoretical insight to the Christian community at large. In concert with likeminded scholars around the globe, Christian academics must do their utmost to bring the renewing power of the gospel to bear on the prestigious, powerful and pivotal domain of culture represented by the universities. Here too the claims of Christ must be honoured and His Kingship advanced.

Academic Freedom

The document makes reference to a letter sent by the board to the AUCC about academic freedom. The AUCC was uncomfortable with the presence of two institutions, Trinity Western University and Redeemer College, as members of the organisation because of the faith statements on which these two schools were founded. It was proposed to make institutions with a faith statement "qualified members" and to preclude them from voting on certain issues. Our board wrote a letter and proposed that "for regular admission in the AUCC the criteria of academic freedom be understood in terms of the definition given by Lovejoy in his article 'Academic Freedom' in the Encyclopaedia of the Social Sciences Vol. I, 1937:

> Academic freedom is the freedom of the teacher or researcher in higher institutions of learning to investigate and discuss the problems of his science and to express his conclusions, whether through publications or the instruction of students, without interference from political or ecclesiastical authority, or from the administrative officials of the institution in which he is employed, unless his method by qualified bodies of his own profession is considered to be a) clearly incompetent or b) contrary to professional ethics.
> '...to this definition should be added, *or c) contrary to the central characteristic of the institution, or d) contrary to the coherent value system of the institution's overall academic program.*'"

The AUCC responded by allowing institutions with a faith statement to remain regular members, but they would be identified with an asterisk in AUCC publications, with a note that these institutions had a faith statement. The asterisk reminded me of the Star of David that the Jews had to wear in the Nazi-occupied territories during the Second World War. I remember that the Jews wore those stars with pride, but it was a constant irritation to the Nazis. It did not take long before the Jews were persecuted. Many died in concentration camps.

It was indeed an honour for us to be identified with an asterisk, but it was a constant irritation to some members of the AUCC. A few years later, the board of directors of the AUCC tried again to make us second class members. At that time I recalled the story of the Jewish star and reminded the members of its consequences. The proposal of the board to take away our voting rights was defeated, but the asterisk stayed.

Instead of making us "qualified members" the board appointed Dr. Lee, president of McMaster University, to compose a statement defining academic freedom. His proposed statement was discussed many times at AUCC meetings. Dr. Lee's statement emphasised not only academic freedom, but also institutional autonomy. It was a balanced document, which was finally adopted by the AUCC. The following are the principles of that statement:

1. The AUCC believes that the principles of academic freedom and institutional autonomy are essential to the fulfillment of the role of universities in the context of a democratic society.
2. The AUCC believes that academic freedom is essential to the fulfillment of the universities' primary mandate, the pursuit and dissemination of knowledge and understanding. Freedom of inquiry is fundamental to the search for truth and the advancement of knowledge. Freedom in teaching, justified by the special professional expertise of the faculty members, is fundamental to the protection of the rights of the teacher to teach and of the student to learn. Academic freedom is essential in order that society may have access to impartial exper-

tise for knowledgeable contents on all issues studied in universities, including those surrounded by controversy.

3. The AUCC recognizes the obligation of universities to ensure the academic freedom of individual faculty members to conduct inquiries, to make judgments, and to express views without fear of retribution. The practice of tenure is one important means of meeting this obligation. In addition, decisions relative to appointments and the granting of tenure and promotion must be conducted according to principles of fairness and natural justice.

4. The AUCC recognizes the obligation of universities to respect the right of students to be treated according to principles of fairness and natural justice and also to pursue their education according to the principles of academic freedom.

5. The AUCC recognizes that historically the universities of Canada have struggled to achieve institutional autonomy and must continue to do so. The Association affirms that this autonomy provides the best possible condition for the conduct of scholarship and higher education essential to a free society. As centres of free inquiry universities have an obligation to society to resist outside intrusion into their planning and management and to insist that institutional autonomy be recognized by governments and others as the necessary pre-condition to their proper functioning. Institutional autonomy includes, *inter-alia*, the following powers and duties: to select, appoint and discipline faculty and staff in accordance with the institution's mission (statement); to select, admit and discipline students; to set and control curriculum; to create programs and to direct resources to them; to certify completion of a program of study and grant degrees.

6. The AUCC recognizes that the academic freedom of individual members of universities and the institutional autonomy accorded to the institutions themselves involve the following major responsibilities to society: to conduct scholarship and research according to the highest possible standards of excellence so that society may benefit; within the constraints of the resources available to them, to ensure high quality education to as many academically qualified individuals as possible; to

abide by the laws of society; and to account publicly through Boards and audits for their expenditure of funds.

We discussed that statement internally. We appreciated the emphasis on both academic freedom and institutional autonomy. Hence our board decided that we could live with these principles. At the same time it gave us an opportunity to formulate our own mission statement. We worked on such a statement for a long time. In 1988 we accepted a statement which expressed that we were a teaching institution, but it did not include research. Finally, in 1991, the following mission statement was adopted, which expressed both teaching and research:

> The mission of Redeemer College is: first, to offer a university-level liberal arts and science education which is Scripturally-directed and explores the relation of faith, learning, and living from a Reformed Christian perspective; and, second, to support research and creative endeavour in this context.
>
> Central to this mission are the following objectives: to equip students for lives of leadership and service under the Lordship of Jesus Christ; to advance knowledge through excellence in teaching and in scholarship; to be an academic community in which faculty, staff and students can develop intellectually, socially, and spiritually; to reach out through academic service to society; and in all these things to glorify God.

The Pascal Centre

In the late 1980's, the College was privileged to engage in something special. On August 17, 1987, I received a visit from Jitse Vander Meer, our biology professor. He presented a proposal to start a centre to study the relationship between faith and science. He wanted to give his time and energy to this study, organise conferences where this important question would be discussed, publish articles and eventually publish books on that subject. I liked his proposal and appointed a committee, which recommended that we start such a centre.

Jitse Vander Meer, watched by student Mary Bom,
as he conducts research using the electron microscope.

While we studied this proposal, Jitse heard that Dr. Arthur Custance had died. Jitse had met Dr. Custance, a well-known scientist, who had spent his life studying questions of origin and creation from a biblical perspective. He left behind a very valuable library which was coveted by many universities. Jitse and our librarian, Dan Savage, visited Dr. Custance's secretary, Ms. Evelyn White. They explained the purpose and vision of Redeemer College to her and asked her about the possibility of donating this library to Redeemer College. She promised to think about it, but did not make a decision.

When the plans to start a centre of faith and science were well advanced, Jitse went to see Ms. White again and told her about our plans. She indicated that if such a centre were established, she would donate the library to Redeemer College. The College council and the academic council endorsed the plans. The proposal was approved by the board and a centre to study faith and science was opened. The College then became the owner of Dr. Custance's library. I want to congratulate Jitse on his work during these early years. The centre adopted the appropriate name, "Pascal Centre,

Centre for Reformed Studies in Science and Religion." During my presidency, it organised important international conferences and published papers which were delivered at those conferences and it has continued that tradition.

I was very aware that we needed God's blessing on all our activities. It is easy to look at our accomplishment and pat ourselves on the back, forgetting that the Lord directs and guides us. I spent much time in prayer, alone and with members of the administration. We always asked the Lord to bless us before we commenced any meeting. But we also needed the prayers and financial support of the community. I often reminded them of that need. In my 1988 membership report I was able to report many good things, but then I continued:

> Of course that does not mean that there are no concerns. Every day we are reminded of our dependence on the Lord. Unless God's people continue to support us, and unless those who have been blessed in a particular way come through with additional large contributions, we will not be able to maintain Redeemer College.

Finances

The financial position of the College weighed heavily on all of us, including the board. Pretty well every meeting the finance committee of the board expressed some concern about the ever growing debt load, even though it had been planned that the debt would continue to increase for some time.

During the first few years of occupying the new campus, we were not very concerned about the capital budget; it was the operating budget that created anxiety. Our business community was repeatedly asked for additional funds to keep our operating budget within sustainable limits. Some of our business people asked: "How long do we need to help you?" I usually answered: "As long as you are willing, and as long as the Lord gives you the means to do so." Nevertheless, it was necessary to pay careful attention to such remarks. The only way to solve the problem was to increase the number of students to 500 as soon as possible. And grow we did, even to the point that we built new residences and some apartments for married students. In

1986 we welcomed 275 full-time equivalent (FTE) students. That number increased to 361 FTE in 1989. Unfortunately, in 1990 there was a slight decrease when we registered 359 FTE students.

There was no magical way to reach the 500 student goal quickly. Everybody worked hard, but we needed to look for new ways to balance the budget. We launched a fundraising campaign. We knew of successful campaigns at Calvin College and Dordt College, but we were hesitant to follow their example because the Canadian situation was different from that in the U.S. Our immigrant community was not as settled and established as the supporters of Christian education in that country. Therefore, we believed that we could not expect extraordinary donations if we launched a capital fundraising campaign.

However, a campaign would at least help to promote the College in communities where it was not well known. It was an unfortunate fact that our college was "the best kept secret." We needed to change that impression. How should this be done?

In 1987, the board decided to establish Redeemer Foundation. Such a foundation would become the fundraising arm of the College. It took a while before the foundation became established. Bert Bakker became the foundation's first president. Under his leadership, the foundation identified new sources of income for the College. Since the College's board had decided to launch a capital fundraising campaign, it requested the new foundation to become involved.

The LIFT Campaign

Prior to the discussions at the board level, Dick Kranendonk and Bill Smouter had been searching for an agency that could help us raise funds in addition to the donations we were already receiving. Among these agencies one company caught their attention: "Community Charitable Counselling Service of Canada, Inc" (CCS). Its vice-president, Mr. Vincent F. Seale, was asked to present his company to Dick, Bill and myself. We were impressed that this company had helped churches as well as universities in their capital fundraising endeavours. They were acquainted with the Christian mind. Moreover, they conducted thorough preparatory work, before beginning an actual campaign. The result of this procedure was that when a goal was set, the goal was invariably reached. McMaster University had exceeded its $25 million goal with the help of CCS. After several meetings we asked Mr. Seale to prepare a proposal which I would present to the board.

Mr. Seale proposed a feasibility study to determine the actual potential for fundraising, and to establish the best and most effective manner of meeting the overall development needs of Redeemer College. He explained that when the study was complete, a report would be written by CCS which would answer such questions as:

- What should Redeemer College do next?
- How much money can be raised through a special campaign and/or other fund-raising strategies?
- To what extent would corporations, foundations, parishes and other potential donors provide support?
- What leaders can be relied upon to represent the College?
- What methods and procedures would be necessary to raise the required funds?
- How much time will be required?
- What timetable should be followed?
- Exactly how much will it cost to raise the potentials?

The feasibility study would include interviews with many individuals who knew the College and who could be potential supporters. The study personnel would work closely with college administrators and together they would prepare a case statement for the study. The study participants would concentrate on interviewing 10-15 internal leaders to familiarise themselves with the College, the College's plans and its financial requirements. After that initial approach the study would interview between 70 and 90 people in the external constituencies. A completed study report would be presented to the board. The report would include answers to the relevant questions and would make specific recommendations for the future.

The board and the Redeemer Foundation accepted the proposal, and CCS conducted its study in December 1988 and January 1989. On February 18, 1989, CCS's feasibility study report was presented to the board and accepted. The report indicated that there was much support for the College and that it should be possible to raise a minimum of $5 million. The board went on record to commence a financial plan to raise that kind of money. Encouraging indications early in the campaign made the board increase that figure to $10 million. CCS was hired to assist us and assigned Mr. Gregory J. Hatton as their full-time on-site representative. Greg worked from an office at the College and developed the actual campaign. He composed the case statement, introduced the plan and advised us step by step how to proceed.

The first order of business was to appoint a campaign committee, consisting of: Justin D. Cooper, Henry R. De Bolster, Dick L. Kranendonk, William Smouter, Gilbert Langerak (college accountant), William Grin (member of the support community), Debra J. Van Noord (alumna), C. Kees Vreugdenhil (treasurer of the board), Cornelis G. Kors (dean of students), John C.Kuurstra (chairman of the board) and John Zantingh (vice-chairman of the board)

Kees Vreugdenhil, left, speaking to Robert Lowe,
who later became chairman of Redeemer Foundation.

Kees Vreugdenhil accepted the appointment to serve as chairman. Kees did a lot of work, was always available, and he and I made many visits to potential donors. I want to thank him for his untiring efforts. My thanks are also extended to the president of Union Gas, Kees' employer, for giving Kees the time to chair our campaign. Our campaign needed a name. Daina Doucet, our publication director, suggested the name: "Leadership Investment for Tomorrow" (LIFT), which we unanimously accepted.

The campaign committee met to identify the needs that Greg Hatton should include in the case statement. We decided to focus on six areas. The paragraph in the brochure dealing with this need read as follows:

The Need

Redeemer College is not willing to compromise its commitment to a quality university education from a Christian perspective. To maintain the university's approach to academic excellence while continuing to prepare its graduates for leadership roles in society, several major projects need immediate attention and require support from the private sector. For this reason, Redeemer College has undertaken the Leadership Investment For Tomorrow campaign to raise $10 million for six critical areas of need. The areas of need include:

I	Academic Programs and Teacher Education	$ 2,750,000
II	Residence Expansion	1,250,000
III	Pascal Centre	1,000,000
IV	Library, Research and Academic Activities	500,000
V	Scholarships	1,500,000
VI	Capital Debt	3,000,000
	Total	$10,000,000

It took all spring and early summer to get the material ready for distribution and to plan the actual campaign. The first people to be approached were the members of the board, the faculty, the staff, the alumni, the students via the student council, and those whom we believed could contribute major donations to the campaign. The intent was to make a specific proposal to each prospective donor personally.

It was my suggestion that we should try to get some of our business people together for a dinner and to explain what we were doing and what we expected from them. After the dinner we would make individual appointments with these people and ask for a definite donation. This suggestion was accepted, and those who had supported us in the past and had the potential to be major donors were invited to the dinner. I hoped for twenty-five to thirty people, however, we were delighted to welcome sixty-eight people.

On an evening in early August, we presented the case to a distinguished group of people. We told them that we hoped to raise half the target or $5 million from them if the campaign were to succeed. In order to reach that goal, we would need gifts from $100,000 to $1 million. Dick Kranendonk and Bill Smouter did an incredible job presenting these facts. I spoke to the audience about the challenges faced by the College, about the necessity of Christian higher education, and asked the group to become the funding agency of the College in a similar way the government funded the public universities. I challenged them with Mordecai's question to Esther: "Who knows but that you have come to your position for such a time as this?" I was privileged to conclude the evening by committing all of us into the hands of our faithful heavenly Father. As they left, I asked whether I could count on their support. Except for one person, all encouraged me to visit them. One person asked me to come the following day. It was a special evening where we experienced the presence of the Lord.

The following day, I visited the person who had asked me to visit him. I was hardly seated when he said how moved he had been the night before and how he wanted to be the first person to commit himself to a donation of $1 million. I was stunned and I thanked him profusely. As I left his office, I thanked God for His unspeakable grace, and when I came back to the College, I jumped for joy when I related my visit to the members of my administration. What a wonderful beginning!

We continued the dinners throughout the fall of 1989 and visited everyone of the guests personally. It was an unforgettable experience. I am not a natural fundraiser, and it was with a trembling heart and with a feeling of anxiety that I made my calls. Those whom I visited were aware of the purpose of my visit. Before I would leave the office, I took time to pray. Yet most of the time I was humbled when I arrived and met the people. It seemed as though I were doing them a favour. I would ask—usually a very large amount—and either with a smile or a tear, I would be told that they would gladly contribute. The love for the Lord and His Kingdom was very evident in these gifts and pledges for Redeemer College. As early as October 28, 1989, I could report to the board that more than $4 million had been given and pledged.

Peter Turkstra and his wife Tina, speaking to Dick L Kranendonk just prior to the August 1989 LIFT campaign dinner.

Several board members helped in the campaign, especially in visiting members of the faculty and staff. Debra Van Noord, an alumna, who had volunteered to help as well, met with the alumni. All other visits were made by members of the administration, Kees Vreugdenhil and myself. In April 1990, we had reached the $10 million goal. Of this total, $1 million had been contributed by the board, the students, the staff, the alumni and the faculty. The campaign was an overwhelming success—not just because of the substantial donations. Many volunteers in local congregations agreed to regularly publish the activities at the College in their church bulletins and helped in the local phase of the campaign. We officially ended the campaign on November 1, 1990, in the presence of the College community, many volunteers and local politicians. We thanked the internal and external campaign participants, especially the CCS. We presented plaques to Kees and Debra, and we returned thanks to God as we sang: "Praise God from Whom All Blessings Flow." The total collected and pledged was $11.9 million. The results were overwhelming, but we had to keep in mind that the pledges needed to be collected over a five-year period.

More needed to be done to balance the operating budget. The ancillary services department did a wonderful job renting out the College facilities. This activity brought in significant additional funds. But the primary income source for the operating budget was student tuition. We kept the tuition as low as we could because we wanted the education at the College to remain affordable. Yet it was necessary to announce to the students that the tuition would be increased by 10 percent for the year 1990/91. The hefty increase in tuition undoubtedly caused enrollment to decrease that fall. Even though the decrease was only two students, we were disappointed, since we had counted on a small increase. As a result the financial pressures continued.

The Voortman brothers. Left Bill, a member of the board of Redeemer Foundation, right Harry, a member of the feasibility study committee.

Steve and Renee

During this same time, some joyful and some sad things happened in the student body. Steve Kouwenhoven, a pre-seminary student, became very ill. The doctors diagnosed a malignant brain tumour which was inoperable. Steve completed his studies, and even though he could not be present at the graduation exercises, Cor Kors, student life director, and I went to Steve's home and conferred his degree on him just a few weeks before his death. He was sadly missed by all, but his memory remains alive in the bursaries and scholarships that have been established in his name.

The B.S.C. degree conferred on Steve Kouwenhoven in the presence of his parents Simon and Martha.

Another student, Renee Hogendoorn, who had just finished her first year, was involved in a car accident and killed instantly. When these things happen, we grieve, but never as those who have no hope. We are convinced that the Lord took care of Steve and Renee and received them home in eternal glory. Yet, they left an empty place among their loved ones and in the College community.

Among the many good things we experienced, I want to mention our first major scholarship winner. Sharon Timmerman won the Queen Elizabeth Silver Jubilee scholarship award in 1987. That was very special because the AUCC selected only five students from all the universities in Canada for this scholarship.

Even though the College's finances were on our minds all the time, we did our work with pleasure. I was able to carry our concerns to the Lord and was convinced that we did the work of the Lord and that He would take care of us. He would not forsake the works of his own hands. That was evident to me time and again. The donations from our support community kept coming in and, a couple of years later, the RRSP investments of our members and supporters were such that we were able to discharge our bank debt. All the remaining debt was then held by our members and supporters. That was a great relief. There was no longer an outside body that could exercise control.

I wanted to express our thanks and appreciation to our supporters. Most of them would not have had an opportunity to attend classes, but I felt there might be a possibility for them to sample what Redeemer College was all about. In the first year of our existence, I had introduced a senior citizens' day. On this special day, our seniors were invited to visit with us; we honoured them and thanked them for their involvement and their continued support. Usually we met on October 31, Reformation Day, the day in 1517 when Martin Luther nailed his 95 theses to the door of the castle chapel in Wittenberg, Germany—generally recognised as the beginning of the Reformation. We would begin that day with singing and a meditation. A lecture by one of our professors would always be the main event. After the lecture and discussion, an excellent lunch was served. In the afternoon we would sing again and enjoy a relaxing program, frequently concluded by a performance of our concert choir. But I wanted to do more for our supporters.

Milk and Honey Festival

The Institute for Christian Studies in Toronto annually organised a family weekend conference. Calvin College in Grand Rapids,

Michigan, organised an annual summer festival. I wondered whether Redeemer College could do something similar for our supporters. After some discussion, we decided to organise a week's vacation at the College. During that week we would combine a taste of college life with some outings: some intellectual "meat" and some cultural "delicacies" which made Marian De Boer suggest the name Milk and Honey Festival. Our first festival was held during the week of June 5 to June 9, 1989. Fifty-four people registered and enjoyed a most wonderful week. The program developed for that week set the pattern for the future annual festivals. We began the week by eating together. The meals were extraordinary. Most were prepared by our cafeteria staff. On Tuesday and Thursday we visited a museum and attended a play in Stratford or, in later years, in Niagara-on-the-Lake. When the group was on the road, we ate in a classy restaurant. A frequent comment from the participants was: "We never had it so good." Each morning we listened to two lectures by our own professors. One lecture usually dealt with a biblical subject and the other gave the participants a taste of a course at the College, such as history, psychology and political science. On Monday evening, we had a formal banquet and a concert prepared especially for the Milk and Honey Festival. Everyone left enthused and promised to come back the following year D.V. The Milk and Honey Festival became very popular. Each year we welcomed more participants. The festival is geared towards empty nesters, the age group over forty-five. Everyone is welcome. Unfortunately there are no facilities for children. Please consider coming. It gives the College an opportunity to say: "Thank you for your support."

Seminary Program

Another exciting development was the establishment of a fourth-year pre-seminary program in cooperation with Calvin Seminary in Grand Rapids, Michigan. This fourth year at Redeemer College would be the equivalent of the first year at Calvin Seminary. The program was considered because our pre-seminary students who wanted to take their seminary training at Calvin Seminary wanted to stay in Canada another year. Because of visa restrictions, it was impossible for spouses of Canadian students to obtain employment in the USA. The cost in the U.S. became a barrier, especially for the married students, and a postponement even by one year would make it financially easier.

I went to Grand Rapids and met with the president of Calvin Seminary, Dr. James De Jong, to discuss this possibility. At first he was somewhat hesitant. He was afraid that this move would be the beginning of a separate seminary in Canada, and in his opinion, that would not be beneficial for the Christian Reformed Church and the Seminary. We came to the conclusion that it would be wise to have representatives of the two institutions meet together and look at the advantages and the disadvantages. This was done with the result that an agreement was reached to develop an additional year at Redeemer as the first year of Calvin Seminary. The basic commitments were that the strength of existing Calvin Seminary programs would not be compromised, while Redeemer College would maintain control of the program with full consultation and cooperation of Calvin Seminary. Some courses such as preaching, public worship, teaching ministry and church and its ministry would be taught by seminary professors. All other courses would be taught by Redeemer professors.

We started the program in September 1988 with ten students. Even though the courses were taught well and appreciated by the students, there was a complaint about the overall program. Most of the negative comments were related to the design of the program as a fourth (or fifth) year at an undergraduate institution. The students concluded that they would not recommend the program to other students. In the second year we enrolled eight students, who agreed that the education they received was good, but the same complaints surfaced again.

We took these comments seriously and asked ourselves what we should do. It was clear that if we were to continue seminary-level instruction, it should be part of a full seminary program, which is distinct from an undergraduate degree program. But Redeemer College was not in a position to make such a decision on its own. The Canadian Christian Reformed Churches would have to be involved. Moreover, the enrollment for the next few years would be very small. In September 1990, only two students qualified for the fourth-year pre-seminary program. To my regret, we had no choice but to eliminate the program. I look back on those two years with pleasure and gratitude because I was privileged to teach New Testament preaching. I enjoyed that immensely. I still hope that, sometime in the future, it might be possible to revive the program, even though the format would need changes.

We had to say farewell to one program, but welcomed another in September of 1990. Until that time we shared an elementary education program with Calvin College. Students would take three years of study at Redeemer College and then transfer to Calvin College to finish their studies. The board decided to launch the entire elementary education program at Redeemer College. Consultations with the Christian Teachers Associations and with the Ontario Alliance of Christian School Societies resulted in the decision that students graduating from Redeemer College would receive the Christian School Teachers' Certificate. Because of these assurances, our education graduates would be certified to teach in the Christian school system. If students wanted to teach in the public school system, they would have to enrol at a certified university for another year. Redeemer College had the authority to confer the degree of Bachelor of Christian Education, but was not allowed to promise its students the Ontario Teachers Certificate. (I will deal with government relations and accreditation in a separate chapter.)

Two other events took place during those first years on the new campus which are noteworthy: the establishment of RUNA and the celebration of the "charter plus ten."

RUNA

It was the custom for the presidents of the Reformed Christian colleges to meet at least once a year to discuss questions of mutual interest and to help and support each other. At one of these meetings, Dr. John Hulst, president of Dordt College, suggested that we begin a Christian university, to be called Reformed University of North America (RUNA). That was easier said than done, and we discussed this matter for several years. Not everyone was in favour of starting such an institution. Many felt that we did not have the necessary resources. I remember well that one of the presidents asked a very penetrating question. He asked: "If you were a student and had the choice of going to Harvard or to a small beginning Reformed Christian institution, where would you go?" That question haunted me, not only in connection with the establishment of a Christian university, but also in connection with choosing an undergraduate institution. When you are a student coming out of high school and you are offered admission to a prestigious university, would you consider coming to Redeemer College, knowing that it is a young institution, which does not have all the courses a secular university is able to offer? Would you consider an institution that does not have the physical facilities of well-established colleges and universities? These are very real questions, which many high school graduates face. They are difficult to answer. Each person must decide what the answer is for him or her. In chapter 9, I want to come back to this issue and discuss it.

At the time of my retirement, the group had decided to support the idea; more specifically, it decided to encourage the Institute for Christian Studies, which was already involved in graduate work, and to urge colleges that had the ability and the necessary resources to begin graduate programs. Both Calvin College and Dordt College had already introduced master of education programs. The annual meetings would be used to stimulate each other and to encourage each other in the work we do at our individual institutions.

The other noteworthy event was the celebration of the "charter plus ten." We received our charter in 1980 and we wanted to give expression of our gratitude for that event when ten years later the College had been in operation for eight years. We organised a very simple celebration, invited some guests, reminisced, and gave thanks to God for His blessings.

South Africa

That same year, I received an invitation from Dr. Carools Reinecke, the Rector of the Potchefstroomse Universiteit vir Christelyke Ho'r Onderwys (Potchefstroom's University for Christian Higher

Education) in South Africa to visit the University. That trip was the journey of a lifetime. My wife Cobie and I travelled to South Africa at a time when everyone spoke of a new South Africa because of the agreement to end apartheid made by Mr. De Klerk, the then president, and Mr. Nelson Mandela, who became president a few years later. The University had started racial integration a few years earlier and continued that process even during the few weeks of our visit.

I had an opportunity to speak with some members of the faculty, and discussed the question of fundraising with the administration. The University received government funding, but it was in danger of losing that support. My wife Cobie and I received a warm welcome and spent some unforgettable days in Potchefstroom. We also visited the former rector of the University, Dr. T. Van der Walt, who had initiated my visit to South Africa and who lived in Johannesberg. I was a guest at the University of South Africa in Pretoria, and both Cobie and I spent some leisurely days in the Paul Kruger National Park. The second week we travelled to Cape Town, visited the University of Stellenbosch and the Cape of Good Hope.

While in Potchefstroom, I met Dr. Elaine Botha. She, together with Al Wolters, had reminded Dr. Reinecke of the plan to invite me to visit the University. Cobie and I had a wonderful time with her. I was delighted when she accepted an appointment at Redeemer College.

The College choir performing at one of the Stained Glass concerts.

On the Sunday of our visit I was privileged to preach in one of the churches. It was enriching to experience the communion of believers, to sing together and to pray together. Cobie and I are extremely grateful that we were given the opportunity to visit that beautiful country, and I thank Dr. Reinecke again for his kind invitation.

When we returned from South Africa, Dick Kranendonk and Bill Smouter informed me that they had been busy investigating new possibilities for increasing enrollment and for balancing the budget.

Boris Brott, Christiaan Teeuwsen and Henry R. De Bolster at the conclusion of one of the Stained Glass concerts.

SEVEN

The Brookview Trust

The failure of the Brookview Trust was the most emotionally-charged problem I encountered during my presidency of Redeemer College. When I recollect my personal feelings, I still have a tendency to get uptight. Writing about that venture, its failure and its aftermath may help me come to terms with my anxieties. By the grace of God, it will help me put this episode in perspective. One reason for my anxieties is the risk we took in this venture. However, the greatest effect of this episode was the highly-charged emotional outbursts that swept the College, and especially the faculty.

There is no doubt that errors in judgment were made by all those actively involved in this sad and unfortunate episode at the College. Ultimately, I personally felt the brunt of the weight because I was the president. I was responsible and accountable for all the activities at the College including the whole Brookview Trust affair.

The history of my years at the College would not be complete without dealing with the trust. Since ten years have now passed, it may be possible to take an objective look at this time period without any emotional baggage taking control of the facts and their interpretation. The story I will tell includes the historical context in which the trust was proposed and accepted by me and the board.

Historical Setting

In chapter 5, I related that the College, for better or for worse, had adopted a debt-financing plan to build the campus. The price-level- adjusted mortgage bonds were the primary financing instrument. The source of funds for debt repayment was to be an inflation adjusted portion of the annual tuition and residence fees. This amount was set at $1,525 for each student in residence and $475 for each student's tuition in constant 1984 dollars. Consequently, these debt repayment amounts were to be adjusted for inflation each successive year. Because of the restriction on the repayment program, adopted by the board, we all knew that the debt load would increase for at least twelve years.

To achieve the debt repayment objectives, it would be crucial to reach our enrollment and student/faculty ratio projections. In 1985, when the financing plan was approved, it was projected that there would be 360 students and 24 full-time faculty by the academic year 1990/91. The 360 student number was reached in the year 1989/90, but the enrollment slightly decreased to 359 the following year. The number of faculty had increased to 33 full-time and a little more than 20 part-time instructors for an overall full-time equivalent (FTE) faculty of 36.5 members. Previously, we had projected a student/faculty ratio of 15 to 1 for the year 1990/91, instead the ratio was 10 to 1.

Also keep in mind that tuition had been raised substantially. This led many students to complain about the high cost of education. Such complaints had been especially strong by students who could not complete their degree program in four years because the College could not always offer the range of courses each semester that would permit students to complete their degree requirements within four years. There also were students who could not handle a five-course-per-semester workload. We felt that the students had a legitimate complaint and should not be financially penalised if they needed one or two additional semesters to complete their degree requirements. Consequently, the College adopted a tuition structure permitting students to pay on a per-course basis. This meant that students would not normally pay for more than forty courses to complete their degree program.

But this decision had a negative effect on gross tuition fees actually collected. As a result of this flexible tuition program, there were only 348 FTE student tuition payments received. Thus, the student/faculty ratio in terms of tuition revenue had actually decreased to 9.5 to 1. Moreover, it was felt that student retention would suffer if we were not able to offer more majors. This meant even more pressure to add professors. Hence there was a strong possibility for a still lower student/faculty ratio.

Furthermore, all the beds in the residences were not occupied. Because we had to increase tuition and housing substantially, many students decided to live off campus. The student life department attempted to make up the shortage by trying to attract students from public institutions to the residences. Even though this brought in a few students, the effort did not succeed in filling our residences.

Since salaries are the single largest cost of operating an educational institution like Redeemer College, it is not difficult to understand that we began to experience serious budget pressures. Dick Kranendonk and Bill Smouter both expressed concern about the continued faculty and program expansion. They informed me that we should have at least $700,000 more in tuition and/or residence revenue. The only way out of this dilemma seemed another increase in tuition fees, which could cause more students to withdraw. I was convinced that to increase the tuition and fees further was out of the question. I asked Dick and Bill to look for another way to solve our financial challenge.

Their advice in the fall of 1990 was to make tuition more competitive with those at public universities. They were of the opinion that we would be able to increase our enrollment to about 500 students in 1991/92 if we would dare to lower the tuition. As a result of natural retention increases, they projected that overall enrollment would be 850 within four years. At 500 students paying reduced tuition, they told me, the College would be in exactly the same financial position as it was at that moment. By taking this reduced tuition approach, we would reach a student/faculty ratio of 14 to 1, but still substantially below the 17 to 1 target. They concluded that the capital debt could be retired if the student/faculty ratio were increased to 17 to 1, a target that could be reached with an enrollment of 850 students. The projections they presented, together with budget costs assuming 850 students and a student/faculty ratio of 17 to 1, seemed reasonable and realistic to me.

Their advice became even more attractive when Dr. Richard Allen, one of the local MPP's, was appointed Minister of Colleges and Universities in Ontario. The NDP had won the election, and Richard Allen was a friend of the College. He knew us well and had been a guest lecturer on a few occasions on the subject of the social gospel in one of John Bolt's courses. When interviewed by the *Hamilton Spectator*, he said that Redeemer College "had a solid reputation and would have a good chance if the new government makes a move" to allow new regular degree-granting institutions in Ontario. This statement was interpreted by all of us as an indication that there was the political will, at least by the minister, to change the nomenclature of our degree to a B.A. If that change would come through, the enrollment projections would be more than reasonable, perhaps even conservative.

After a lot of prayer and thought, I decided that I could not present such a drastic tuition and residence cost reduction to the board because we were already faced with a substantial deficit. We were neither able to decrease nor increase the cost, which made it all the more difficult to find a solution. New outside funding sources seemed to be the only way. I asked Dick and Bill to try to find a way whereby the $1.1 million projected shortfall over the next three years would be covered.

Establishment of the Trust

When I returned from my South Africa trip, Dick and Bill informed me that a group of people, who wished to remain anonymous, were prepared to establish a trust fund with Redeemer College and the Redeemer Foundation as the only beneficiaries. The purpose of the trust would be to make tuition, food and housing at Redeemer College competitive with such fees at the public universities in Ontario. They informed me that the trust would have four trustees, of which they (Dick and Bill) were two. The other two trustees would have to remain anonymous. They believed that the trust would generate sufficient income to provide the College and the foundation with about $2.2 million annually. The College would be able to reduce its tuition, food and housing fees and be financially competitive with the public universities. The foundation would have a new source of funding to provide scholarships and bursaries.

I was flabbergasted and asked them who these people were and how it was possible to be able to do what we had only dreamt of doing up to that moment. They repeated that they were not able to give me the identity of these people, except that they loved the College and Christian education. I was assured that everything was in order and that Herman Faber, a lawyer and a member of the board's executive committee, would be retained by the settlors to prepare the trust agreement. He would have full knowledge of the trust and its operations. He would be required to maintain confidentiality and anonymity of the settlors and the other two trustees. However, he would be able to inform me if he saw anything problematic with the proposed structure or the expected income for the College and the foundation. All I could do was rejoice greatly and thank the two men for their involvement.

It was very important to me that this news came from both Dick and Bill. Dick, as I mentioned before, was the creative person, who often came forward with new ideas. Bill, however, as the former banker, was known as a conservative person in the administration. He wanted to be convinced that new ideas would work and be of value to the College. Only after the two agreed would they come to me with their plans. Therefore, when both Dick and Bill informed me of the trust, I was delighted and joyfully accepted that news and thanked the Lord for His wonderful provision. I truly saw it as an answer to prayer.

I phoned the members of the executive committee immediately and shared the good news with them. Except for one member, all accepted the news with gratitude. They advised me to accept the gracious offer. One member of the executive committee had misgivings and wondered whether such an offer could possibly be true. When I told him the details as I knew them, he cautiously expressed his support.

In the last week of November, the trust agreement was prepared and properly executed. Herman Faber had identified no problems with the legal structure, and Dick and Bill assured me that the short-term income from the trust would be more than sufficient to overcome any tuition and fee reductions, even if the trust would not be able to fulfill its commitment in the long run. After all, the total support needed by the College over the next three years would only be about $1.1 million. The administration and the executive committee agreed that the down-side risk would be minimal compared to the up-side potential.

I called both staff and faculty together to inform them of these new developments. Quite a few questions were raised. Some faculty members could not believe what they heard and asked me if I would be willing to take full responsibility for this trust. I answered in the affirmative. After the meeting with faculty, I wondered why I had answered their question so positively, since I had no confirmation about the trust other than the one I received from Dick, Bill and Herman Faber. I decided to contact an outside professional to confirm the legality and structure of the trust. I phoned a solicitor in Mississauga. He confirmed his familiarity with trusts in general and was positive in his remarks about the Brookview Trust information that I was able to provide to him. I had no reason not to trust my administrators, the lawyer for the trust (who was a member of the executive committee) and the outside confirmation I obtained. The anonymity condition was no problem for me or the executive committee. I remembered clearly the $1 million which was donated anonymously a few years earlier. At that time, the money was also not immediately received by us, but we trusted that it would come.

On November 30, I authorised the following news release:

FOR IMMEDIATE RELEASE

Ancaster, Ont., November 30, 1990—Henry R. De Bolster, President of Redeemer College, today announced some exciting news about tuition and the reduced cost of a Redeemer College university education.

In making the announcement, he said, "Through the services of a group of people who have set up a trust fund, we are able to assure ALL students that they will now be able to attend Redeemer College at a cost which is comparable to that at public Ontario universities. To be more specific," he added, "for the 1991/92 academic year, the cost for students will be $5,990 for tuition and housing or $4,450 for tuition alone. Students will be requested to pay the $5,990 or $4,450 to the trust fund at the beginning of the academic year."

When asked whether there were any strings attached or any other commitments to be made by the students or their parents, Mr. De Bolster said that the only condition will be that the student complete the entire academic year.

Students will be able to use all sources of funds from OSAP, scholarships and/or bursaries to pay towards their total required payment. Any remaining balance would have to be covered from summer earnings, personal savings, or from any other sources available.

By arrangement with the trust fund and the Redeemer Foundation, Redeemer College will receive the full cost for housing for each student living in College housing and the full cost for tuition for each student enrolled on a full-time basis. The student will receive a tuition receipt for the full amount actually paid to the College as tuition.

De Bolster stated, "This breakthrough in tuition cost means that the cost of tuition and housing at Redeemer College compares favourably with that charged by Ontario universities. For example, the 1990/91 charges at a nearby public university are $1,910 for tuition and $4,123 for food and housing on the 6 day meal plan for a total of $6,033. This is expected to increase by at least 5 percent for the 1991/92 academic year bringing the total comparable cost to at least $6,335."

He concluded his announcement by remarking, "This exciting development will make a Christian university education at Redeemer College accessible to many more students for whom finances might have been an obstacle in the past. Let us together praise the Lord for his wonderful ways and blessings.'

This announcement caused a lot of excitement both inside and outside the College. There was a lot of press exposure and the reaction was one of awe and wonder. There was another reaction from some students which was unexpected. They came to my office to tell me how grateful they were, but that they would skip the second semester and be back in September to benefit from the reduction. I went to Dick and Bill and informed them that some students planned to withdraw for the second semester. I asked them whether there was a possibility for the trust fund to include the second semester of the 1990/91 academic year in its generous offer, so that we would not lose these students. They consulted with the other people involved in the trust and informed me that for the second semester it would be possible to reduce the cost for housing and tuition from $5,215 to $3,680 and for tuition only from $3,477.50 to $2,910. I was then informed that the press release did not include the word "food," but that food was included as well and that the name of the trust was Brookview Trust.

None of the students left, and we started the second semester with joy and gratitude. For the first time, I did not have to worry about finances. The board shared in this joy and passed a resolution saying, "that the Board of Governors hereby goes on record as acknowledging and accepting with gratitude the commitment of the Brookview Trust to make possible for students to pay the full cost of education ($10,000) and the full cost of room and board ($3,650) for the 1991/92 academic year while at the same time the students will be required to use only $5,990 out of their own resources as payment to the Trust."

Because of the broad public exposure, applications for the 1991/92 academic year dramatically increased. It did not take long for all of us to realise that the enrollment projection of 500 students for the next year was not only realistic, but that it could be exceeded.

Everything went well during the next six months. We all lived in the bliss of the trust. The April 1 edition of the student spoof paper called the *Clown*, announced, in fun, the failure of the trust, and I remember saying to Dick and Bill how funny that article was. Then a terrible thing happened. The economy took a turn for the worse. The recession became severe, especially in the real estate market. Housing prices plummeted to lows that had not been seen for a long time. As a result of this strong recession, bank interest rates were suddenly lowered significantly, while inflation continued to rise.

The Collapse of the Trust

On May 31, 1991, Herman Faber, the solicitor for Brookview Trust, delivered a letter to me which read as follows:

> Please be advised that I am the solicitor for Brookview Trust, which was created to help offset the tuition, food, and housing costs at Redeemer Christian College. I was advised by the settlors of Brookview Trust on May 31, 1991 that the Trust is depleted due to serious investment reversals. A brief explanation is attached.
>
> As solicitor for the Trust, I wish to acknowledge and emphasize that to the best of my knowledge no one, including the employees of the College who agreed to serve as Trustees, has been negligent in terms of the causes that resulted in these recent events.
>
> The settlors and trustees deeply regret this development and pray that the activities of Redeemer Reformed Christian College may continue, with the Lord's help.

The attached explanation read as follows:

> It is with deep regret that the settlors of the Brookview Trust have asked me to inform you that the Trust has become financially incapable to perform its objectives of supporting the College and Redeemer Foundation.
>
> When the Trust was established last year with and by knowledgeable people, after lengthy negotiations, there was nothing to indicate the economic conditions that ultimately forced the complete collapse last week of the Trust.
>
> The fundamental contributing cause was a sudden, unexpected inability of the Trust to realize what prior to last week had appeared to be totally realistic gains of sufficient proportion to achieve its objectives.
>
> It would be totally unrealistic, given the prolonged and continuing deep recession, which has also severely affected the tradi-

tional business support community of Redeemer College, to hope that the Trust would be able to make compensating alternative arrangements to offset the devastating loss it has suffered.

It is therefore with extreme regret that the Trust announces its total collapse. Holding out any hope at this time, or even delaying its notification of this sad turn of events, would be a disservice to the College and the students for whom the existence of the Trust had made a university education an opportunity that had come within their reach.

The settlors of the Trust have appreciated in the past that their anonymity has been respected and preserved and they request that this anonymity continue to prevail.

It is difficult to relate my emotions of that moment. The words "numb" and "devastated" do not adequately describe how I felt. It was awful. When the letter from Herman Faber came, I had asked Dick and Bill to come to my office and I found them equally devastated. As trustees they had received prior notice. I asked them how this collapse was possible after all the confidence I had expressed in the trust through them. They felt terrible, apologised to me and offered their resignations. In answer to my questions, they told me the same things that I had read in the letter from Mr. Faber. When I asked what had happened to the fees of the students that had been deposited in the trust, they assured me that none of the students' payments had been lost, since those payments had already been received by the College in the previous months. The trust operated properly from January to May 1991. All this took place late Friday afternoon, May 31. I did not accept their resignations.

I immediately notified all the members of the executive committee and suggested that we should meet as soon as possible. It was decided to meet D.V. the following Tuesday evening June 4. The chairman suggested that we invite all the board members to this special meeting of the executive committee. Accordingly, I phoned the members of the board and invited them to come to the meeting.

That weekend I did not sleep much. My thoughts churned around and around and always came back to the same questions: *Why did it happen? What went wrong? Was I correct in accepting the anonymity, and, because of that, not being able to dig more deeply into the people behind the trust? What are the consequences of this disaster for the College? Did I betray the trust of the community that so faithfully supported Redeemer? Should I resign?* It was a nightmare.

Before the meeting of the executive committee, I met with senior faculty and staff members and announced the failure of the Brookview Trust. Many questions were raised, but because of the anonymity agreement, it was not possible to give information other than to talk about the general economic situation that had gone sour and the resulting losses which many of our supporters had suffered. The impression was that those who were involved in the Brookview Trust had been badly affected by the economic situation. The reaction of faculty and staff was devastating, but their reaction was supportive. It made me feel a little better to experience that we were together in this thing and that we would survive by the grace of God.

The executive committee meeting of June 4 was a good meeting. I informed the committee of the events that had taken place, and since I felt very much responsible as president, I tendered my resignation. Dick Kranendonk and Herman Faber answered the questions of the members present. Once these initial questions were out of the way, the executive committee passed a motion not to accept my resignation. It also decided that the board intended to honour its commitment to the students. The administration was mandated to develop positive alternative plans and to present these plans to the board's finance committee, which would meet the following Saturday. A board meeting was tentatively scheduled for June 15. The executive committee composed an announcement for the board, the faculty, staff, and student senate.

The next day I met with the faculty. I read the executive committee's announcement and gave everyone an opportunity to comment. Many faculty members used that opportunity to express disappointment. Others stated that they had serious concerns about the administration and called for the resignation of the president and the vice-presidents involved. Most of them asked for an inde-

STEPPING FORWARD IN FAITH

pendent investigation. The next day, I wrote a memo to the faculty thanking them for their openness, candid remarks, the questions they raised and the criticisms they offered. I thanked them for their cooperation and for their willingness to stand together "so that we continue to have the confidence of the returning students as well as the new applicants and their parents." I was convinced that if we were to get out from under this miserable dilemma, we would need to stand together. It is all right to criticise internally but to the outside you should show solidarity. The way I was educated at home when I was a child held very true at the College: we are family, and the family solves its problems internally. That was, I believed, the mood of that meeting with the faculty.

I held similar meetings with the staff, the students who were on campus during the summer months, and the student senate. These were sad meetings, where many tears were shed. All those present expressed their disappointment. Still, there was the determination to continue together. The student senate went on record to express confidence in the College administration.

Not everything was black and dark that week. I received several encouragements by letter and by word of mouth. It was especially moving to receive support from an unexpected source— the annual Milk and Honey Festival. On the last day of the festival, I informed the participants of the shocking news that the Brookview Trust had failed. One of the participants, a widow, wrote me a note of appreciation and included a cheque for $20,000. I also received a phone call from one of our major supporters. He wanted me to come as soon as possible. I went to see him that same day. I expected to hear about his disappointment with what had taken place at the College. Instead, he shook my hand, told me of his continued support and presented me with a cheque for $100,000.

That Saturday the finance committee and the executive committee met in a combined session. They listened to my report, looked at the alternative plans and made the following decisions, which were communicated in a news release dated June 10, 1991:

> Ancaster, ON. The Executive Committee and the administration of Redeemer College acknowledge that the Brookview Trust

Fund (BTF), established by a group of independent businessmen for the express purpose of subsidizing tuition, housing and food for Redeemer College students, has been forced to shut down as of May 31, 1991. The assets placed in the Trust were rendered valueless due to the prolonged recession. Prior to this failure, the BTF had fully met its obligations to the College for the second semester of the current 1990/91 academic year.

The BTF made it possible for the College to reduce tuition, housing, and food to students to a cost comparable to public universities. This new lower cost plan has contributed to a 74 percent increase in admissions applications when compared to last year.

In order to offset the loss of assistance by the BTF to the students and therefore *nullify* its impact on the College's financial situation, while at the same time keeping costs down for students, the College intends to do the following:

1. To keep the tuition for 1991/92 at $4,450 as committed and to keep the food and housing cost within the $1,540 to $3,650 range.
2. To step up fundraising efforts and encourage its supporters to honour their LIFT pledges to the College on a timely and generous basis. The College will also make a special appeal for funds to the supporting community through churches and personal contact.
3. To establish a task force of board, staff, faculty and students to come up with a reduced budget for 1991/92 by June 21, 1991.
4. To defer any capital building projects (i.e. new student residences) at this time.
5. To request students and parents to attend a special meeting on June 22 at 2:00 p.m. in the College auditorium where they will be briefed, updated, and have opportunity to share suggestions and questions.

Adopting the above measures enables the College to assure its supporters that its overall financial position remains the same as it was before the BTF was established.

The combined meeting also asked Mr. Bert Bakker, our solicitor, to investigate the circumstances surrounding the establishment of the special trust fund and its collapse and to report to the executive committee his findings at the next meeting of the committee. Bert Bakker had a meeting with Dick Kranendonk, Bill Smouter and Herman Faber, but felt that our auditors, Ernst & Young, would be better equipped to investigate the financial set-up of the trust. The executive committee agreed and asked Ernst & Young to audit the Brookview Trust and to inquire into the circumstances surrounding the setting up of the trust and to report to the executive committee. Some members were also concerned that the Brookview Trust might have been one of the parties that had pledged to the LIFT campaign or that it might have had other involvement with the campaign. Ernst & Young was asked to look into these concerns as well.

Ernst & Young conducted the investigation quickly and well. A "private and confidential" report was given to the executive committee at its combined meeting with the finance committee on June 21. Dick and Bill also sent a "private and confidential" memo to the executive committee regarding the report prepared by Ernst & Young. The meeting decided to keep the two reports private and confidential. For that reason I am not able to quote these reports, but the following news release accurately summarises the report from Ernst & Young:

What Happened?

On the 31st day of December 1990, an irrevocable trust under the name of Brookview Trust was set up with four Trustees, two of whom were financial administrative officers of Redeemer College. The beneficiaries of the Trust were Redeemer College and the Redeemer Foundation.

Contrary to public perception, the assets deposited into the Trust were a minimal amount of cash in order to set up a proper bank account with a chartered bank. No other gifts of any kind were made to the Trust.

At the same time, the Trustees of Brookview Trust, in their capacity as Trustees, borrowed money from a private Ontario company. The money was borrowed at interest and was used to purchase a large block of valuable common shares in the same private company.

According to the Trustees, this large block of common shares being acquired would realize a substantial capital gain over time. At the end of the year a part of the shares would be sold and the proceeds paid out to Redeemer College.

However, during the period that the Trust was functioning the economic condition in Ontario deteriorated. By May, the Trustees were made aware of the impact that increasing inflation coupled with declining interest rates was having on the investment returns of the company concerned. The Trustees contacted the auditor of the company and the solicitor of the Trust to determine the extent to which the Trust would be affected by these economic factors.

As a result of their review, the loans of the Trust were called and the investments were liquidated, leaving a zero balance in the Brookview Trust.

OBSERVATIONS

1. In accepting the representations of the Trustees, and the conditions of the total anonymity of both the settlors and the assets placed in the Trust, the Board of Governors and the College placed total reliance on the Trustees of the Trust. In hindsight, an error was made in a premature publication of reduced tuition, food and housing costs which the Board of Governors would not have made had they known that the income of the Trust was to come from the sale of common shares which were projected to rise in value.

2. No evidence was found of any personal benefit received or accruing to the Trustees of the Brookview Trust.

3. The statement made in the first press release of the Brookview Trust failure that "the assets placed in the Trust were rendered valueless due to the prolonged recession" was found to be subject to misinterpretation. The misunderstanding was that the shares owned by the Trust were valueless, whereas in fact they were all sold to pay off the loans (plus interest) of the Trust.

4. There were no LIFT campaign funds transferred to the Trust for investment, nor was the Trust a pledger to the LIFT campaign.

CONCLUSIONS

1. The Board of Governors and the Administration of Redeemer College regret that the financial plan devised did not work. Therefore, the College regrets that it could not fully fulfill its promises to students, alumni, faculty and staff.
2. Students are now asked to pay a total of $7,700.00 for tuition, food and housing instead of $5,990.00.
3. Just as before the establishment of the Brookview Trust, Redeemer College remains an academically and financially viable institution.

There is no doubt in my mind that Dick and Bill, together with the other trustees and the settlors of the trust, wanted to ease the financial burden of the College. It is true that they took a risk in doing so, because they "counted the chickens before they hatched." But let me remind the readers that it was and is impossible to avoid having to plan on receiving certain levels of donation income to sustain day-to-day operations. We planned on the basis of what we had received in the past, trusting that the Lord would provide. All our planning had risk factors. The financial structure at the College necessitated a creative financial approach. We made a conscious, communal decision to build a new campus, and to build it on credit. We had Dick, who was creative, and Bill, who counterbalanced that creativity. The two of them were constantly forced to do their planning for the future, faced with pressures to expand the academic programs at the same time. In planning, you always face an inherent risk, even when you plan on the basis of past experience. This time they could not plan based on past experience since there was none. Hindsight is always 20/20 vision. When a plan backfires it is easy to say that the planners should have been more cautious. Since this was such an extraordinary initiative, more caution should have been taken by all those involved.

An Ernst & Young partner and the solicitor for the College were present when the reports were tabled. The report came as a shock. Much grief might have been avoided had Dick and Bill given us these details immediately after the trust's collapse. A lengthy discussion followed. It was a most difficult meeting because questions were raised that could not be answered. Dick and Bill had made a commitment to maintain the confidentiality and anonymity of the settlors and the other trustees. They had requested, but had not received permission from those parties to make a full disclosure. A disclosure of the identity of the other parties probably could have helped to clear the air.

Some board members were of the opinion that Dick and Bill were obstinate and had placed their loyalties with the wrong parties. I fully understood their frustration, but there was nothing that could be done. Dick and Bill declared that for them the true test of trust and confidentiality comes when "the chips were down" and when maintaining confidentiality can cause personal hurt. I had to agree with them. What would have happened if they had betrayed their confidence? What would confidentiality at the College mean after it had once been betrayed? To betray a confidentiality always causes damage and liability. The Bible makes the necessity of confidentiality very clear when it says in Psalm 15 that the one who may dwell in the Lord's sanctuary is the person "who keeps his oath even when it hurts."

The board members who wanted to know more did not accept that it was a question of confidentiality. They did not believe Dick and Bill's explanation. They perceived that Dick and Bill did not want to answer the questions so that they would not have to reveal what the Brookview Trust truly was and what it had done. These distrusts created a foul atmosphere that had to be dealt with. The climax came at the meeting of the executive committee on July 9. Dick, Bill and I were asked to leave the meeting to give the executive committee opportunity to discuss in private session what needed to be done about the crisis. We were gone for a long time. It was good for the committee to take its time to look at all the facets of the issue and to take leadership. It was time to deal decisively so that the Brookview Trust affair could be put behind us. Too much work was waiting. My time was spent on damage control instead of preparing for another academic year. When I rejoined the meeting, the chairman informed me that the committee had passed a motion "expressing confidence in the continuing leadership of the president." I was relieved and expressed my sincere thanks to the members. The committee was not ready to pass a similar motion with regards to Dick and Bill. I begged the committee to leave the administrative team intact. Now was not the time to dismiss anyone. The committee listened to that argument, but felt that something needed to be done. The following three motions were passed:

A. That D. Kranendonk and Bill Smouter be reprimanded for their lack of disclosure, and failure to fully inform the Executive respecting the Brookview Trust.
B. That new policies be developed in cooperation with our auditors regarding the financial management of the College.
C. That the duties of the Vice-President of Administration and Finance, and the Vice-President of Advancement, be reviewed in consultation with our auditors for the purpose of possible restructuring, which could involve the addition of the position of financial comptroller or the equivalent.

The executive committee felt that something needed to be done because of the increasing pressure they experienced and the rumours that had started both inside and outside the College. I agreed that a reprimand was necessary. Dick and Bill humbly accepted it when they returned to the meeting. I believed that the action by the executive committee should have been the end of the discussions around this sad and unfortunate affair. The investigation had taken place, the facts that could be revealed were known, steps to avoid anything like that in the future were taken, the financial structure of the College was going to be considered, disapproval was expressed and penalties were handed out. That should have been the end, but it was not.

The Aftermath

Ten days later, on July 19 the executive committee met again. There was a letter from a board member, who was also a member of the executive committee, asking the executive committee to rescind the decisions taken at the last meeting in order to discuss this matter of the Brookview Trust again and to dismiss one of the administrators who had been a trustee of the trust. There was also a communication from a number of faculty members expressing their increasing lack of confidence and their dissatisfaction with the administration for the following reasons:

1. the demise of the Brookview Trust
2. the conflict of interest that occurred with Vista and Brookview Trust [Vista was a company originally set up to provide afford-able housing for faculty members. Dick and Bill were directors of Vista as well, HRD]
3. they feel misled by the administration
4. they object to the speculative type of financing policy fol-lowed by administration. They feel that the calls for caution have been ignored.

The committee rejected the request from the board member and received the communication from the faculty members as informa-tion. Before I continue the story of the decisions by the executive committee and the board, I want to relate the conflict I encountered with the Redeemer Foundation board. Right after we received the letter from Herman Faber, there was a meeting of the foundation board. We, the administration, deliberated whether we should inform the foundation of the shocking events. I suggested that we should wait until the board members had been notified. I told the foundation board that it was difficult for us to meet because of some unforeseen events that had taken place, and I asked that the meeting be adjourned. I promised to inform the members of the foundation board of the events sometime later. Because of the rapid succession of meetings, I totally forgot about the foundation board.

The foundation board members heard of the Brookview fail-ure from their chairman, Bert Bakker, who, as our solicitor, was involved from the beginning. I wished I had called the members of the foundation board, but I had not. I felt bad and apologised at the next meeting of the foundation board. Unfortunately, the members had not only heard from Bert Bakker, they had also been told by employees of the College who had given their own inter-pretation of the events.

One board member was very angry and did not want to accept my apology. He asked the foundation board to meet without the members who were employed at the College. He wanted to meet only with outside members, of which there were four, and to exclude, Dick, Bill and myself. The chairman allowed this request. The four board members walked out and left the three of us as if we did not belong. I was astounded! Later, the chairman offered his apologies, which I accepted, and the angry member resigned from the board. Yet on September 12, another meeting was held of "out-side Trustees of Redeemer Foundation" and "outside members of the Executive Committee" of the College's board with the auditor. The meeting dealt with financial matters which concerned both the College and the foundation but which had nothing to do with the Brookview affair. However, the fact that "inside" members were not invited revealed the tensions of that time.

Between July 19 and the next meeting of the executive commit-tee on August 28, the executive committee members stayed in touch frequently by telephone. The committee wanted to carry out its decision to develop new policies for the financial management of the College. The administration made several suggestions and the executive committee decided on the following:

1) Effective immediately and until further notice, Dick Kranen-donk's responsibilities of financial management will be shared with an ad hoc committee consisting of Mr. Nick Van Duyvendyk, retired Assistant Deputy Minister of Transport and former chairman of the Board of Governors of Redeemer Col-lege; Mr. Martin Bosveld, Accounting Instructor, Kent County Board of Education, presently Treasurer of the Board of Gover-nors; and Mr. Kees Vreugdenhil, Director of Information Resources at Union Gas Ltd. and former treasurer of the Board of Governors. This committee will report to the President.

2) The above committee will also review the financial management of the College and the duties of Dick Kranendonk and Bill

Smouter, with a view to a possible restructuring of the financial administration of the College, in accordance with the instructions of the Executive Committee.

3) This committee will be asked to submit a report to the President by November 15, 1991, for presentation to the Executive Committee of the Board of Governors on November 23, 1991.

4) During the study, D. Kranendonk will not use his title of Vice-President (Administration and Finance).

This was quite a penalty, which both Dick and Bill accepted. Yet at the same meeting of August 28, a communication was received from the faculty which contained two motions that they had passed:

A) A motion of non-confidence in the financial administration of Redeemer College,

B) The faculty requests a meeting of the full Board of Governors, before September 28, 1991, to consider the crisis of financial leadership and trust at Redeemer College.

The executive committee called a board meeting for September 14, 1991. The faculty were allowed 30 minutes to present their concerns. To help restore confidence at the College, I met that summer several times with faculty, staff and student senate. My most difficult meetings were with faculty. It did not seem possible for several faculty members to put this matter behind them. They continued to ask for the dismissal of the administration. It became clear to me that the Brookview Trust was not the only matter that bothered them; they did not like the way the administration had done its work. They reminded me of the changes in tuition policy that had been made in the past. The administration was accused of causing the debt load of the new campus. They ignored the fact that the College would not have been able to grow and expand its academic programs without financial creativity. The new campus would not have been built. The result would have been that tuition and residence fees, earmarked for debt reduction, could not have been redirected to allow for the academic program expansion. Significant pressure for expanding the curriculum and course offerings had been put on the financial administrators by the faculty and academic administration of the College. In short, without the creative policy proposals of the financial administration, the College would have remained small. Also, it would likely have lost its membership in the AUCC with all the consequences that would have entailed. It appears that faculty had forgotten that all financial policy proposals had been approved by the appropriate internal committees and the board. Faculty confidence and trust in the administration was gone. Al Wolters correctly observed at one of these meetings: "You cannot demand trust, it must be earned." The decisions of the executive committee did not satisfy the faculty. That is why they presented the above noted motions.

The staff was much more forgiving than the faculty. Disappointments were expressed, but there was a determination by the staff members to move on.

The student senate met often during that summer. At their request, I attended their meetings several times. Even though they had difficulties with the events and even expressed that they had no confidence in the financial administration, they nevertheless continued "to look forward to the restoration of confidence within Redeemer College, and through prayer and hard work, to play a major part in that process." I want to make special mention of the president of the student senate that year, Ben Westerveld. Ben showed a lot of leadership. He came to my office weekly and did much to restore a good relationship between the administration and the student body.

However, restoration of trust and confidence was a long way off. The situation at the College worsened. Rumours started circulating within the College that the trustees of the Brookview Trust had been involved in fraud. These rumours eventually made their way outside the College. I received phone calls from our support community urging me to get rid of these Brookview people because they were frauds. I do not know whether our auditors heard these rumours, but the audit that year was a stringent one which took much longer than in previous years. The results were as we knew and expected. The financial records were found to be in order and no trace of fraud was found. The rumours were painful. How do we deal with each other as Christians, and how do we deal with each other at a Christian college? Is there not such a thing as forgiveness? Apparently some people were determined to get rid of one or both financial administrators at any cost. Some said that the president should also be dismissed because he would no longer be able to function effectively at the College.

When the students came back from summer holidays, they were thrown into this horrible mess. The student paper, *The Crown*, also became involved. The editor of the paper could not welcome the new students at the beginning of a new academic year as she had wanted to because of what had happened during the summer.

The editor of *Calvinist Contact* (now *Christian Courier*) wrote an editorial in which he said that "it appears that the very desire to address the financial pressures of an institution has led Redeemer's leaders to wander from the path of faith, prayer and acts of integrity into the unholy way of impatience and an 'I'll-fix-it-myself' kind of mentality."

This was the atmosphere in which the board met on September 14, 1991. I wrote in my report to the board: "The main reason for this special board meeting is to review the actions of the executive committee as they relate to the Brookview Trust failure. It is my prayer that this meeting will serve the College well so that any lingering issues can be clarified. Perhaps it will be possible to put the trust failure to rest." I was able to report that we had an increase in enrollment from 359 to 488 FTE students in spite of the turmoil we went through. It was a cause for thankfulness. However, the meeting was filled with anxieties because of the Trust and its aftermath.

The faculty had been asked to present their concerns to the board. The four division chairmen functioned as spokespersons for the faculty. Many faculty members were present at the meeting, but they were not permitted to speak. One division chairman was the primary spokesman. In no uncertain terms he expressed his displeasure with the administration. I have never been in a meeting where such harsh words were spoken without a trace of charity. The request was to fire the president and the two vice-presidents who had been the trustees of Brookview Trust. He stated that it was no longer possible for the faculty to work with them.

The board discussed the presentation of the faculty and the activities of the executive committee since the previous board meeting. After a long and difficult discussion, the board decided to approve the decisions of the executive committee, except for the penalties imposed on Dick Kranendonk. The board was of the opinion that a reprimand was insufficient and that a resignation was required. A motion was made and passed to ask Dick Kranendonk for his resignation as vice-president of Redeemer College effective January 1, 1992. It was a sad moment and a sad decision. I felt that Dick was used as a scapegoat to satisfy the administration's critics. Since my resignation had been requested as well, I asked the board to express itself on that issue. A motion went on record, with two votes against, that the board "expresses its confidence in the continued leadership of the president." No action was taken regarding Bill Smouter. Sad as it was, we had finally reached closure of this matter: at least, so I thought.

That same evening, I, together with my wife, visited Dick Kranendonk and his wife Henny. I informed Dick of the board's decision. He was not surprised and indicated that he would give me an answer soon, which he did. We prayed together and I left Dick and Henny in the hands of the Lord.

I confirmed our conversation with the following letter:

Dear Dick:

At its meeting of September 14, 1991, the Board of Governors of Redeemer College asked me to request your resignation to be effective on or about January 1, 1992. This letter is to confirm that I asked for your resignation and I did so with deep sadness and received your resignation with regret.

This letter will confirm that your resignation was not requested because you engaged in any unlawful activities, such as fraud or misappropriation of funds. The failure of the Brookview Trust entailed an error in judgement shared by more than one person.

Also, I want to confirm that your resignation was not requested because of incompetence. On the contrary, you have worked long and hard since 1980 to help build Redeemer College. Your service to the College has been exemplary, and more often than not you served beyond the call of duty. You were instrumental in the building and financing of the campus. Your commitment to the cause of Christian education, and to Christian higher education at Redeemer College was total. You will be sorely missed.

In final analysis, it appears the board had a need to take some decisive overt action in addition to what the executive committee had already done. They chose to ask for your resignation. You already know how sorry I am about this turn of events. I want to thank you for your willingness to resign for the good of the College.

I want to thank you personally for your advice, support, and friendship, and for all the work you have done during these last twelve years. They were exciting and challenging years.

May God bless the work of your hands in whatever field you choose to go.

With warm greetings,
Henry R. De Bolster
President

When I told Bill Smouter that Dick had been asked to resign, he wanted to do the same thing. He felt that he was as much to blame as Dick. However, it was Dick who persuaded him not to resign. Dick said that for the good of the College he should stay. I am glad that he stayed.

I used the following weeks to speak with each faculty member individually and to ask each the same question: "Now that we have this Brookview affair behind us, and the board has made its decision, what must I do to help you work together with me?" Most of the faculty members were ready to move. Since the board had reconfirmed my presidency, they had no problem working with me. Some had supported me throughout, expressed full confidence and were more than willing to help and advise me. I want to thank them very much.

A few faculty members indicated they could no longer work with me and would leave the College for employment elsewhere. Only one faculty member left that year and he came to tell me that his departure had nothing to do with the Brookview Trust failure. Some faculty members indicated that I should have resigned but were willing to accept the decision of the board.

Slowly the atmosphere changed. The annual meeting of the membership at the end of September went well. The members were satisfied with the explanations given and the decisions taken by the board. It was heartwarming to hear Al Wolters move a vote of thanks to Dick Kranendonk for all he had done for the College. His remarks were greeted by the warm round of applause by the members present.

Yet it took a year before I could say that we were back to where we used to be. *The Crown* found it necessary to remind all of us of the "scandal" of the Brookview Trust in each issue published that year. No one acknowledged that the number of students had increased to record numbers, and that tuition and fees had been decreased drastically. This illustrated how deep the wound was that had been inflicted on all of us. Yet it was a fact that the magic 500 student mark had almost been reached in spite of the turmoil of that summer.

A few questions remain. The first one is: "Was the premise and structure of the trust sound, and were I and, on my recommendation, the executive committee correct in accepting the trust and its terms at face value?"

The executive committee and I were assured by Dick and Bill that the premise of the proposed trust, in their view, was sound. They firmly believed that the trust could produce the anticipated benefits. We had also been reassured by the fact that one of the members of the executive committee was appointed as the trust's solicitor. He had full knowledge of the legal structure and assets of the trust. In view of the endorsement of two senior and trusted members of the administration and the verbal report to me by the trust's solicitor, I believe it was reasonable for me and the executive committee to accept the Brookview Trust.

I cannot imagine how a charity would ever reject its beneficial interest in a legitimate trust. A charity may refuse to accept a contribution when it believes that the donor is, for whatever reason, not capable of making the gift, or legally not competent to do so, or when the donor attaches unacceptable restrictions to the gift. To the best of my knowledge, a charity has no power to deny anyone their right to set up a trust of which the charity is the beneficiary. In this case, the solicitor reported that all the terms of the trust were normal. The restriction was that the funds should be used only to reduce tuition, food and housing costs for the students. That restriction was not problematic. Therefore, the College had thankfully accepted the trust and advertised the benefits that students would receive from the trust.

All of us went wrong when we began spending the funds before the trust had actually distributed its income to the College. The tuition, food and housing costs for students for the winter semester of the 1990/91 academic year should not have been reduced before the funds came in. But the response to the announcement had some immediate consequences! The number of students increased that winter semester and the number of applications for the next year increased dramatically.

A second question is: "What was the actual cost for the College as a result of the Brookview Trust failure?"

It is difficult, if not impossible, to determine with any degree of certainty what the costs or benefits of the trust's failure were. It depends on the factors that are taken into consideration. It is easy to come up with costs and benefits once there is agreement on the variables that need to be taken into account. I am sure that there is considerable disagreement on the question of the effect that the trust had on the enrollment of the 1990/91 winter semester. It is impossible to determine how many students would have withdrawn if the tuition, food and housing costs had not been reduced for the second semester. The shortfall in tuition income could have been significant, if the students who intended to withdraw for the semester had followed up on their intent. Another factor was the elimination of the per-course charge for tuition. This meant that all students once again paid for a full load of courses, although at a reduced rate. When these factors are taken into account, I estimate that the net revenue reduction for the College in the winter semester 1990/91 was probably less than assumed at the time of the trust's failure.

If the reduced amount that the students paid and what the trust had promised to pay are the only factors taken into account, the result is a shortage of $426,000. However, if the fee income less the financial aid cost in the 1989/90 fiscal year's audited financial statements is compared to the same numbers in the audited financial statements for the 1990/91 fiscal year, the net result is a difference of $58,515. Since the actual revenue producing enrollment and campus housing occupancy had declined over the two previous years, it may be difficult to argue that the negative effect of the Brookview Trust's establishment and failure was more than that amount. Some would say that the results of the trust's failure were felt in the 1991/92 academic year as well, since it was necessary to draw up a new budget based on the reduced tuition cost. But all agreed with that decision because we did not want to lose students by raising the tuition and fees to their former levels.

In that connection, I have often asked myself a number of questions. What would the enrollment have been in September 1991 if the Board of Governors had not increased fees by $1,700? What if the energy that was consumed by anger and resentment had instead been channelled into a constructive evaluation of the lesson we should have learned from the increased enrollment? The enrollment, in a very concrete way, demonstrated the price sensitivity of total fees including tuition, housing and food. I know that the answers to these questions cannot be determined with any degree of certainty. Don't get me wrong: I am not posing these questions to minimise the hurt and frustration we all felt. Neither am I trying to point fingers at anyone. However, I do believe that we were so focussed on ourselves and the failure of the Brookview Trust that we did not properly evaluate and interpret the results of the experiment, unintended though it was. We did not behave as might have been expected of an academic institution whose scholars are trained to make objective evaluations and interpret such observations without the interference of personal emotions. That was our problem. Our emotions controlled all of us.

This then is the story of the Brookview Trust. The pain came back as I recalled these events. I am certain that these pages will revive some old hurts and open some old wounds. God is gracious and He forgives. It is my prayer that we have also forgiven one another. A crisis such as this serves as a reminder that God accomplishes His purposes through weak vessels. Brookview Trust taught me and others valuable lessons that will be of benefit to the future of Redeemer College. I thank God that Redeemer continues its mission of educating young men and women for the glory of God, for service to God's people and to the world in which we live.

EIGHT

Government Relations

In this chapter I will expand on the discussions the College had with the government of Ontario, the letters to and from the Ministry of Colleges and Universities (later the Ministry of Education and Training), and the letters from the government ministers who served at various times during the years in question. I will share the frustrations we experienced in our dealings with the Ontario Council on University Affairs, and quote the decisions of the various government bodies during the years 1985 to 1994.

While our membership application was being considered by the Association of Colleges and Universities in Canada, a ministry representative visited us at our request. We asked him to recognise Redeemer College as an undergraduate university. He was impressed by what he saw. Nevertheless, he reiterated the government's position not to permit new, free-standing, secular degree-granting institutions to be established. He conceded that the government's denial to change the nomenclature of our degrees would be more difficult to maintain should we be admitted as a member of the AUCC. We had the distinct impression that he considered our chances of being admitted to the "exclusive club" of universities remote at best.

The Conservative Government

In 1985, Redeemer College was admitted as a member of the AUCC. I immediately wrote the following letter to the Honourable Mr. Keith Norton, Minister of Colleges and Universities:

Ancaster, April 10, 1985
Dear Mr. Norton:
As president of Redeemer Reformed Christian College, I

respectfully ask that you carefully read and act upon the requests made by this presentation, namely:

1. that the name of our institution be changed to Redeemer Reformed Christian University,
2. that the powers of the academic council be expanded to include the power to grant degrees, and
3. that various housekeeping amendments to clean up the general provisions of the Charter be passed.

Redeemer College has received full recognition by and membership in the Association of Universities and Colleges of Canada. The AUCC in its official report states that:

It is the judgment of the visiting committee that the courses constituting the Bachelor of Christian Studies Program are comparable to courses leading to a Bachelor of Arts in Canadian Universities,

Academic standards for promotion and graduation are comparable to Canadian Universities, generally.

In summary, the visiting committee was impressed with the quality of the faculty, the competence of the administrative staff and the attention paid to good planning and development in their academic programs. We were particularly impressed with the commitment of all sectors of the College: students, faculty, support staff, administrative staff, and the supporting broader community to the idea of developing their own higher education institution of high academic quality.

We are aware of the concerns of the ministry which find expression in the longstanding "Robarts policy" not to allow any further free-standing publicly-funded institutions to be established in Ontario. As we understand it, this policy has as its purpose to prevent a proliferation of duplicate programs in Ontario which would further dilute the public resources available for university education. We understand, respect, and accept this concern.

In relation to Redeemer College, we wish to draw a few important factors to your attention which will enable the ministry to maintain its policy and at the same time allow a necessary measure of academic freedom. These factors are:

1. Our institution has an expressed policy of not accepting public funding for operating purposes. We are prepared to have our commitment to that policy enshrined in the Charter.

2. The education at our institution, while comparable to that in Canadian universities, is at the same time distinct since all courses must be "permeated by Scripturally-directed Reformed Christian perspectives in accordance with the Statement of Basis and Principles as set out in the by-laws of the university." This distinctiveness has been enshrined in the Charter, and we wish to maintain it so that our institution will not *duplicate* what is offered at the public universities. Our religious-philosophical distinctiveness is our *raison d'être* without which we should not have the right to operate.

On the basis of the above factors and for the sake of academic freedom and the economic contributions made by our institution to the province of Ontario, I humbly request that you support the desired amendments to our Charter.

Sincerely,
Henry R. De Bolster
President

We delivered this letter to the ministry. It gave us an opportunity to elaborate on our request. We spoke with Mr. J. MacKay. He suggested that we should ask Dr. Lee, president of McMaster University, to write a letter on our behalf. Dr Lee also was the president of the Council of Ontario Universities, the organisation whose support would be needed to get a positive response from the ministry. We promised Mr. MacKay that we would send him more information about the College. In turn, he promised to give his attention to our submission. The following day I visited Dr. Lee. He was willing to write a letter in support of our request to expand the College's degree-granting powers. He did not agree that the word "University" should be added to our name. He was of the view that the College was too small to be identified as a university. The degree change was the vital issue for us. We were very grateful for his willingness to write a letter of support to the ministry.

However, before Dr. Lee wrote his letter we received the following response from the minister, dated May 13, 1985:

> Thank you for your recent letter concerning your institution's desire to amend the Redeemer Reformed Christian College Act, 1980, such that Redeemer Reformed Christian College be empowered to call itself a university and grant non-religious degrees.
>
> The fact that Redeemer College has received provisional membership in the Association of Universities and Colleges of Canada (AUCC) is certainly a development of which you, your colleagues and the College's supporting community can be proud and I would like to take this opportunity to extend my congratulations to you.
>
> Membership in the Association, whether provisional or full, may not be sufficient grounds upon which the government could base a recommendation to the Legislature that Redeemer College's statutory charter be amended in the manner that you have suggested. As you are aware, it has been the government's longstanding policy that no new free-standing, secular, degree-granting institutions be established. It has been our policy to advise institutions that wish to offer secular degree programs, to affiliate with one of the province's established degree-granting institutions. I have asked my staff to review the Association's eligibility criteria and to advise me in this regard.
>
> I wish you and your colleagues at Redeemer College every success in your future endeavours.
>
> Your very truly,
> Keith Norton
> Minister

Clearly, the Conservative government of the day had no intention to grant our request. However, there was one item in this letter that caught our attention.

The quote of the Robarts policy was "that no new free-standing, secular, degree-granting institutions be established." We noticed the comma after the word "secular." We interpreted this wording to mean that the policy does not allow *new secular degree-granting institutions* to be established. In the same paragraph, the minister spoke of offering *secular degree programs* as if the word "secular" modified the "degree" rather than the "institution." Ever since that letter, the latter interpretation has been used by the ministry to inform us that we could not grant a B.A. degree because we were a Christian institution. A "B.A.", henceforth, was considered to be a "secular degree." In later years we were told that a university education at a Christian institution was a contradiction in terms.

The Liberal Government

Dr. Lee wrote his letter to the minister on June 26, 1985. In the meantime, a provincial election had taken place with the result that a Liberal government had been elected. Dr Lee's letter arrived on the desk of the new minister, Mr. Gregory Sorbara. Dr. Lee wrote:

> ...As you and members of the Ministry staff will know, McMaster University has provided some informal assistance to Redeemer College in its early formative years. Some of their students take McMaster courses as part of their College programme. Also, quite a number of their graduates have come to McMaster to proceed to degrees here. In both categories their students have performed well.
>
> We also have examined the report of the site consultants for the Association of Universities and Colleges of Canada on the basis of which the College has been admitted to provisional membership in the Association.
>
> On these two grounds we do not object to the request of the College for degree-granting powers. In doing so, we note the firm assurance of the President of the College to the Ministry that neither now nor in the future will they be seeking public funding. It is on this explicit understanding that we support the application...

It must have been Dr. Lee's letter that made the new minister take note of our application degree-granting powers. We received a letter from Mr. Sorbara, written on September 31 [sic], 1985:

I am writing further to your institution's request to amend the Redeemer Reformed Christian College Act, 1980, such that Redeemer Reformed Christian College be empowered to call itself a university and grant non-religious degrees.

Given Ontario's longstanding policy that no new free-standing, secular, degree-granting institutions be established, I am reluctant to consider your institution's request without first reviewing the entire policy regarding the establishment of new private universities. I have therefore asked the Ontario Council on University Affairs to conduct a review of this matter and advise me accordingly. I am confident that Redeemer Reformed Christian College will have the opportunity to present its views to the Council.

The Ontario Council on University Affairs

When we received the minister's letter, we were somewhat encouraged. It was not an outright rejection, and we understood that the minister needed some time to be fully informed about our request. We did not think it was unreasonable for him to ask the OCUA for advice. This council consisted of 22 members from outside the immediate university communities. No administrators were on that council. Faculty members, business people and representatives of labour unions were appointed by the minister as a cross section of the population to advise the minister on matters he chose to place before them.

I contacted the chairperson, Ms. Marnie Paikin, and requested a meeting with her on November 21, 1985. At that meeting, I had an opportunity to personally inform her about the College. I gave her copies of the *Charter*, the *College Calendar* and correspondence relating to the *Charter*. She listened but was non-committal and advised me that OCUA had many items on its agenda. The matter of private universities would not be discussed for some time. But she did promise to visit the College and to expedite this matter as quickly as possible.

Ms. Paikin visited our campus on February 17, 1986. It was immediately clear that she had not read any of the material I had left with her because she asked why Redeemer College, as a Bible college, would want to grant B.A. degrees. Her question gave us another opportunity to tell her that Redeemer was not a Bible college, but a liberal arts institution. Because of that confusion, we needed a change in our name as well as expanded degree-granting powers.

On may 5, 1986, we were pleasantly surprised to receive a communication from the OCUA asking for more information. Finally there was some action. We mistakenly concluded that the item of private universities had been placed on the agenda for a speedy resolution. The letter read as follows:

> The Ontario Council on University Affairs, at the request of the Minister of Colleges and Universities, is conducting a review of government policy with respect to the establishment of new private universities. Given the longstanding provincial policy that no new free-standing, secular degree-granting institutions be established there are a number of issues on which the Council is seeking input from universities, private colleges and other interests. Your response to any of the following would be helpful.
> 1. What are the advantages and drawbacks of the existing policy which requires new institutions to affiliate with an existing university in order to obtain degree-granting powers? 2. Should new institutions be granted degree-granting powers? If so, why? If not, why not?
> 3. If new degree-granting institutions were established what sort of process would ensure a high standard of program quality?
> 4. If you are of the opinion that the current policy should change, how would graduates of new private degree-granting institutions be assured that their programs were of sufficient quality to gain admittance to a graduate program at a publicly-funded Ontario university?
> 5. Would the existence of new degree-granting private universities affect the enrollment, funding, student assistance and university finances of the existing system? If so, how?
> 6. Should new privately financed degree-granting institutions expect access to public funding directly through grants and/or

indirectly through government assistance programs (i.e. OSAP for students' tuition fees)?

7. If you believe privately financed degree-granting institutions should be eligible for indirect government funding through OSAP, should there be a limit to the amount of OSAP available to students of these institutions?

Council would also appreciate receiving information on any of the following questions regarding the affiliation process.

a) the basis on which requests for affiliation are accepted or denied

b) the number and year of requests that have been received from private institutions seeking to affiliate; and

c) the types of institutions requesting affiliation (i.e. religious, business, professional, technical or special colleges).

Your response to the above or any additional issues you would like to address is a valued aspect of Council's decision-making process. Please make your submission by July 31, 1986. I look forward to receiving your comments.

Yours sincerely,

M. Paikin,

Chairman

It is interesting to note in the first paragraph of this letter, that the comma after secular had disappeared.

We responded to this invitation by making a two-volume submission to OCUA regarding the Robarts policy on the establishment of new free-standing, secular degree-granting institutions. The summary of the submission gave an overview of the contents as follows:

SUMMARY OF THE BRIEF

PART ONE of this Brief will show the history of the College, identity of the College, resources of the College, and the progress the College has made in its five years with a restricted degree-granting charter. However, on the basis of its experience, the College has found it necessary to apply for a change in its degree-granting powers which reflect more accurately the objects of the College as set out in its charter and the College's educational programs based thereon. Such a change in degree designation will allow the Ontario universities to treat the College's graduates in a manner consistent with their transcripts. Most Ontario universities presently treat the College's degrees in a manner similar to degrees from Bible Colleges because both are empowered to grant only religiously designated degrees. However, the universities readily acknowledge that Bible College programs have a very different nature and focus than the programs at the College.

PART TWO of this Brief will deal with the questions posed by the Council. It is the conviction of the College that the Council should recommend the modification of "the long-standing provincial policy that no new free-standing, secular degree-granting institutions be established." PART TWO proposes to the Council policies and procedures whereby new degree-granting institutions can be established. These policies and procedures are in response to the questions posed by the Council, and are presented in the light of the experience of the College as an institution with a limited degree-granting charter. The College is convinced that the policies and procedures proposed in this Brief if adopted as government policy will assure academic and institutional accountability of all applicants for degree-granting charters (be they of a religious, philosophical or unique service nature) both at the time of their initial application and during their continued existence.

While we were waiting for an answer, we continued our discussions with the government about OSAP grants for our students. Early in 1987, we received word from the ministry that our students qualified for these grants. This gave me an opportunity to write the minister to thank him for this decision and to remind him of our request for the *Charter* amendments. I reminded him that we had been waiting for almost two years and that OCUA had been studying this matter for more than a year. In his letter of response, he told us that he had given a copy of my letter to the Council, which did not help very much. When I phoned Ms. Paikin she always gave the same answer: "We are very busy and as soon as we deal with this matter you will hear from us."

The Brief to the Minister

The waiting game was frustrating and it did not change when, in the fall of 1987, Ms. Lynn McLeod became the Minister of Colleges and Universities. We met her shortly after her appointment. The meeting was arranged by Mr. Chris Ward, our local MPP. He became the Minister of Education in the same Cabinet shuffle. We met Ms. McLeod in the hallway near the Legislature, and we had a short but amicable conversation. I promised to send her a brief about the College. I also mentioned our frustration with the delay of our request for a *Charter* amendment. She encouraged me to give her as much information as possible. In the brief that I sent her, we changed strategy and explained who we truly were in more detail. Thus far, we had cooperated with the minister and accepted the fact that we might have to wait until the minister received the advice of OCUA. It seemed as if we might have to wait a very long time and in the end OCUA might deal only with the general question of private universities. The danger was that OCUA might recommend against the establishment of new private universities. Such a recommendation would also likely mean a negative response to our request. Since there was a new minister we decided to try to by-pass OCUA for the direct attention of the minister. Therefore, in the letter to the minister on December 21, 1987 I wrote:

Thank you very much for taking the time to talk to us last Thursday afternoon. To meet you and find a listening ear greatly encouraged us.

Further to our meeting, please find enclosed a Brief which basically asks you to grant an amendment to our Charter that will extend our degree-granting power and will change our name. We make this request on the basis of the identity and standing the College has obtained over the past seven years.

We wrote this Brief out of a sense of frustration. We placed the same question before the Minister of Colleges and Universities 2 1/2 years ago. The delay in receiving an answer was caused by the minister's decision to ask the Council of University Affairs (OCUA) for advice because of the long-standing policy, which says that "no new, free-standing, secular, degree-granting institutions be established in Ontario."

This referral has not only delayed our request unnecessarily, but more importantly, the "longstanding policy" in no way addresses the uniqueness of Redeemer College.

Our submission does not mean to say that the study by OCUA re the "longstanding policy" should not continue. There are institutions to which the policy applies. However, our request should be judged by itself for the following reasons:

1. the College already is a free-standing chartered institution.
2. the College is not a secular i.e. publicly-funded institution, nor does it request to become one.
3. Religiously the College is not a secular institution.
4. the College already has degree-granting powers, albeit limited.

In addition, we want to point out that our program, though unique, nevertheless is comparable to programs given at publicly-funded Canadian universities. The quality and content of our programs have been judged and approved by our peers—the university community—to qualify for admission to ordinary membership in the Association of Universities and Colleges of Canada (AUCC).

We also show in our Brief the economic benefit our college brings to Ontario. Moreover, we do not divert students from Ontario universities. On the contrary, we bring students back to Canada who otherwise study in similar colleges and universities in the U.S.A. and other countries.

By granting our request, you do not compromise the above mentioned long-standing policy, neither will you set a precedent.

Needless to say, we are very much disappointed that the government has not as yet supported our private initiative. We do not ask for operating funds. We have proven ourselves. We ask for equity. The students who attend at great financial sacrifice to receive an education which has been judged by the university community to be comparable to its own, should receive the same degree given by a university for a similar program. Being forced to give a different degree is clearly discriminatory.

We are grateful for your appointment. We pray that God will bless you. We have high hopes that you will take us out of the labyrinth in which we have been placed. We expect a positive reply from you in the very near future so that our solicitors and yours may sit down to draft an amendment to our charter. This will enable us to develop as a contributor to the educational community as well as to provide an economic benefit for the province.

I wish you a very blessed Christmas and a Happy New Year.

Sincerely,
Henry R. De Bolster
President

At the fall meeting of the AUCC, I had asked several presidents to write a letter on our behalf to the newly appointed minister. Several took the time to write. I want to share one example of such a letter. The letter was written by Dr. David L. Johnston of McGill University in Montreal on December 22, 1987:

Re: Redeemer College, Ancaster, Ontario
Dear Madame Minister:

Reverend Henry R. De Bolster, President of Redeemer College, advises me that Redeemer College is seeking general degree granting powers from the province of Ontario so that it will be able to grant a B.A. and B.Sc. degrees. He advises me that the impediment is an appendix to a review of the "Robarts Policy" of 1965 which states that: "No new, free-standing, secular, degree-granting institutions be established in Ontario." President De Bolster points out

that Redeemer College does not fit into the category circu
by the Robarts Policy in that it is chartered as a free-sta
degree-granting, university-level institution. It is not secular a
does not ask for public funding.

I have had the opportunity to see the teaching and research of
Redeemer College and as a member of the Association of Universities and Colleges of Canada, participated in the decision to
receive it as a full member of the Association, one judged to be
offering university-level programs. This is an institution which
pursues its educational mission with remarkable commitment and
dedication and I am delighted to see it playing a vital role in
enhancing the diversity of university-level institutions in Canada.
From it we all gain.

I hope that this letter may be helpful to you and your colleagues in your decision on this matter.

Yours sincerely,
David L. Johnston

On February 17, 1988, I received a reply to my letter of December 21, 1987. The minister wrote:

I understand your frustration with the time it is taking to consider your application. I wish to assure you that the council has
assigned a high priority to the completion of the review, and that
the advice of the council will be given expeditious consideration. I
regret, however, that until such time as I have received and
reviewed the council's advice, I cannot consider the application by
Redeemer to be granted full university powers.

What a disappointment. The minister did not wish to deal with
this matter apart from OCUA.

The Presentation to OCUA

In the meantime, in June 1987, Ms. Paikin had been replaced as
chairperson of OCUA by Dr. Paul Fox. Late April 1988, I received
a phone call from Dr. Fox telling me that he had appointed a sub-

ı the matter of private universities and that
r George, would contact me.

ater became president of McMaster Univer-
ge in August. He was impressed by what he
expedite the matter referred to his committee.
ʒe would be able to make a presentation to the
committee arouɪ..ɪ ..ɪe middle of November.

We received several communications inviting us to appear before the committee, but each time the meeting was postponed to a later date. Finally, on December 16, 1988, we received a letter indicating place, time and the expected content of our presentation. The letter was signed by Dr. H.V. Nelles, interim chairman of OCUA, who had succeeded Dr. Fox. We were to meet with the committee on January 31, 1989, from 4:00 p.m. to 5:00 p.m. We were told that:

The purpose of these hearings is to discuss policy-related issues only and is not intended to be a forum in which organizations argue the merit of their own individual cases.

Organizations will be invited to make an initial presentation of no more than 15 minutes in duration, focussing on the policy-related issues listed below. The remaining 45 minutes will be spent in a discussion with the Committee which will include, but not be limited to, the following:

1. Your organization's views on and/or experience with the "Robarts Policy" of affiliation.
2. Societal needs which are currently unmet by the existing post-secondary institutions in Ontario.
3. If you have advocated that new institutions should be granted degree-granting powers:
   (a) What would be the appropriate evaluative criteria for the granting of university status and/or degree-granting powers?;
   (b) Would your organization be in favour of an externally administered system of program evaluation?;
   (c) If not, how should institutional and program quality be demonstrated?

4. Should the existing policy be modified to permit institutions without university status to grant, for example Bachelor of Arts, Bachelor of Science, or Master of Arts degrees without university status?

5. If the existing policy were changed to permit the establishment of free-standing secular degree-granting institutions:

    (a) Should private post-secondary institutions receive public funding of any sort, directly through grants or indirectly via student aid?;

    (b) How should these institutions relate to the administrative and regulatory apparatus of the existing, publicly-funded university system?; For example, what should the policy be with respect to the transfer of students' credits from free-standing institutions to publicly-funded institutions?;

    (c) What should be the Government's role in relation to free-standing secular degree-granting institutions?

We arrived at the meeting at the appropriate time and were cordially welcomed by Dr. George. There were several other people present to hear the presentations that were to be made that day. There were representatives from other institutions and organisations which had already spoken. Furthermore, there was a representative of the AUCC, as well as a number of lawyers and interested spectators. When it was our turn to present our views, I addressed the meeting as follows:

Mr. Chairman, members of the committee, my name is Henry R. De Bolster, president of Redeemer College. Please, allow me to introduce to you the other members of our delegation. With me are Dr. Jacob Zeyl, assistant dean of arts and sciences and associate professor of classics and chairman of that department at Sir Wilfrid Laurier University, Dr. Albert M. Wolters, professor of religion and theology at Redeemer College, both of whom are members of our academic council; Dr. Justin Cooper and Dr. Dick L. Kranendonk, Redeemer College vice-presidents for academics and administration respectively; and Mr. William Charlton, of the law firm Ross & McBride, our legal counsel.

As representatives of Redeemer College, we welcome this opportunity to present to you, the free-standing institutions committee of the Ontario Council on University Affairs, our views on the issues raised in your letter of December 16, 1988. Each question will be dealt with in turn.

(1) Affiliation:

On the basis of our experience over the past twelve years, it has become clear that the current policy requiring new institutions to affiliate with an existing publicly-funded university, has significant limitations. Specifically, the policy presupposes that the institution seeking affiliation offers a limited and specialised program which complements courses and programs offered by the host university. Universities have been unwilling to affiliate with an institution wishing to provide a full liberal arts program, considering this to be an unnecessary duplication of their own similar courses. In effect, the policy of affiliation is biased against the establishment of a liberal arts institution or any institution which intends to provide a complete academic program, integrated on the basis of specific religious, philosophical or other principles.

From a financial viewpoint, it is indeed ironic that the requirement of affiliation has discouraged initiatives to establish university-level institutions which would be privately funded. Under the present policy, an affiliated institution would receive provincial grants on the formula basis, causing a further drain on public funds.

(2) Unmet Societal needs:

The existence of institutions like Redeemer College, the Institute for Christian Studies, and programs offered in Ontario by out of province institutions under the Ministerial Consent Policy is evidence that there are educational needs which are not being met by existing, publicly-funded universities. For example, Redeemer College serves primarily students who previously obtained their Christian liberal arts education outside the province and, in most cases, outside the country.

(3) Degree-Granting Powers:

We have previously advocated that legitimate, free-standing, privately-funded institutions should be given degree-granting powers. We remain committed to this position, but recognise the need for well-defined criteria and procedures to ensure that academic standards are maintained by any institution which has either the power to grant specific degrees (i.e. Bachelor of Arts, Bachelor of Science) or general degree-granting powers (specific degrees are not designated in the charter). These include:

(a) Evaluation Criteria:

(i) Societal Need and Community Support:

The institution must give evidence that:

- its proposed degree program(s) serve(s) a societal need not currently being met by existing institutions, and
- it has the support of the community it is seeking to serve by offering a degree program(s).

(ii) Quality of Faculty:

The institution must be committed to academic quality by:

- employing as faculty members only those who have appropriate academic qualifications,
- establishing appropriate provisions for faculty promotion and tenure,
- providing for a large component of full-time faculty,
- establishing a sabbatical leave policy and giving evidence that eligible faculty members received sabbatical leaves, and
- adopting a statement of academic freedom which is appropriate to its mission and which is implemented in its teaching and research.

(iii) Resources:

The institution must show that:

- it has the financial resources to remain financially independent of government funding for the operation of its academic program(s),
- it has realistic enrollment expectations for each proposed degree program,
- it has a permanent physical plant including library, computer and laboratory facilities and resources appropriate to the degree programs it offers or proposes to offer;

(iv) Quality of Academic Program(s):

To ensure academic quality, the institution must have an academic council or senate:

- which is independent of the Board of Governors,
- which has final authority for academic matters,
- which has a membership consisting of qualified academics, representatives of the Board of Governors and representatives of the student body,
- which has external members with the rank of associate or full professor employed at other accredited university-level institutions, and
- which has an appropriate initial and ongoing review mechanism for all academic programs offered by the institution.

(v) Recognition by Peers:

To achieve general degree-granting (university) status, the institution must have earned recognition in:

- that each of its degree programs meets appropriate standards of academic quality,
- that it has achieved ordinary membership in the Association of Universities and Colleges of Canada (AUCC),
- that it has satisfactorily completed the external review procedure in (3)(b) below. In the case of graduate programs the institution must meet the requirements of the appraisals committee of the Ontario Council on Graduate Studies (OCGS), the graduate studies arm of the Council of Ontario Universities (COU), and
- that it has operated with a specific degree-granting charter for at least five years.

(b) External Evaluations:

We are in favour of external evaluation. However, we do not deem it necessary to establish a new agency to *administer* such external evaluations. Rather, a pre-determined evaluation procedure can be arranged and paid for by the institution itself. Evaluation would take place when a new institution is first established, and at the time of a general degree-granting application. The procedure would include the appointment of an external review committee of university presidents and vice-presidents (academic) nominated by the institution and approved by the COU. This committee would verify that the criteria listed under(3)(a) above, as established by the government (see (5)(c)(i) below), are satisfied. The external review committee would report to the academic council or senate of the free-standing institution with a copy of its final report to the provincial body authorized in (5)(c)(ii) below. In the case of graduate programs, these should be subject to the same initial and periodic reviews by OCGS as programs at the publicly-funded universities.

(c) Demonstration of Program Quality:

The above method of maintaining program quality parallels the approach taken with the programs of publicly-funded universities, without creating a new bureaucratic agency. Beyond this, a new institution would demonstrate the quality of its academic programs in the same way that all academic institutions do, for example, by the performance of its students and graduates in employment and at other universities and by the research carried on by faculty.

(4) Existing Policy Modifications:

Traditionally, the power to offer academic programs and to grant degrees in a broad range of disciplines in the arts and sciences has constituted university status. If the assumption behind the committee's question is that all institutions with university status should be publicly-funded, our response is that the method of funding should not determine the institution's status. If degree-granting powers without university status implies the offering of programs in a limited range of disciplines, our response is that institutions which teach in only one or two disciplines should not be given the power to grant degrees, but that those institutions which intend to teach in a broad range of disciplines should be given the right to grant specific degrees. However, our preference is that all institutions which have taught in a broad range of disciplines for at least five years be given the right to apply for general degree-granting powers (university status), on the condition that the objects and purposes of the institution be restricted in the institution's charter so that every degree program must be approved in accordance with the internal review procedure outlined above in (3)(a)(iv) before the institution is authorized to offer that program.

(5) **Existing Policy Change:**

If the existing policy were changed to permit the establishment of free-standing, degree-granting institutions, either with specific or general degree-granting powers, the following should apply:

(a) The private, post-secondary institution should not receive direct public funding for the operation of academic programs. However, its faculty should be eligible to receive research funding, and its students should be eligible for student aid on the same basis as students at the publicly-funded universities. Provincial and federal financial support for students at privately-funded institutions is already in place for private trade schools and Bible colleges.

(b) The new privately-funded institution should in some way be involved in appropriate administrative and regulatory bodies relevant to the maintenance of good academic standards and relations in the province and should share in any related costs. However, involvement in any regulatory apparatus specifically related to funding would be unnecessary.

With respect to credit transfer, a new institution should also be involved in any body which deals with credit transfer, and on the basis of its degree-granting status, its students and credits should be treated the same as those from any other university-level institution, regardless of its mode of funding, or of its religious or philosophical basis.

(c) The government's role in relation to free-standing degree-granting institutions should be to guarantee that standards of quality are maintained, while respecting the essentially private, self-governing character of these institutions as centres of higher learning. This can be achieved if the government:

(i) establishes, from time to time, the criteria and evaluation procedure under which a privately-funded, free-standing institution can be granted either specific or general degree-granting status and can be authorized to offer a given degree program; and

(ii) authorizes the Minister of Colleges and Universities, via an appropriate existing body such as OCUA, to ascertain that an appropriate evaluation procedure has been followed in accordance with (5)(c)(i) above.

We believe that the proposals outlined in this presentation will preserve the high academic standards in this province, while at the same time allowing for the development of new initiatives in university-level education.

In this presentation we tried to accomplish two things:

1. We wanted to make sure that OCUA would know who we were, taking away the caricature they had formed of us; and
2. We wanted to demonstrate that it would be possible for the government to change its policy without threatening academic quality.

A discussion followed after our presentation. A few members of the committee asked us some questions for clarification. None of the questions were difficult to answer. The main discussion centred around the question of academic freedom. Dr. Nelles frankly told us that academic freedom was an impossibility at a Christian college. When we presented our point of view, he did not listen to our arguments. He had made up his mind and kept repeating that academic freedom could be a reality only in secular institutions because in these institutions there were no obstacles and the neutrality of the university guaranteed academic freedom. Our legal counsel, Mr. Charlton, interjected at that point telling Dr. Nelles that the public universities had their own paradigm. Mr. Charlton knew Dr. Nelles since they attended university together. I did not think that Mr. Charlton's interjection changed Dr. Nelles' mind, but it gave us another opportunity to tell the committee and everyone else in the room our version of academic freedom.

Mr. Charlton wrote us on Feb.2:

I would like to congratulate you and your colleagues on your presentation. Our student-at-law says that your proposal was the best one prepared by the participating institutions. Your answers to the questions put to you by the Committee members generated a significant exchange of ideas; Mr. Nelles was no match for you.

Soon after the meeting with the OCUA committee, we received an invitation from Harry Fernhout of the Institute for Christian Studies, to meet on April 5, 1989, with the various institutions which were participants at the OCUA hearing to consider whether the participating institutions should/could act together on areas of common concern. At that meeting, Justin Cooper reported that the Ontario Council of Deans of Arts and Sciences was examining the matter of credit transfers from independent and other institutions. This council and its counterparts were interested in becoming a type of accrediting board. He also mentioned that the COU had established a committee to advocate COU's opposition to expanded degree-granting rights for independent institutions. It was agreed that efforts to develop a public debate on the issues should be initiated and that letter writing to politicians and others should be a concrete strategy for all participants.

Mr. Nick Van Duyvendyk, a former chairman of the board, had worked together with Mr. Dalton McGuinty's father on the Ottawa Board of Education. Mr. Dalton McGuinty was a Liberal MPP. We asked Nick to speak with Mr. McGuinty about our request, which he did. He was able to arrange a meeting with him to explain our frustrations. Mr. McGuinty promised to raise the subject of Redeemer College with Chris Ward and Lyn McLeod, and he expressed his willingness to meet with representatives of the College. In his letter of May 3, 1989, to Nick, he wrote this significant sentence: "Funding for Alternative and Independent Schools and Colleges such as Redeemer is an idea whose time has surely come. But it must be pursued delicately—not with an axe, but a razor."

On July 24, Dick Kranendonk, Justin Cooper and I met with the deputy minister of Colleges and Universities, Dr. Thomas Brzustowski. Before we entered the meeting room, we prayed together as we always did before we met with ministry officials.

We prayed that the Lord would give us wisdom and that the hearts of those with whom we would meet would be receptive to our presentation. The meeting with the deputy minister and his staff was pleasant. He was well informed and very complimentary about the work at Redeemer College. He understood our frustrations, but was not able to do much since he was waiting for the advice from OCUA.

Finally on October 30, 1989, OCUA released a "Discussion Paper on the Issue of the Establishment of Freestanding Secular Degree-granting Institutions in Ontario." Specifically, the paper dealt with the policy change that would be required to allow Redeemer and other similar institutions to have expanded degree-granting powers and to include the word "University" in their name. It was clear from the paper that the committee interpreted the Robarts policy to say: "no new, secular degree-granting, institutions," placing the comma behind "degree-granting" instead of placing the comma after the word "secular." Throughout the discussion paper, there was a notion that institutions whose faculty members must subscribe to religious principles should have their degree-granting powers restricted to "religious degrees." One section in the paper argued:

> …that no religious test should be required of any professor, lecturer, teacher, officer, employee, servant or student of an institution offering secular degrees.
>
> Should religious tests be required, the institution should be offering religiously designated degrees which reflect the educational perspective from which knowledge at that institution is transmitted.
>
> On the other hand, institutions with a pronounced religious character offering secular degrees should be permitted to establish hiring requirements in *religious fields* to sustain the mission and to make certain religious requirements of their students…

The committee released this discussion paper to the public for its comments. The committee itself seemed to have made up its mind. The questions on which the committee wanted to hear the views of our support community were:

1. Does the existence of Redeemer College make education more accessible for the Christian community in Ontario?
2. Does Redeemer College provide quality education and is the College and its support community committed to a high standard of educational quality?
3. Does the education at Redeemer College lead to sectarianism?
4. Is the type of education provided by Redeemer College and other privately-funded Christian institutions worth the extra cost as compared to the education provided by the publicly-funded universities?
5. Should the particular religious commitment of an institution be identified by the type of degrees it is allowed to offer?

It was incomprehensible that a group of educated people would identify the nomenclature of a degree by the perspective from which education was given rather than by the content of the academic program. The latter had been the practice throughout the centuries. We suggested in our letter of response that "a more helpful classification would be: university degrees, Bible college degrees, seminary degrees, and, perhaps, professional degrees." The emphasis on secular degrees proved that education had been secularised to the point that education given from a Christian perspective was regarded as inferior and not worthy of university recognition.

The NDP Government

Then something unexpected happened. That fall an early Ontario election was called. To the surprise of most, the NDP won and Dr. Richard Allen, former professor at McMaster University, was appointed Minister of Colleges and Universities. Was this the answer to our many prayers? Dick Kranendonk and I went to see him and congratulated him at the Queen's Park open house. Dr. Allen had been at Redeemer College in the Spring of 1986 to speak to John Bolt's senior social ethics class about how the social gospel had shaped his vision of public service and the importance in politics of personal integrity and commitment to justice. Would he dare to "take the bull by the horns" and give a positive answer to our request for a *Charter* amendment?

We were grateful that both John Bolt and Dr. Lee wrote the minister immediately. John Bolt reminded Dr. Allen of his visit to the College and wrote:

> From our conversation that day, and the course of your own political career, I believe that you have shown yourself a person who exemplifies a combination of integrity and commitment to justice. I believe, therefore, that you have and will utilize the opportunity now to address what has been a serious injustice in the Ontario university and college world. You have perhaps suspected by now that I am referring to the stonewalling that Redeemer College has received during the last decade from both the previous conservative and liberal governments with respect to its charter change.

Dr. Lee wrote:

> When membership in the AUCC was being negotiated, I was on the AUCC Board of Directors and was able to help bring the College into that body....I have had great personal satisfaction in seeing how well this fine young institution has developed....So far as Redeemer is concerned, I hope very much that you can devise a policy that will do two things for them: grant the designation "university college"; grant them B.A. and B.Sc. degree-granting powers. In my view they fully merit both.

The positive response from the minister did not come as we had fervently hoped. The minister was quoted in the *Hamilton Spectator* of October 6, 1990, as saying that "Redeemer College will be a front-runner if the Ontario government decides to recognise private universities. The Ancaster-based Christian college has a solid reputation and would have a good chance if the new government makes a move." But there were too many "if's" in his statement.

Early in December we received an invitation from the deputy minister to meet with him and his staff on December 11th. Dick, Justin and I met with Dr. Bzrustowski, Mr. Fleischer, Mr. MacKay, and Mr. Mac-

Intyre. We had a productive meeting and were informed that the government was working on changing the Robarts policy. The meeting left us with the distinct impression that the College would eventually be granted full degree-granting powers through a new accreditation policy. However, the policy needed prior approval by Cabinet. Once this occurred, we could expect further action by the ministry leading to a change in our charter, possibly in the fall of 1991. A ray of hope?

We were informed that OCUA was going to advise the minister regarding the Robarts policy by the end of 1990. However, we did not hear anything at all, not even after we wrote a letter of inquiry to Mr. Fleischer at the ministry in April 1991.

The first communication from the ministry came in November 1991 when we were informed that the new deputy minister, Dr. Bernard J. Shapiro would visit us. We were pleased to welcome him, since he was the first high ranking official from the ministry to come to our campus. We hoped to hear from him what progress had been made regarding our request. Dr. Shapiro visited us on November 26, 1991. He was very interested to hear first hand from faculty, students and administrators what Redeemer College was all about, but he could not give us an indication when we could expect to hear from the minister. He sympathised with us that it had been more than five years since we made application to the minister and that we still did not know what the changes, if any, were going to be made to the Robarts policy.

Following Dr. Shapiro's visit, I approached the minister and met with him on December 20, 1991. We had a good and frank discussion. After December 20, we met again on several occasions and I got the impression that he was as frustrated with the course of things as we were. He implied that the hold-up was both at the Cabinet and the ministry. We considered what could be done to expedite matters. He suggested that our solicitor might meet with the legal department of the ministry and formulate some pertinent questions to initiate the process of drafting an amendment to our charter. He was going to pass the information on to Dr. Shapiro. On January 14, 1992, we received a fax from Dr. Allen's office, in which one of the minister's assistants passed on the information that Dr. Shapiro had been informed of our discussion and was going to explore the possibilities with their legal department.

Not hearing of any further progress, I wrote a letter to the minister on March 13th, reminding him of the fax of January 14 and informing him that Dr. Shapiro had not been in touch with us. When we tried to contact Dr. Shapiro, we were told that he was on vacation until March 25. I said in my letter:

> In light of the discussion between us, could I ask our lawyer to be in touch with your legal department to initiate the process of drafting an amendment to our charter? As you know, we are very anxious to see some movement on our request for a charter change.

I concluded the letter by asking the minister for a response "within the next few weeks."

By early May, I had not received an answer from the minister nor from the ministry. I contacted our lawyer, Bert Bakker, early in May and advised him of my consultations with the minister. I asked him to contact the legal department of the ministry and discreetly inquire about the possibility of meeting with them. I impressed upon him the sensitivity of this matter. He assured me that he would be very discreet. To my amazement I received a letter from the minister, dated May 20, informing me as follows:

> I refer to the discussions recently held between my ministry's legal counsel and Mr. Bert Batcher (sic), who identified himself as counsel for Redeemer College, regarding your request to amend the *Redeemer Reformed Christian College Act* to permit Redeemer College to grant secular degrees...
>
> I have been astonished to learn that Mr. Batcher advised our counsel that it was your opinion that I have agreed to Redeemer's request for secular degree-granting powers. I presume that was his misinterpretation of some communication from yourself.
>
> In any case, I regret to advise you that I cannot agree to your request for expanded degree-granting powers.
>
> Cordially,
> Richard Allen,
> Minister

This response stunned us. It was the last thing we expected to hear from the minister who had been so sympathetic to the College. Something had happened to trigger this letter. I tried to reach him as soon as I received his letter, but I was unable to talk to him. I wrote him, apologizing for the misunderstanding and the embarrassment I might have caused him. I stated that I hoped to meet with him in the near future. It was not until September that I was finally able to meet with Dr. Allen. He had accepted our invitation to be present at our 10th anniversary. We had a private conversation and concluded that we should continue our dialogue. At that time, he also told me that he did not make a decision regarding OCUA's report. For the record, the report of OCUA was received for information. A few years later, we heard that the report had not been favourable to us. The report had recommended in favour of private universities that were not religious schools.

Soon after that meeting, the premier shuffled his cabinet and combined the Ministries of Education and of Colleges and Universities into one portfolio, the Ministry of Education and Training. The premier appointed Mr. Dave Cook as the minister, and the new minister replaced Dr. Shapiro, the deputy minister, with Dr. Charles Pascal.

Instead of approaching the new minister, I decided to contact Premier Bob Rae. I wrote him and again explained who we were, what we hoped to achieve, and the treatment we had received from the former governments. I told him that Dr. Allen had encouraged me to write to him. I asked him to meet with me and the administrators of the College. Mr. R.J. Whynott, the chairman of the Regional Municipality of Hamilton-Wentworth also wrote the premier on our behalf, urging him to meet with us.

The premier responded that he was too busy to meet with us and that he had forwarded our letter to the minister, Mr. Dave Cook, with the advice that we follow up with the minister. When we contacted him, he informed us that he had no time and referred us to the deputy minister. It was ironic that the minister wrote in his letter:

> May I take this opportunity to offer my best wishes to you on your impending retirement. You are to be congratulated both for the

leadership that you have provided to Redeemer College and for the contribution you have made to the post-secondary education sector in Ontario.

Nice words, but rather meaningless without some positive action.

Before Justin and I met with Dr. Pascal, I contacted the education critics of the opposition parties: Mr. Dalton McGuinty of the Liberals and Ms. Dianne Cunningham of the Conservatives. Both responded favourably—easily done when in Opposition— and both of them asked me to let them know the outcome of our meeting with Dr. Pascal.

On June 14, we met with Dr. Pascal, the deputy minister and Mr. David Scott, the minister's policy advisor. Dr. Pascal complimented us for a job well done in bringing Redeemer College to its present state. He promised to revisit our application for charter change and inquired about the history we had with the governments and the ministry. We received the impression that, even though he showed interest, the requested changes would not be imminent. We kept both Mr. McGuinty and Ms. Cunningham abreast of our contacts with the government, but we did not hear from Mr. McGuinty again.

Ms. Dianne Cunningham invited me to visit her to tell our story. I saw her several times either by myself or with Justin Cooper. We used these visits to convey the urgent need for a positive response. She informed us of a publication by the Conservative Party: "New Directions Volume II: A blueprint for learning in Ontario," in which the Conservative Party went on record favouring private universities. She was convinced that her party would win the next election and that I would be the first president of a government-accredited private university. It all sounded good, but we hoped that the present government would make a favourable decision, thereby making a decision by a future Conservative government unnecessary.

On July 14, Dr. Pascal wrote:

the ministry's policy with respect to the degree-granting status of institutions in Ontario is determined at the political level. Accordingly, the Honourable David Cooke, Minister of Education and Training, will be writing to you directly with respect to the above-referenced policy and its specific implications for Redeemer College.

When I read this letter, I contacted our support community and faculty, staff and students at the College, urging them to write letters to the minister asking him to do justice regarding our application for a *Charter* amendment. I also asked them to send a copy of their letter to their member of the Legislature.

The long expected reply from the minister was dated October 1, 1993. The minister wrote:

> I am aware that denominational institutions in Ontario used to grant secular as well as theological degrees and that such degree-granting authority continues to be available in other jurisdictions. I am also cognizant of the reputation that Redeemer has for providing a quality post-secondary education. Still, it is the position of this government that the public good is served by allowing only publicly-funded institutions to grant degrees with secular designations, such as the Bachelor of Arts, and by allowing privately-funded institutions to grant only degrees that are of a theological designation. As such, this government would not support an application to the Legislature to expand the authority of Redeemer to grant other than degrees of a theological designation.
>
> I understand your disappointment with this policy and regret that a positive response to your wish to expand Redeemer's degree-granting authority could not be forthcoming.
>
> Sincerely,
> Dave Cook
> Minister

The response made us both angry and disappointed. After all these years, the government did not understand or did not want to understand the nature and purpose of Redeemer College. I wrote the following letter to the minister on October 15:

Dear Mr. Cook:

I received your letter of October 1, 1993, and am very disappointed that in spite of our best efforts the ministry still does not understand the nature and purpose of Redeemer College. I am especially disturbed that this misunderstanding is reflected in the reasons given for the ministry's rejection of our request for charter and name change.

Redeemer College is not a denominational college. In fact, twenty-seven different denominations are represented in our student body. Furthermore it is widely recognised and generally accepted that degree designation is determined by program and not by religion. Ontario is the only jurisdiction which maintains the misconception that the B.A. degree is a secular degree. May I urge you to read the document written by our vice-president, Dr. Justin Cooper, regarding this matter. I include it for your information.

May I also remind the minister that the Institute for Christian Studies in Toronto has received from your ministry the privilege of granting degrees without religious connotation. This contradicts the notion that your ministry would deny our request on the basis that only publicly-funded institutions are to grant degrees with secular designations.

The programs we presently offer are not theological programs but are in fact equivalent to the B.A., B.Sc. and B.Ed. degree programs offered by other universities. To require a liberal arts/undergraduate institution like Redeemer College to grant theological degrees is absurd and inconsistent with the nature and purpose of our institution. Since our founding, it was never our intent to duplicate Bible colleges, since they are plentiful in Ontario and do an outstanding job in their own sphere and for their own intended purpose. Instead we are the only independent, free-standing university in Ontario which holds membership in the AUCC, unlike Bible colleges, who are not admitted as members into the AUCC.

Redeemer College is a valuable employer of more than 100 persons in the Hamilton/Ancaster area and our graduates become producers in the Canadian economy or become excellent students in the publicly-funded universities where they train for the professions. I enclose a list of the admissions of our graduates again.

It is my firm conviction that government is instituted for the protection of its citizens against discrimination. Redeemer College seeks that protection and defence of government in our calling to be Christians in education and in a university. According to a lead article in *MacLean's* of April 12, 1993, "God is alive—Canada is a nation of believers" there are many Christians in Canada who would look to government for protection and encouragement.

Redeemer College has attempted to deal with this matter patiently. However, we note that we have not been heard. It is very discouraging to receive a letter from the minister that shows a lack of understanding of the facts and our intent and purpose. You are now not only hearing this from me but from over 500 other citizens across the province, who represent a cross section of Ontario society, and among whom are professionals, academics, politicians, corporate executives and students. They, as well as we, are making it abundantly clear that Redeemer College is an undergraduate university which offers a legitimate liberal arts program and is acknowledged by the AUCC to be a university-level institution.

I therefore place before you once more the request that Redeemer College be allowed to give the correct nomenclature for the degrees Redeemer College already gives, namely the B.A., B.Sc. and B.Ed. degrees.

For your information, I include the calendar, Dr. Cooper's paper, a list of graduate placements and our new view book. Please use your influence to revisit our request for charter and name changes.

A copy of your letter of October 1 has been sent to the education critics of the other parties. I look forward to hearing from you and perhaps meeting with you in the near future.

Sincerely,
Henry R. De Bolster
President.

Copies of this letter were sent to the premier, Dr. Charles Pascal, Mr. Dalton McGuinty and Ms. Dianne Cunningham. We never received a reply to this letter. We received copies of letters

People socializing during one of the Stained Glass concerts.

of members of the Legislature in response to our request for support. Mr. Cam Jackson, MPP for Burlington South, who had always been ready to listen to me and to give his support, wrote:

> I continue to stand by the College in opposing the NDP decision to withhold that right (of granting B.A.'s and B.Sc.'s) as unjustified discrimination against Redeemer College.

It was of special interest to hear the opinion of the leaders of the Liberal and Conservative Parties. Ms. McLeod wrote on December 13, 1993:

> My colleagues and I in the Liberal Caucus believe that only publicly-funded institutions should grant degrees with secular designations. At this time, we would not support a move to expand Redeemer's degree-granting authority.

Mr. Michael (Mike) D. Harris, leader of the Conservative Party, wrote on December 16, 1993:

> My Party and I believe the restriction on private, degree-granting universities should be lifted. However, anyone wishing to start a private university should be subject to intense scrutiny to ensure its financial viability and to maintain consistent standards in post-secondary education.

It was clear that we would not receive support from the NDP and Liberal Parties, but that the Conservative Party, if it won the next election, would consider granting our request: the authority to grant the B.A. and B.Sc. degrees. In final analysis, it was in God's hand, and He would grant us our legitimate rights at His time.

NINE

The Years Until My Retirement

In chapter 7, I mentioned that an "operations review committee" had been established to address issues of financial administration at the College. Its members were Mr. Martin Bosveld, Mr. Nick Van Duyvendyk and Mr. Kees Vreugdenhil. This committee reported to the board in November 1992. It suggested ongoing monitoring of spending on all budget accounts; a study by faculty to reach a student/faculty ratio of 17 to 1 by the year 1992/1993 and an increase in tuition, room and board by $1,000. The committee also recommended the appointment of a comptroller and a structure that would allow each department to propose and review the financial responsibilities within its own department to be compared to approved budgets.

Structures and Finances

In August 1991, I appointed a task force made up of a cross-section of the College—faculty, staff, administration and students—to study the structures and processes of decision-making at the College. I wanted to make sure that the authority and responsibilities at the College were recognised by all and that we would make changes where needed. This committee reported in March 1992 and recommended some changes. For example, the task force wanted to change the College council to faculty council with the vice-president (academic) to chair the council. The vice-president (administration and finance), the vice-president (development), the registrar, and the dean of students would be non- voting members of the council. The task force also recommended more participation on the administrative council by faculty. It proposed changing the name of the administrative council to president's advisory council.

On the academic side, the committee recommended changing the academic council's name to "senate." The report ended by stating:

> It is hoped that in making the recommended changes to the structure and decision-making process at Redeemer College that a more participatory and consultive style of management will enable a greater number of college members to be engaged in the decision-making process in a manner appropriate to their office. It is our belief that these proposals will encourage the various groups in the College to work together more efficiently and more harmoniously as we continue the mission of Redeemer College.

The board referred both reports to an *ad hoc* committee of Mr. Bill De Jong, Mr. Nick Van Duyvendyk, Dr. Justin Cooper and Ms. Marian Brink. This committee reported to the board in October. It recommended acceptance of the report of the operations review committee to appoint management committees in each administrative area. This board mandated change worked well. It assigned responsibility for budget compliance to each area of the College.

The task force's report was received for information with a note of thanks for a thorough job. The *ad hoc* committee accepted some of the task force's recommendations, like changing the name of the College council to faculty council. It advised implementing the consultative principles, procedures and structures in a manner appropriate for each college department. The recommendation to change the name of the College council to faculty council was implemented. The faculty decided to meet whenever its members felt the need to discuss matters of mutual concern with the understanding that the vice-president (academic) would be invited to its meetings. This process helped to restore confidence within the College community, and it assisted the administration in making some difficult decisions regarding budget matters.

When the Brookview Trust failed, the board's executive committee and the finance committee reviewed its effect on the 1990/91 budget and considered what effect this would have on the College's operations for 1991/92. This review concluded that "the lower than expected enrollment of students in September 1990 and the lower participation of those students in the housing program resulted in a loss of income estimated to be about $362,000 for tuition and $85,000 for housing for a total of $447,000. The inability of the trust to continue its contributions had no direct adverse effect on the 1990/91 budget."

As far as the 1991/92 budget was concerned, the committee concluded that the current economic recession was primarily to blame for the exceptionally high budget deficit. It noted that in 1990:

a) The Board was able to make an arrangement whereby the difference between the interest paid on its borrowing (the cost of the Series "G" Bonds, which had been issued the previous year) and the amount it collected on its lending would result in a net saving to the College for the 1991/92 fiscal year of about $870,000. As a result of the unique situation that the rate of inflation plus 4 percent (the interest we paid to our Bond holders) has been higher than the prime interest rate at which the College borrows its funds from the bank, the College had to retract the series "G" Bonds. However it must be remembered that this action resulted in a budgeted revenue shortfall of the $870,000 plus the interest cost to finance this shortfall in an estimated amount of about $40,000 for a total budget deficit effect of about $910,000.

b) In addition, because of the economic situation, many of the contributors to the LIFT campaign will not be able to make their pledge payments as originally planned. The new budgeted shortfall as a result of this factor will be a direct $200,000.

c) As a result of the interest and inflation rates over the past six month period, the College will incur an additional budget deficit as a result of its series "A" to "F" Mortgage Bonds. Instead of saving the College about 3 percent or $315,000 in interest for the 1991/92 fiscal year on the $10.5 million in Bonds, we now have to assume an additional cost of about $53,000 plus the financing cost of this shortfall of about $18,000 for a total budget deficit effect of about $386,000.

d) The donation and church receipts for the 1991/92 fiscal year are expected to be about $175,000 lower than earlier budgeted.

e) The effect of the Trust Fund on the currently projected $1.9 million deficit, therefore, will be about $110,000. It was hoped and expected that the Trust Fund would produce a significant budget surplus with which we would be able to address the cumulated capital and operating debt of the past nine years.

The report concluded:

> The foregoing analysis has been prepared to help place the effect of the Trust in its proper perspective. The risk for the College of accepting the Trust and the condition of its total anonymity was minimal. The potential benefits were great. However, after the Trust was established, we began to count on the Trust to offset the negative economic effects of the other factors. This we can no longer expect.

As a result of this report, the executive committee appointed a task force consisting of two board members, three faculty members, three staff members, and two students to present the finance committee with a new budget for 1991/92. The task force recommended increasing the food and housing cost for the students by $1,100 and reducing the expenditure side of the budget by $576,373. To achieve this goal, all expenditures were re-evaluated and reduced. No new purchases were allowed, all faculty and senior staff would accept a 5 percent decrease in salary, while the president offered a 10 percent decrease in his salary. All sabbaticals would be on hold until further notice.

We were greatly assisted by a committee of four which I appointed to help us in our financial planning. These four people were Nick Van Duyvendyk and Kees Vreugdenhil, who had already served on the operations review committee, Mr. Bill Voortman, a well known businessman, and Mr. Simon Kouwenhoven, a senior vice-president at the Bank of Montreal.

The year 1991/92 was the most difficult year I experienced. Financially, the burden of the recession weighed heavily on the College, even though all did their best to keep expenses down. Our business community sympathised with us, but many of them were hurting as well, sometimes even more than we were. They could not donate to the College as they had hoped and pledged. Emotionally, it was not only the finances that made the year so difficult, but it also was the resignation of Dick Kranendonk, the loss of confidence in the administration by some of the faculty members, the continued mention of the trust failure by the student paper and the publications in the Christian press. At times, accusations were hurled at me when I spoke with people outside of the College. I was told that they had heard of the awful events from persons within the College. It was encouraging that the board had expressed its confidence in me as president: otherwise, I am sure I would not have been able to survive that difficult year.

At the end of the year, we pulled together and with restored confidence and renewed energy we gave thanks to the Lord. In my annual report to the membership I wrote:

> During the past year I have spent much of my time moving the institution forward in the wake of the Trust failure. The aftermath of this episode was much more severe than I anticipated and, therefore, in the short history of Redeemer College, the year just behind us was the most challenging and difficult year we have experienced. Many meetings were held with faculty, staff and students in order to restore confidence and heal relationships. Many visits were also made to members of our support community. The Executive of the Board and the Board itself set new policies and assisted me in restoring confidence in the work to which Redeemer College is called.

A Balanced Budget

We were grateful that Mr. Bert Seinen accepted our invitation to join us in July 1992 as senior director of administration and student life. Bert was an administrator at a college in Slave Lake, Alberta, and was willing to come for one year. That year went by very fast and we were sorry to see him go back to his job in Slave Lake so soon. During that year the recession ended. Consequently, there was a remarkable improvement in our financial position. Our deficit decreased from over $1.5 million at the end of the fiscal year 1991/92 to $70,000 at the end of 1992/93. In July 1993, we welcomed Mr. Lloyd Hack, who had accepted the position of vice-president (administration and finance). He informed me that it was his goal to help achieve a balanced budget by the time of my retirement. When he joined the administration, we were well on our way towards balancing the budget. Indeed the following year, when I retired, our deficit had shrunk to $48,000, less than one percent of the operating budget—a near balanced budget.

Christian Education Policy

When the College began recruiting faculty and staff, it was decided that those who were hired by the College should support Christian education at all levels. During each interview, the prospective staff or faculty member was asked to support this policy. All agreed, but at times it created difficulties. A few faculty members had decided to leave the College because they could not live up to their commitment regarding Christian education. I felt strongly about this policy because the majority of students came from families who had decided that Christian education was essential for their children. These families had made financial sacrifices to provide their children with that kind of education. I wanted these students and families to know that we, at the College, were of the same mind and held to the same principles. This policy worked well until one staff member, who had enthusiastically endorsed this policy, no longer wished to support Christian education, but who did not want to face up to the consequences of that position. It became clear that some other staff and faculty members agreed with this staff member's position. Moreover, this person had consulted others outside of the College. Therefore, I decided to appoint an *ad hoc* committee to study this matter and to make recommendations. This committee consisted of D. Benner, M. Buma, D. Loney, W. Smouter, W. Van Dyk, J. Vriend and J. Ellens as chairman. The committee met many times and made the following unanimous recommendations:

Policy Statement on Support for Christian Education

1. While we affirm that the fundamental responsibility for giving a Christian education to children lies with the parents, the nature and confessional basis of Redeemer College as a constituency based, Christian educational institution makes it appropriate to expect that its faculty and administrators—level administration B and up—should be committed to, and should demonstrate support for, distinctly Christian education.

2. Since the College does not desire to step outside its legitimate sphere of responsibility in this matter, it does not seek to dictate precisely how its faculty and senior administrators are to honour the principle of Christian education in their own homes and families.

3. However, as members of a college community, we do hold one another accountable to show in word and deed that we support Christ-centred education; the commitment to Christian education implicit in our professional service must also be demonstrated explicitly in our personal lives.

4. There are a number of ways in which commitment to Christian education may be demonstrated and it is important that each new employee be given opportunity to express his or her understanding of the principle and for its outworking in the education of his or her children. In order to guard against misunderstanding, this matter should also be addressed at times of reappointment or review.

5. For faculty members and administrators—level administration B and up—who are parents, support of Christian education normally means enrolling one's minor children in Christian schools at the elementary and secondary levels. However, it is recognized that in certain cases Christian schooling may be impossible or inappropriate for some children. Such situations shall be discussed with the Vice-President or the President or both. In cases of disagreement, no decision will be made without prior advice from an appeals committee which includes one's peers.

I received these recommendations of the committee and forwarded them to the board with my recommendation of support.

On April 24, 1992, the executive committee adopted this policy statement, and the board approved it the next day.

The Institute for Christian Studies

From the beginning of my presidency, the College had contact with the Institute for Christian Studies (ICS). At my inaugural, Dr. Bernard Zylstra its president, brought greetings on behalf of ICS. Bernard and I had many conversations about the future of Christian higher education and particularly the future of our institutions. The ICS had gone through some difficult times. The solutions to their problems had caused controversy in the Reformed Christian community. There was disagreement in that community about the content of publications of some of their senior members (professors). Since both the ICS and Redeemer College were primarily supported by the same Reformed constituency, I told Bernard that a close relationship of the two institutions would be impossible as long as those publications were endorsed by the ICS. I did not want to divide our support community over the ICS issues. Despite our institutional disagreements, Bernard and I had a very cordial relationship. We joined with the ICS in mourning his untimely death in 1985. During Bernard's presidency, the two institutions never corresponded with each other at the board level.

His successor, Dr. Clifford Pitt, contacted me soon after his appointment. I attended his inaugural and congratulated him on behalf of Redeemer College. Dr. Pitt had been caught by the vision of the Kingdom of God. His enthusiasm was evident whenever he spoke of the Kingship of Christ in all areas of life. When he got to know Redeemer, which taught the same emphasis on the Kingdom of God, he hoped that the two institutions would establish a close relationship and cooperate on matters of Christian higher learning. He asked his board to contact the Redeemer College board to accomplish that goal.

On October 7, 1985, the ICS board of trustees wrote:

Dear Colleagues in Christian Education,

We as board members of the ICS have wondered how to establish better avenues of communication and possible cooperation with Redeemer College. Many of us support Redeemer financially, our constituencies overlap, our educational philosophies run parallel, and above all we hold in common the pursuit of higher education in the name of and in obedience to Jesus Christ. We rejoice in the impressive progress Redeemer has made in its short history, and we wish you continued progress in the future.

We invite you to meet with us to discuss common concerns, concerns each of us may have about the other, and to explore what, if any, future contacts might be mutually profitable.

We are aware that at least some of the Redeemer community may prefer to have no such contact with us. Though we regret that, we hope there will be at least an opportunity to discuss these matters. We suggest that:

1. representatives of Redeemer College meet with representatives of the ICS to discuss areas of common concern, such as:
   a) institutional relations
   b) comparison and possible coordination of educational programs
   c) coordination of contacts with governmental and church bodies
   d) exchange of staff and/or courses
   e) mutual support of institutional goals
2. each institution appoint seven representatives for such a meeting, the representation to consist of:
   a) the President of the institution plus another member of his staff
   b) three members of the Board of Trustees/Governors, including the chairman
   c) two members of the faculty
3. each institution appoint two members of its Board to form an ad hoc committee to:
   a) set the agenda for such a meeting
   b) decide a time and place, and make arrangements for the meeting
   c) arrange for persons to make presentations at the meeting
   d) appoint a chairperson for the meeting
   e) be prepared to advise about possible future meetings

Our specific goals in requesting this meeting are:

1. to do all possible to foster more open and more cordial contacts between our two institutions;
2. to listen seriously to concerns your community may have about us, to be candid about concerns we have with respect to you, and to strengthen mutual understanding and trust;
3. to assure that in our contacts with governments we come with a unified approach if at all possible, lest opposing forces try to "divide and conquer" us;
4. to do all we can to foster mutual support of our educational goals and programs;
5. to work towards stronger ties and more serious cooperative efforts between all our reformed educational institutions; and
6. to do all we can to encourage our reformed colleges to help us in our recruitment of students.

We trust this proposal will meet with a positive response from you.

Yours in Christ,
Herman D. Praamsma
Secretary
Board of Trustees
c. President H. De Bolster

The board met in January, discussed the letter at length and decided to send the following response:

Dear Members of the Board of Trustees:

The Board of Governors of Redeemer College has discussed your letter of October 7, 1985. It is your wish to establish better avenues of communication and possible cooperation with Redeemer College. Your proposal is to establish a Board/Faculty/Administration Committee to accomplish that goal.

We propose a better and more common avenue. We believe that contact between the administration of the ICS and Redeemer College is a more appropriate way of doing so. As a matter of fact this is the way contact is maintained between Calvin College and

Redeemer College and Dordt College and Redeemer College and between other similar institutions.

It is our understanding that this is already happening between the Presidents and we encourage our administration to continue that contact.

Yours in Christ,
Mrs. Ineke Bezuyen, Secretary
the Board of Governors of Redeemer College

On March 17, 1986, the ICS board of trustees wrote another letter, once again asking for a meeting as proposed in their October 7, 1985 letter. Redeemer's board maintained its policy "to instruct college administrators, and especially the president, to maintain and nurture contact with other institutions," and advised the ICS board accordingly. Dr. Pitt and I met whenever we spoke at classical meetings of the Christian Reformed Church, and we made it a point to meet whenever we were in the neighbourhood of each other's institution. The meetings were cordial, but no progress was made to come closer together. The ICS maintained its support of its senior members, and we maintained that as long as those members continued to speak, teach and publish their controversial views, a closer cooperation would not be possible.

The meetings between Dr. Pitt and myself remained informal. We discussed many matters pertaining to our institutions and Christian higher learning in general. We kept each other posted on developments with the government. However, the ICS board of trustees wanted more than just meetings between the two presidents. On June 5, 1987, the ICS board wrote us another letter signed by Mr. Fred Reinders, chairman of the board, and Dr. Clifford Pitt. Mr. Reinders was one of our supporters and had been involved in the construction of the campus. He had informed me of his election as chairman of the ICS board and conveyed to me that it was his goal to work towards a close relationship between the two institutions. I told him of our misgivings, but he assured me that changes were taking place at the ICS. He had informed the senior members in question not to publish anything without his permission. He was sure that a different principial direction prevailed. The ICS board wrote:

> We are most anxious to pursue this initiative of our board for some sort of affiliation between our two institutions... our Board suggests the formation of a joint committee of ten to explore further this possibility.

The proposal read:

Whereas the ICS Christian community desires to heed God's call to work together in unity with Redeemer College in the cause of Christian higher education and thereby to begin to give joint testimony to the world, to the wider Christian community, and to our own Reformed constituency of our fellowship in Christ through common service,

and whereas there is wisdom in sharing resources, avoiding costly duplication, promoting administrative efficiency, and recognizing that all of this could be destroyed in a sinful spirit of competition

and given that both institutions have overlapping responsibilities in providing Christian higher education, serve constituencies which overlap in many ways, seek support and funds from many of the same people, and have boards and staff's sympathetic to both institutions,

further observing that ICS is blessed with and can therefore offer Redeemer Christian College the benefits of a supporting community which has had the ability to maintain the difficult project of a free-standing graduate institution of high quality for over twenty years, a comparatively large number of excellent graduate students devoted to the perspectival and foundational exploration of learning as Christian believers, a highly competent faculty which has gained many years of valuable experience in the practice of Christian scholarship, an international base for attracting students and disseminating ideas, and respect from traditional institutions of learning and reputable international scholars,

mindful also of the fact that classes of the Canadian segment of the

Christian Reformed Church have clearly indicated their desire for our cooperation and that an undergraduate institution and a graduate institution especially when they are as naturally close to each other in aims and purposes as our two institutions, can only benefit from complementing each other.

Be it resolved that the Board of Trustees of the Institute for Christian Studies humbly requests the Board of Trustees of Redeemer College to join together in a commitment:

to develop concrete, practical, and achievable ways of closer cooperation to orient this process to the shared and declared aim of some sort of affiliation as soon as appears wisely and practically achievable to adopt a mutually agreeable time table and agenda for the serious and speedy implementation of this resolution and to appoint a joint committee of ten, five to be appointed by each board (three from its own members, one from its administration, and one from its faculty), to meet in July of 1987 and thereafter at least monthly but not beyond November of 1987 to determine the above mentioned time table and agenda.

Our board did not answer this letter until November 9. However, Mr. Reinders and Mr. Van Duyvendyk had made contact and decided, in consultation with the presidents, that further informal meetings of the presidents, together with the academic deans as well as the chairmen of the boards, would be more beneficial. This was communicated to Mr. Reinders and the board of ICS. These meetings took place regularly, and from our point of view, they confirmed our concerns about the Institute. The representatives of the Institute felt differently. Our board received another letter dated June 20, 1988, with the request "to meet as boards together formally, to discuss items of mutual concern and benefit." Our board was not ready for such meetings. The board's secretary wrote on October 16, 1988:

> Please allow us to explain why we believe that meetings between the full boards at this time would not be fruitful:
>
> 1. There are some questions of academic credibility that must be addressed in the informal meetings.

2. There are issues of concern relating to academic freedom and institutional autonomy which must be discussed at the level of the informal meetings before we as board wish to address them.

We do not wish to go into the specifics of the above two points, but our chairman and president are quite prepared to discuss them in the informal meetings with your chairman and president. To meet as boards would not resolve the above issues, but would only serve to:

1. Confuse the issues because the competence for dealing with them is at the administrative level.

2. Give the impression to our support community that there are no major issues of concern between our respective institutions.

3. Potentially further complicate matters if a large group attempts to address issues of major concern which can be more constructively handled by a small group.

In view of the above we ask you not to request meetings between the two boards until such a time as the informal discussions convince us that such a meeting would be productive and necessary.

The last letter our board received concerning this matter was dated November 29, 1988, and read as follows:

Dear members of the Board of Governors,

Thank you for your letter of November 9, 1988, in which you responded to the request of the ICS Board of Trustees for Board-level discussions between our two institutions. Your letter was discussed at the meeting of the Executive Committee of our Board of Trustees on November 21, 1988.

While we are disappointed in your judgement that Board-level discussions would serve no useful purpose, we are encouraged by the fact that you have directed your Chairman and President to continue discussions with their ICS counterparts. We agree that such discussions are a fruitful source of communication.

In your letter you characterize these meetings of our respective Chairmen and Presidents as "informal." We are not sure what this term implies from your point of view. However, we want you to know that for our part, we expect our Chairman and President to keep us fully informed of these meetings, so that we can respond as Board when necessary. Your letter clearly indicates that you wish to do the same.

Your letter suggested two areas of concern that need to be addressed by the respective Chairmen and Presidents. We are quite willing to accept these agenda items. In fact, we are eager to learn what you mean by the "questions of academic credibility" and the issues of "academic freedom and institutional autonomy" which, you suggest, need to be addressed.

It is our understanding that in one of their previous meetings the Chairmen and Presidents agreed that matters concerning academic interaction between our institutions should be handled directly by the respective Vice-Presidents (Academic). Since the two points listed in your letter seem to be academic in nature, we request that the two Vice-Presidents (Academic) be included as participants in the discussions.

1. We have some concern about the extent to which Redeemer College presents itself as a university in its promotional materials. We feel that this may raise serious questions in the minds of public authorities, with implications for other institutions.

   Also, we wonder whether your use of the term university implies an intention to develop graduate-level programs.

2. We would like to discuss the matter of our respective appeals for funding from the classes of the Christian Reformed Church. We were pleased to hear that President De Bolster indicated to Classis Toronto that Redeemer College does not make an exclusive claim on regional classical funds for Christian higher education. However, various classes are persistently urging our respective institutions to show increased cooperation in this area. We believe that our Lord is speaking to us through the admonition of the classes, urging us to open a window of cooperation. In our judgment, the voices of the classes must be taken seriously,

so that an opportunity to work cooperatively rather than competitively is not missed.

With you, we commit ourselves to encouraging the continuation of the informal discussions which have already begun. We have instructed the Chairman and President to arrange for further discussions at the participants earliest convenience.

We trust that God will richly bless these efforts with the presence and power of the Holy Spirit.

Sincerely,

Herman Praamsma,
Secretary
Board of Trustees

In our informal discussions, we placed our concerns on the table. As far as academic credibility was concerned, we wondered whether the ICS had sufficient instructors to teach the different subjects of a range of programs leading to a Master's degree. We raised concerns about the publications of some senior members on hermeneutics, homosexuality and the use of inclusive language. There were concerns in the minds of the ICS representatives about these publications as well, but they were of the opinion that they could do no more than what had been done. This opinion did not help us erase our concerns. We urged the Institute representatives to deal with this matter conclusively so that it would be possible for Redeemer College to have a close relationship with ICS.

We also dealt with the concerns of the Institute. We assured the chairman and president of the ICS that we had no intentions to develop graduate-level programs. We were an undergraduate university, and we were thankful to be able to launch the programs we offered. We had a lengthy discussion about the distribution of classical funds. We explained that even though we had no authority to direct funds one way or another, we were of the opinion that the synod of the Christian Reformed Church in North America did not have institutions like ICS in mind when it transferred "the moneys saved from the Calvin College quota" to the regional colleges. That quota was originally set for Calvin College, which was an undergraduate institution. When the synod of the Christian Reformed Church allowed the "moneys saved from the Calvin College quota" to go to the regional colleges, it did so because those students now attending the regional colleges would otherwise have attended Calvin College. In other words the funds were for undergraduate institutions and not for graduate institutions.

The Institute felt it could do no more than it had done regarding the concerns we expressed, hence our relationship, cordial as it was, did not proceed any further. When Dr. Pitt was succeeded as president by Dr. Harry Fernhout, the same cordial relationships continued on a personal and informal level until the day I retired. I know how disappointed some of the Institute people were, especially Mr. Reinders, who had hoped to bring the two institutions together.

The Dooyeweerd Centre

Dr. Herman Dooyeweerd was undoubtedly one of the most influential Christian philosophers of the twentieth century. He wanted to bring to expression the scriptural truth that all things belong to Christ and that therefore all of creation must listen to and obey the laws of the Lord. These laws he described in what became known as the Philosophy of the Law Idea, or Cosmonomic Idea. Dr. Dooyeweerd developed his philosophy in The Netherlands; consequently many of his works were written in the Dutch language. After his death, his children were convinced that all the major works of their father, which had already influenced many scholars throughout the world, should become available in the English language, so that Dr. Dooyeweerd's thought would receive well-deserved attention and hopefully wider acceptance. Up to that time, Dr. Dooyeweerd's philosophy had been available to the English speaking world primarily through the four volume work *A New Critique of Theoretical Thought*.

Mr. Herman Dooyeweerd Jr. contacted me and explained the hopes and dreams of the Dooyeweerd family. They wanted to establish a centre of translation and study, and he thought that Redeemer College would be the place for such a centre. I was honoured by his request and promised to discuss his desires with the College community.

Both the administration and the board were enthused about the request, but felt that because of the financial burdens of the College we could not make any further financial commitments. However, there would be a possibility to operate the centre in the same way as the Pascal Centre. The Pascal Centre did its own fundraising and was not financially dependent on the College. We spoke with Herman Dooyeweerd, who immediately agreed that the College should not become financially responsible for the centre, and he pledged that the centre would take care of its own fundraising.

The board discussed the establishment of the Dooyeweerd Centre at several meetings, and on November 27, 1993, the board decided to approve the Centre for a two-year initial period to be reviewed in April 1996. The College had received more than 60 letters from all over the world expressing support for this initiative. The establishment of the Dooyeweerd Centre was a prestigious accomplishment, and is the only centre of its kind. The objectives of the centre are:

> translation and publication of Dooyeweerd's major works and eventually his *opera omnia* and of other major works in the neo-Calvinist movement which are related to Dooyeweerd's thought;
>
> development of undergraduate courses to eventually expand the body of scholars conversant with Dooyeweerd's philosophy, its context in the neo-Calvinist movement and the continuing school of thought which it has engendered;
>
> and promotion of in-depth study at the graduate and post-graduate level to foster scholarly study of Dooyeweerd's thought, including its development in the context of the neo-Calvinist movement, and the development and application of his thought to all fields of human endeavour.

RUNA

In chapter 6, I promised to return to a question that had been raised by one of the college presidents during the discussion about the establishment of a Reformed University in North America. But before I do so, I will first relate the development of RUNA. After a few years of discussing this matter, it was finally decided to begin with an Association for a Reformed University. All the Reformed colleges were asked to become members of that Association. Once a year the members would meet to promote the cause of a Christian university and to listen to papers given by faculty of the participating institutions. Redeemer College decided to become a member on April 24, 1993.

The question posed by the president at that earlier meeting was: "If you were a student and had the choice of going to Harvard or to a small beginning Reformed Christian institution, where would you go?" In my mind I could see someone ask: "When you are a student coming out of high school and you are offered admission to a prestigious university, would you go to Redeemer College, knowing that it is a young institution, which does not offer all the courses a secular university offers, and which does not have the physical facilities that are present at well-established colleges and universities?" And I would add, "where the cost is considerably higher?" Many students contemplating university are faced with these questions. They are difficult ones—so difficult that I am amazed that so many students decided to come to Redeemer College. I suppose the decision depends on one's priorities, but above all, on one's commitment. I would like to compare this decision with the commitments made by the immigrants from The Netherlands shortly after World War II. I am one of those immigrants. I remember the discussions about establishing Christian schools. Dutch immigrants came to this country with next to nothing. Canadian dollars were scarce and the government in The Netherlands only allowed each emigrant to take along $10. You immediately needed a job to be able to provide for your family. Wages for recent immigrants were low. I remember working at Stelco, in Hamilton, in 1952, and earning a salary of $160 a month. Yet many of us were convinced that we needed to establish a school where Christ would be the centre of education. Why? The public school was not bad, and it was free. If we would start a Christian school, we would have to pay personally for the education of our children. Moreover, where would we find experienced teachers? The obstacles were numerous. Besides, we were not united about the need for Christian education. Some objected to starting our own school; others thought the public school was a good school for their children. The primary concern was: Who was going to pay for such schools?

It required determination, faith and perseverance to start and maintain a Christian school. It took even more of a commitment to send one's children to such a small, fledgling school with benches discarded by the public school. What motivated us to do it? Why do we continue to have these schools? Let me assure everyone that it was not a protest against the public schools to protest against the quality of their education. The reason for the financial sacrifices to send their children to the Christian school was because they remembered the promises made at the time of the baptism of their children. They had promised to educate and to have their children educated in the Christian faith. They wanted their children to know the Lord and to learn about the fullness of God's creation from a biblical perspective. This world belongs to God, and we wanted God to be number one in our and our children's lives. A Christ-centred education was the only alternative—not an option, but a necessity. If sacrifices needed to be made, so be it. God would help and bless and as forgiven and delivered children of God we knew we were here to glorify God and, with all our shortcomings, to make use of the means that became available to live a godly life in the midst of a world that either rejected the Lord or ignored Him.

I believe that we face the same dilemmas today. The questions have not changed and the answers must still be given based on the principles we hold. Is a Christ-centred education a priority, or is it an option? As far as Redeemer College was concerned, its education programs were of high academic quality. It is not a question of getting a better education elsewhere. I dare say, that the quality and dedication of the faculty, the small classes, the close contact with the professors, and the teaching of all classes by the professors, rather than teaching assistants, speak for themselves. It is a question of commitment and a humble acknowledgement that a Christ-centred education was necessary to be prepared to face life with its many trials. Young people may not be aware of all these consequences, but we older ones should help our young people make the right decisions. They will never regret it.

This is the way I felt. For that reason I was able to give all my energy to Redeemer College. I believe that God gave us a jewel for the Christian community to use. Surely, studying at Redeemer costs more than studying at a secular institution, but the benefits cannot be measured in dollars and cents. I know that Redeemer College does not teach all subjects. For certain professions you may have to attend public institutions, but may I urge everyone seriously to consider spending at least one year at Redeemer College! Get the proper foundation based on the Scriptures, and you will be able, with God's continued help and grace, to face the post-modern world with its philosophies.

To get back to that president's question: "If you were a student and had the choice of going to Harvard or to a small beginning Reformed Christian institution," my answer should be obvious: go to that small Reformed Christian institution, at least for one year.

With grateful hearts we celebrated our tenth anniversary in September 1992—a moving event. Ten years had gone by since our humble openings on Beach Boulevard. We had experienced many obstacles, many difficulties, but through them all the Lord sustained us. I was very conscious of the fact that the Lord had caused us to succeed. Many supporters and guests expressed their gratitude and joy, and wished us growth and recognition. We prayed that God would give us both through the Holy Spirit, and that we would receive these blessings in dependence on the Lord alone.

Retirement and Appointment of the new President

On January 26, 1991, the board had reappointed me for a fourth term. Because I was already 66 years old at that time, the board decided to reappoint me for a three-year term starting August 1, 1992. When I received this reappointment I fully intended to serve the next three years and to retire in July of 1995 the Lord willing. However, with the trust failure everything changed. I offered my resignation in June 1991, which the executive committee rejected. The board met in September to review all the activities of the executive committee, and until that time I wondered whether the board would ask for my resignation. I was relieved and thankful that the board passed a motion expressing full confidence in the president. Until that time, I had not thought much about retiring. Suddenly the possibility of leaving the College became a reality. I asked myself whether the time had come to step down. I struggled with that question for quite a while, especially since a few faculty members insisted that I should retire. I prayed and asked the Lord for wisdom and insight in this matter. I was very pleased when several faculty members, members of the administration and staff urged me to stay. Members of the board and those who served on the executive committee, also assured me of their confidence. I decided not to resign but to wait for an appropriate moment to leave the presidency at the end of my current appointment term.

While I contemplated retirement, I realised that it was necessary to determine what kind of president my successor should be and what his or her position description should be. The job description dating back to my first appointment needed to be updated. I approached the board and asked them to appoint a committee to look into these matters. The board appointed an ad hoc committee to prepare a job description for a new president. This committee, which had representatives from all the different areas of the College, reported to the board on November 28, 1992, as follows:

Position Description for the President of Redeemer College
The President is the chief executive of the College, appointed by the Board of Governors to direct the overall operation of the institution. The President is directly accountable to the Board of Governors for the exercise of executive authority in conformity with policies established by the Board. The task of the President is to carry out the responsibilities generally associated with that office, and to demonstrate leadership in such a manner as to ensure the integration of each part of the institution into a harmonious

whole. The President provides academic leadership among faculty, promotes the public image of the College, takes leadership in the development of its resources, and safeguards its tangible assets. The President must possess, promote, and articulate the distinctive Reformed Christian vision and worldview with respect to academia as upheld by the Scriptures and as outlined in the College's Mission Statement and its Statement of Basis and Principles.

In the exercise of his office, the President bears responsibility for working constructively with the following groups.

1. Board of Governors
2. Administrators and Staff
3. Faculty
4. Students
5. Constituents of Redeemer College
6. Academic Council
7. Redeemer Foundation

This job description for the president was adopted by the board.

Retirement entered my thoughts again when the board, meeting in November 1992, asked me to give at least a year-and-a-half to two years notice of my retirement. The question I faced was, "Should I serve until my term ends, or should I retire a year earlier?" It was a struggle to come to the right decision. I was helped by the fact that confidence had been restored at the College; once again, there was a good atmosphere, and it seemed that most, if not all, faculty and staff had regained their joy in their work at the College. Financially, we were well on our way to a balanced budget. My hope had been to be able to leave the College when it would be in good shape. The only drawback was the disappointment in not having achieved the desired change in the *Charter*. But that could take many more years. The foundations for those changes had been laid. It had become a matter of keeping the issues before the government while praying that the Lord would change its mind and grant us the requested changes.

After much prayer and discussions with my wife, I informed the board on January 23, 1993, that I intended to retire on July 1, 1994.

I expressed my willingness to continue in some capacity to help the transition and to be of assistance to the new president. The board accepted my request and appointed two committees. The first committee was a presidential search committee, consisting of 23 members, representing all the sectors of the College—board, academic council, administration, faculty, staff, students, alumni and support community. The second committee consisted of three persons: Mr. Nick Van Duyvendyk, Mr. Bill De Jong, and Dr. Justin Cooper. This committee was mandated "to study the president's offer to be useful to the College on a part-time basis." A few meetings later Mr. Bill Smouter and Rev. John Zantingh were added to the committee.

The presidential search committee worked diligently to find the right person to become the next president. The members met many times and spent many hours interviewing different persons and discussing the interviews. On February 12, 1994, the committee presented two candidates to the board: Dr. Elaine Botha and Dr. Justin Cooper. Both candidates were interviewed, and Dr. Justin Cooper was appointed president. Following the announcement to the College community and the support community, Dr. Cooper was formally introduced to the College community by Rev. John Zantingh, chairman of the board, after chapel on February 16, 1994. A reception for Dr. Cooper followed at which faculty, staff and students had the opportunity to congratulate him. It was a joyous occasion. The Lord provided and we thanked and praised the Lord for granting new leadership. We asked that He would bless the president elect. The choice of Dr. Cooper proved to be a good one. During his presidency, the College received government recognition by authorizing the College to grant both the B.A. and B.Sc. degrees. A few years later, the Legislature approved a name change to Redeemer University College.

The committee appointed "to study the president's offer to be useful to the College on a part-time basis" after his retirement came with a lengthy report dated January 24, 1994, which was adopted by the executive committee on February 12. The ad hoc committee wanted to establish the position of chancellor. They stated that the idea of the position of chancellor was not something new. It was included by the board in the list of revisions to the charter in anticipation of a possible charter change with respect to degree-granting and institutional name. The committee said:

There are at least three reasons for establishing the position of chancellor at Redeemer College. One is a matter of general principle and the other two are more specific and contextual considerations. As a matter of general principle, an institution like Redeemer College should have a chancellor, because this symbolic or titular position reflects a proper understanding of what the College is, namely, a multi-faceted institution with a number of dimensions. The position of chancellor is intended to symbolize the totality or organic unity of an institution which is made up of a number of parts (students, faculty, staff, administration, governing bodies, alumni, membership and supporting constituency) in a manner which the office of President cannot, since the President is first of all a servant of the Board. (Thus in some sense a chancellor represents in a university what a titular monarch represents in a country.) This is especially important to Redeemer College, since it is a constituency-based institution.

To put this matter in context, it is common practice for universities to include the position of chancellor in their institutions; some evangelical colleges also have them. Every university has a chancellor, which is an honourary position that includes ceremonial and some fundraising and public relations duties.

Finally, a specific reason for proceeding with implementing this principle at this time is simply that our founding President is about to retire from office, and we need his services in order to ensure continuity in major donor cultivation and fundraising in the transition to a new President, regardless of who is chosen for that position. Rev. De Bolster is willing to make himself available to assist the new President in this way, and the position of chancellor would provide an appropriate vehicle by which to accomplish this. For these reasons the Committee would like to come forward with a proposal to establish the position of Chancellor of Redeemer College.

Recommendations

   1. That the Board of Governors decide, in principle, to establish the position of Chancellor according to the attached position description.

2. That the Board go on record as stating its intention to appoint our founding President as the first Chancellor for a three-year term, effective July 1, 1994, as well as President Emeritus.

3. That these actions be completed at the earliest opportunity by the Board in order to allow time for notification of the other bodies which are part of the College.

Hugh Cook addressing Cobie De Bolster as he presents her with a bouquet.

This proposal received positive responses except from the faculty. The faculty was divided. Some were in favour, but others were of the opinion that Redeemer College was too small to have a chancellor. Moreover, there were some that felt that my connection with the College should cease as soon as I would retire. When I heard the reaction of the faculty, I announced to them that I would withdraw my request for further involvement with the College. We had enough arguments concerning the Brookview Trust. I did not want to leave the College knowing that some had negative feelings about my continued involvement with the College. It was not *my* future that should receive attention, it was the College's future that was important. The executive committee's minutes of March 25, 1994, read: "H. R. De Bolster informs the executive committee that upon his retirement he plans to break all administrative ties with Redeemer College." It was difficult to make that decision, but I was fully at peace with it. I continued as a member of the foundation. In that capacity I assisted with fundraising. At that same meeting the executive committee decided that "the title President Emeritus will be conferred on H. R. De Bolster at the May 28/94 convocation." That decision received unanimous consent.

The board requested that the actual retirement be highlighted during the April 20th closing convocation and the May 28th graduation.

The closing convocation was an in-house ceremony where one of the faculty members, Hugh Cook, spoke words of farewell in the presence of the entire student body. The May 28th graduation was a farewell in the presence of the entire College community. Both events moved Cobie and me deeply. I expressed these feelings in my last report to the board on April 23, 1994. I wrote:

> I want to take this opportunity to express my feelings of joy and gratitude as I reflect on my years with the College. Thank you board members for the solid support I always received from you. I learned from your counsel and guidance. The years I served Redeemer College were the best years of my life and I thank God for the opportunity He gave me to lead this young institution through its infancy. I am more convinced than ever that Christian post-secondary education is not a luxury, but an absolute necessity. There is a crying need in our society for prophetic voices, and I thank God that He gave us Redeemer College where prophetic voices are developed and trained. As I retire, my prayers will accompany the entire College community on a daily basis. My prayers will be especially fervent for you, the board, and the new president.

The board decided to organise two special events in connection with my retirement. The first was held on June 3 in the presence of representatives of the board, academic council, faculty, administration and staff. It was a delightful evening under the leadership of Jim Payton, master of ceremonies. Several speakers took the opportunity to do some roasting and at the end of the evening I felt "well-done." The farewell gift consisted of a computer with a printer, as well as two reserved seats in the auditorium for Cobie and myself whenever an event sponsored by the College would take place. Both my wife and I were overwhelmed by the love expressed during that evening. I was grateful for the opportunity to express my gratitude and appreciation to everyone present for the support given during the years that I was allowed to serve the College in spite of my weaknesses and shortcomings.

On June 14, a farewell was held with the many friends, supporters and guests, who represented the many facets of public life. I was overwhelmed by the presence of so many friends and supporters: especially Rev. Jacob Kuntz, with whom I started the feasibility study for a Christian college; Dr Alvin Lee, the former president of McMaster University, who had been my counsellor so many times; mayor Bob Wade and deputy mayor Ann Sloat, who had been the first ones to welcome Redeemer College to Ancaster; Dr. Tony Diekema, president of Calvin College who had been a listening ear for me many times; Dr. Harry Fernhout from the ICS; and Dr. Boris Brott and his wife Ardyth were also present. Boris Brott was the former director and conductor of the Hamilton Symphony Orchestra. I had such fond memories of them because of the Stained Glass concert series that they had presented at the College. I was pleasantly surprised to see Dr. Richard Allen, the former Minister of Colleges and Universities, who had shown so much interest in Redeemer College, even though he had not been able to convince others of the justice of granting us our charter change.

Everyone present had a special tie with the College, and many of them spoke words of appreciation and support. It was an honour and privilege for me to thank all those present for their support, their love, their prayers, and to ask them to continue their support for the new president and for the College.

I had an opportunity to publicly thank those people who had worked with me on a daily basis. Margaret Buma, my faithful assistant, who was always ready to listen and to encourage me. My wife

Cobie De Bolster presenting a bouquet of roses to Margaret Buma.

presented her with a bouquet of roses. Without her devotion I would not have been able to weather the difficulties we faced. Justin Cooper, who knew the academic side of the College so well, and who was my right hand in everyday decisions. Bill Smouter, the evenly-balanced, yet tireless worker, who always kept the reasons for our existence before us, and reminded us to remain faithful to our roots. Lloyd Hack, who had been with us for only one year, but who had already been of great help to me. Dick Kranendonk, who was present that evening, should have received my thanks and appreciation. I forgot to mention Dick. Without his hard work and devotion, the College would not have been where it was at my retirement. Dick had given all his energy and time to the College. He always looked for ways and means to improve things. He did not always succeed, but he gave himself completely towards the building of Redeemer College. I felt sorry that I had forgotten him. It gives me a feeling of satisfaction that I am able to thank him publicly at this time.

When I left the presidency on June 30, 1994, it was with a feeling of gratitude. Gratitude because God had given me the calling to be president of Redeemer College. I always followed my calling

Justin D. Cooper, the president elect, giving final best wishes to
Henry and Cobie De Bolster.

with trepidation. I never became used to the fact that I was its president. I often had to assure myself of the fact that I had this high
calling. I experienced God's faithfulness, and He gave me the
strength to do my work every day. It was the Lord who, through
His Spirit, gave us the College and made it grow. That knowledge
also gave me the assurance that God will continue to bless the
works of our hands as long as we are faithful to His calling. May
God be near to those who lead the College in future years.

It must be clear that the faculty and I did not always see eye-
to-eye. Therefore, in conclusion let me quote the letter the faculty
sent to me at the time of my retirement. I am very thankful for
that letter:

Dear Henry,

During your final months in office, we as individual members
of the Redeemer community will have ample opportunity to wish
you well in your retirement and to thank you for what you have
done for Christian education and for Redeemer College specifically. But as a faculty we also want to thank you for the work you
have done here over these many years. You have regularly made a
point of thanking us formally for our work, and now the time has

come for us to express our appreciation to you, and also to Cobie, as you begin a new phase in your life.

You entered this task as an ordained minister rather than as a person with a broad background in higher education. We appreciate your boldness in confronting new challenges; not many people would have the courage to undertake such a responsibility without formal training or experience to fall back on. Today people may be inclined to take your record of accomplishment as Redeemer's first President for granted. But many of us remember how the College started out. There were hard lessons to be learned along the way. You were willing to take the personal risks that were involved in learning those lessons.

Through all the turmoil and stress of building the College, you continued your role as an ordained minister, giving spiritual leadership to the College in a number of ways, including regular chapel talks. Your rapport with our primary support community has been of great benefit to the College. And your Reformed understanding of the immensity of the task with which the Lord entrusts us has inspired us, especially at times when some of us were too preoccupied by the details of our own day-to-day work in the College. Your leadership in the purchase and development of our Ancaster campus, complete with its wonderful, spacious auditorium and a first-class organ, is a fine example of your awareness of the magnitude of God's Kingdom. You have reminded us often that the Lord who has given us so much also expects much of us.

There have also been times of great stress, times when we needed to be in prayer on your behalf. Many of us remember the anxious days when you were gravely ill, when it seemed that the Lord would call you home and that someone else would have to pick up your task. But He graciously restored you to health. We also remember, to our sorrow, the disappointment in connection with the proposed Brookview Trust Fund, and the aftermath of that event. For some of us, relations with you were then strained almost to the breaking point. Many of us have put those dark days behind us; for a few there is still healing to be done. We know that those events caused you deep anguish as well, and we note with appreciation that you did reach out to us to seek reconciliation as you continued with your work.

We are not writing this letter to review the past; our purpose is to express our appreciation to you for nurturing the vision of the College and defending that vision in the face of opposition from supporters who may not have understood all of its dimensions. Neither are we writing to say goodbye. It is our hope that you will continue to regard yourself as a full member of the College community. As a young College we are not used to retired members; perhaps the new role will seem awkward for you too. We hope that you will continue to take an interest in the work we do as faculty members, that you will feel free to drop in on us, and that you will not feel that you need an excuse to come to the College or to seek us out as individuals. We would be very pleased to see you continue working for the College in consultation with the Board and the new President. We certainly want you to enjoy your retirement years, and we expect that Cobie has also been looking forward to them as an opportunity for the two of you to enjoy some special times and trips together.

May the Lord richly bless you and Cobie in all that you undertake in the years to come.

Sincerely in Our Lord,
Gene Haas, Chair of Faculty,
Submitted on Behalf of Faculty

Epilogue

As I wrote this short history about the preparations for and the beginning years of Redeemer College, I relived every episode. Some with much pleasure and gratitude, others with a lot of pain. I suppose that is always true in life. We live in a sinful world and we are affected by it. There are things we do well and there are others we do not do so well. We are not immune to our surroundings and our judgments are not always flawless and pure. That was also true of my involvement with the College. I am sorry for mistakes that were made. Yet I thank God for the good things we accomplished. The story you just read related the many challenges we faced and the accomplishments that were achieved.

There are some events that stand out more than others. I was often plagued by feeling of inadequacy because I lack a doctorate. It hindered me more, perhaps, than it bothered others. At times, I was reminded of that educational shortcoming in subtle ways. On the other hand, it never ceased to amaze me that God used my services as president of this important institution, Redeemer, now, University College.

Prayer was the basis of my daily work. Every morning I would ask the Lord for wisdom, insight and dependence on Him. I would ask the Lord to lead the way and to show me how to follow. The Lord performed marvellous deeds. As His servant, this gave me great joy and thankfulness. I wrote that the years at the College were the best years of my life as well as Cobie's. She, too, rejoiced greatly in the achievements of the College. She was the perfect hostess to the guests we received at the president's house and she would speak of the students as her children.

Some things I always regarded as miraculous in the special sense of the word. Let me mention a few. We should never take the 1980

Charter for granted. Without it we would not have been able to open the College, and today we would not rejoice about the subsequent *Charters*. Our admission to membership in the AUCC was, humanly speaking, impossible. The facilities on Beach Boulevard, the acquisition of the library, the student housing on Frances Road, the first faculty members, the devotion on the part of the administration—they are all miracles the Lord provided during the early years.

When we outgrew the facilities on Beach Boulevard, we received that unexpected, incredible gift of one million dollars! This anonymous gift gave us the courage to plan for our new campus. The way we acquired the property where we would be able to build our new campus, and then the new campus itself, is something I will never forget. The Lord directed it all.

I will always remember the emotions I felt when I visited our business people and received large and small donations. The LIFT campaign exceeded our wildest dreams. I found that the joy of giving is a special blessing of the Lord, as is accepting such gifts. I felt very privileged to have had those experiences.

Some disappointments also made a lasting impression on me. No one will ever fully understand my feelings during the time when the Brookview Trust had collapsed. It was utterly devastating. Just as sad was the fact that it seemed impossible for some people to forgive. They failed to remember the good that had been accomplished in the past. I believe that the aftermath of the trust's failure brought greater grief to the College community than the failure of the trust itself.

Let me relate another negative experience. I hope that relating that experience may prevent future similar actions. Sometimes, the administration made a decision or communicated the possibility of making a decision with which a faculty or staff member strongly disagreed. Those faculty or staff members told students, with the result that students would come rushing into my office, angry with me for what they had heard. I had a difficult time understanding such unprofessional behaviour. It would cause students to become upset, while the decision or intended decision did not affect them in the first place.

Disappointments must be taken in stride. they are not pleasant, but they are a part of a growing process given as a lesson for the future. I can testify that my presidency at the College has been a great learning experience. I have learned much, and thank all those who taught me. I received much more than I gave.

Finally, how wonderful that I could live to see the answers to our many prayers for a new Charter. The government of Ontario and the Ontario university community have acknowledged that Redeemer College is an undergraduate university worthy of the name Redeemer College and that the Christian education at Redeemer College is a legitimate education, deserving of the B.A. and the B.Sc. degrees. May God also answer our prayers that Redeemer University College will receive a positive response to its request to grant the Bachelor of Education (B.Ed.) degree. The Lord who has blessed us so tremendously will undoubtedly be with the University in its request for authority to grant the B.Ed. degree.

Redeemer University College has used as its motto "learning is for serving." I pray that Redeemer will remember this motto and continue to prepare men and women to serve the Lord in the Church and His Kingdom for the benefit of society in general.

The title of my book, *Stepping Forward in Faith*, is the motto of the Redeemer Foundation. If we dare to step forward in faith, we have the promise that the Lord will always be beside us. The hymn the College has chosen as its theme song says it all. Let me conclude by quoting the song. that has been my comfort during all those years of serving as the College's founding president.

> *If you but trust in God to guide you*
> *and place your confidence in Him,*
> *you'll find Him always there beside you*
> *to give you hope and strength within;*
> *for those who trust God's changeless love*
> *build on the rock that will not move.*

Welcome to one of the many organisations that use
the University facilities for their conferences.